# Praise for *Radica*

"Weaving together her profound expertise in Dietrich Bonhoeffer and Martin Luther King Jr. with the poignant authenticity of someone who has spent time on the frontlines of lockdown America, Jennifer M. McBride calls us to discover the promise of the gospel in a divided age. Her extraordinary journey to radical discipleship among those in prison challenges us all to a life of costly grace. This is a compelling and beautifully written book for anyone who cares about the future of Christianity."
**Jeffrey C. Pugh**
**Elon University**

"Prisoners need prophetic advocates who will be their voice to teach us about the reality of their lives. Jennifer McBride's powerful account of her work with women in prison raises their insights as she challenges us to rethink what the gospel is all about. This book is full of wisdom, pathos, and hope as it invites us to be transformed into disciples who enter into community with people we readily condemn."
**Helen Prejean, CSJ**
**Author, *Dead Man Walking***

"In her brilliant exploration of the politics of the ecclesial calendar, Jennifer M. McBride shows us the different invitations each church season poses to those who would follow Jesus, and the different truths each season teaches about what following Jesus entails. McBride has named writing this book as an act of worship; in a way, reading it might be an act of worship, too."
**Lauren Winner**
**Duke Divinity School**

"This is an original, wise and inspiring book. McBride draws on her wide and deep theological learning, alongside her experiences of radical Christian practices of community, to present a realistic and challenging account of what discipleship might entail in a profoundly unequal and unjust society."
**Rachel Muers**
**University of Leeds**


"A gritty, honest practical theology rooted in lived experience. A very strong new contribution from the author of the brilliant *The Church for the World*. Strongly recommended!"
**David P. Gushee**
**Mercer University**


"Jennifer McBride writes lived theology in the fullest sense of those words. She has lived into the discipleship to which she calls us. And she has listened deeply to disciples she has walked with along the way: imprisoned women, homeless people, long-time activists, and more. The genius of McBride's work is to respect the theological insights in these lives and to place them in conversation with thinkers like Martin Luther King Jr., Dorothy Day, and Dietrich Bonhoeffer. The result is a book that is both deeply learned and eminently practical. In its method as much as its content, it is one of this generation's most thoughtful and powerful calls to radical discipleship."
**Ted A. Smith**
**Emory University**

# Radical Discipleship

# Radical Discipleship

A Liturgical Politics of the Gospel

Jennifer M. McBride

Fortress Press
*Minneapolis*

RADICAL DISCIPLESHIP

A Liturgical Politics of the Gospel

Cover image: Tree Seasons by Rita Corbin; ritacorbinart.com

Cover design: Alisha Lofgren and Lauren Williamson

Print ISBN: 978-1-5064-0189-8

eBook ISBN: 978-1-5064-0190-4

The paper used in this publication meets the minimum requirements of American National Standard for Information Sciences — Permanence of Paper for Printed Library Materials, ANSI Z329.48-1984.

Manufactured in the U.S.A.

This book was produced using Pressbooks.com, and PDF rendering was done by PrinceXML.

For the women
in the prison theology program:
my teachers, students, sister theologians, and friends.


*"Know it well. Love was his meaning."*
—Julian of Norwich

# Contents

1. Introduction: The Space of Radical Discipleship     *1*

2. Advent     *25*

3. Christmas     *71*

4. Ordinary Time     *101*

5. Lent and Holy Week     *121*

6. Good Friday     *149*

7. Easter     *187*

8. Pentecost: The Birth of the Discipleship Movement     *229*

Acknowledgments     *261*

Suggested Reading     *265*

Index of Names and Subjects     *269*

Index of Scripture     *277*

# 1

---

# Introduction: The Space of Radical Discipleship

"He's talking about us," Natalie says with measured surprise and visible emotion as she looks up from the page I read. It is a passage from Dietrich Bonhoeffer's *Letters and Papers from Prison*:

> From a Christian point of view there is no special problem about Christmas in a prison cell. For many people in this building it will probably be a more sincere and genuine occasion than in places where nothing but the name is kept. That misery, suffering, poverty, loneliness, helplessness, and guilt mean something quite different in the eyes of God from what they mean in the judgment of human beings, that God will approach where humans turn away, that Christ was born in a stable because there was no room in the inn—these are things that a prisoner can understand better than other people; for her they really are glad tidings, and that faith gives her a part in the community of the saints, a Christian fellowship breaking the bounds of time and space (Dec. 17, 1943).[1]

When Natalie looks up, our eyes spark with the kind of connection

---

1. Dietrich Bonhoeffer, *Letters and Papers from Prison*, trans. Reginald Fuller et al. (New York: Touchstone, 1997), 166. The quote appears here as I typed it on the handout. I took the liberty of changing the masculine pronouns to feminine pronouns and not using brackets so that the passage would speak to the women as clearly as possible.

that occasionally happens as eyes lock with a stranger passing by, or that occurs upon a first encounter with someone who is about to become a central figure in one's life, in this case a sister among sisters, fellow pilgrims on a shared journey from suffering, loneliness, and guilt toward belonging, glad tidings, and fellowship.

It was Advent 2008. As a postdoctoral fellow at Emory University, I had been invited to teach a pilot class for a theology certificate program at a women's prison on the German pastor-theologian and Nazi resister Dietrich Bonhoeffer.[2] I did not know what these women would think about this passage from Bonhoeffer. I tried to speak the words "there is no special problem about Christmas in a prison cell" with utmost reverence as one who, in all honesty, had never given much thought to the American prison system, much less to the people inside it. I did not know then that, though fleeting, that spark between Natalie and me captured something of what the New Testament writers call the "fullness of time," a *kairos* moment at once provisional and complete, the gathering of the past and the future into a present pregnant with new creation, the moment when everything opens up and makes room for unlikely connections and community across time, space, and context.[3] Anticipated in that spark would be a communion that would link the likes of Dietrich Bonhoeffer to incarcerated women in Georgia, and that would usher them and me into the beloved community being worked out at the Open Door, an intentionally interracial, residential, Christian activist and worshiping community in Atlanta, Georgia, that for thirty-five years has been engaged in works of mercy and justice focusing on homelessness, mass incarceration, and anti-death-penalty protest.

This book arises out of my overlapping experiences at the women's prison and the Open Door Community. Entering into the surreal world of the prison, "inmate society," as the women in the theology program

---

2. The theology certificate program is housed at Emory University and sponsored by Atlanta's four Protestant seminaries: Columbia Theological Seminary, Interdenominational Theological Center, McAfee School of Theology at Mercer University, and Candler School of Theology at Emory. Names of the women in the program have been changed and quotes are used with permission.
3. See, for example, Gal 4:4 and Mark 1:14–15.

call it, and bringing it home with me every Friday night—"Remember those who are in prison," the writer of Hebrews says, "as though you were in prison with them"—led me to seek out regular worship at the Open Door during Lent 2009. The exhortation in Hebrews was, for me, less of a command and more of a problem. I could not stop remembering them, and I did not know how to integrate my time there into my daily life and relationships the rest of the week. Worshipping at the Open Door—with former inmates, homeless people, academics-turned-activists, seminarians and other students, and residential and non residential volunteers—became that integration. While the women were my guides inside the prison, helping me make sense of what I observed and experienced there, I also needed a church community "on the outside" that understood what I was encountering and that could sustain me as I ventured in and out of the prison.

The biblical and theological reflection in these pages is the fruit of seven years of continual engagement with the women in the theology program and the members of the Open Door. The first two and half years, while living in Atlanta, I was in the prison on a weekly basis, and the Open Door Community was my church home. As the pilot course transitioned into the program's inaugural year, I transitioned with it as unexpected opportunities arose allowing me to remain engaged in the work of teaching and then also directing the program under the vision and leadership of Emory ethicist Elizabeth Bounds. My first sustained interactions with these women consisted of approximately eight to ten hours every Friday teaching the theology foundations course, various electives, and directing afternoon study hall. Even after moving away for an assistant professorship, I have had the opportunity to continue teaching and engaging with the women weekly each summer, during academic year breaks, and through written correspondence.

Over time, as I became immersed in the women's prison, I had a growing desire to become involved in the work of the Open Door beyond weekly worship. I became a full-time community member with the support of a Project on Lived Theology writing grant during the 2010–2011 academic year. My time at the Open Door and my time in the women's prison was seamless for me, and the most important part of my experience at the Open Door remained the way in which I could bring my work at the prison into the daily life of the community.

The period that I served as a full-time participant at the Open Door happened to fall from the beginning to the end of the liturgical calendar, from Advent through Pentecost. This proved to be a welcome coincidence given that one of the most remarkable things about the Open Door is the way its communal life organically connects liturgy with activism and theological reflection. This community impressed upon me that when Christians live a deeply liturgical life, when we structure our existence in the world through the seasons and events that walk us through the Gospel narratives from Advent to Pentecost, we are given the capacity to hear God speak to us in powerful and concrete ways. In light of this, the chapters that follow are structured by the liturgical seasons that move us through the Gospel texts. The Open Door witnesses to the reality that abiding within these scriptures necessitates placing our bodies in the spaces in which, as Bonhoeffer says above, God approaches but humans tend to turn away. What the Open Door provided for me was precisely that space—not only the breathing room in a supportive community to sit with and face the hard realities confronting me at the prison, but also continual openings into the places from which I wanted to shrink yet was compelled to enter because of the promise of Christ's presence there. More specifically, the Open Door provides liturgical space, which is more than, but inclusive of, space that marks time in a particular way. Liturgy is literally "the work of the people," and central to the Open Door is the work of creating space that enables radical discipleship by reducing distance across difference, namely between the "privileged" and the "oppressed"—which, for all of their fluidity and complexity, I define as those who are systematically advantaged and those who are ed.[4]

4. By speaking of the privileged the "oppressed," I do not mean to ignore the multiple identities and roles that individuals play in various social relations. There may be components of a privileged person's identity that make that individual systematically disadvantaged. Likewise, among the oppressed, there are people who inhabit roles of victimizer and victim of social

I focus on the moments in which the Open Door's practice was most transformative for me in order to address the book's primary inquiry: how privileged Christians may grow in concrete discipleship. The purpose of this sympathetic reading is not to deny the real limits, weaknesses, and problems with the Community's inner workings, nor to deny the interconnection between its interior space and outward hospitality. Rather, the sympathetic reading is in the service of a different mode of analysis. This book offers biblical and theological reflection about reducing distance as it draws on anecdotes from my own exper_____nd inside the prison. In other words, it i_____discipleship journey for which I argue. It _____ _____ _____ that reflects the need I had for community and clarity as I deepened my engagement with unjust realities and the people affected by them and asked myself a basic yet perennial question: What is the gospel the church proclaims given these realities, and how may Christians be formed as disciples who faithfully embody it?

Embedded within this movement from Advent through Pentecost is a central argument about formation: in order to be faithful to the gospel proclamation, Christians must become disciples of, not simply believers in, Jesus. These pages aim to facilitate a process of formation, not by offering complete analyses of imprisonment and homelessness (plenty of other resources fill that gap), but by ushering us into a story that leads to deeper engagement with these realities and the people who endure them, a story that when embraced may transform one's disposition and will. The dramatic narrative that holds these pages together is that of the gospel as it liturgically unfolds, a narrative that then brings to light fragmentary stories told about the Open Door

---

harm, as seen by the fact that homeless women are more vulnerable on the streets than men. Although imperfect, it is appropriate, though, to make distinctions between those of us who are systematically advantaged in various ways and those who are in prison or living on the streets. For a helpful discussion of our multiple and overlapping identities, particularly as they correspond to the dominant group or subordinate group in seven categories (race/ethnicity, gender, sexual orientation, socioeconomic status, age, physical ability, or mental ability), see Beverly Daniel Tatum, *Why Are All the Black Kids Sitting Together in the Cafeteria? And Other Conversations About Race* (New York: Basic Books, 1997), 18–28.

Community, people in prison and on the street, and my experiences with them.

Also embedded within this liturgical narrative is a claim about the gospel itself. If the gospel is merely doctrinal, a statement of belief that makes one right with God (as Protestant faith often, albeit unintentionally, reduces it to), then it is a message only for the individual. But since the gospel demands discipleship—that is, following Jesus into the midst of the world as he embodies and proclaims the kingdom of God—it is inherently social and political. It concerns how we structure society in a way that demonstrates love for neighbors, strangers, and enemies, a love that leads to both social and personal transformation. Therefore, each of the following chapters will focus on the social and political significance of the liturgical season. As we walk through the Gospel narratives from Advent through Pentecost, we gain a clearer understanding of the definitive and non negotiable social-structural character of God's good news—good news that has the power to engage and resist even the most unjust realities.

## Performing My Thesis: More on Method

The Open Door served as a vehicle that taught me how church communities may create space and mark time in a way that facilitates radical discipleship. As such, it is a place that enabled me to perform my thesis—to grow deeper in discipleship formation and gain greater clarity about the good news Christians should proclaim and embody. This book, though, is not about the Open Door Community per se. I highlight it as an exemplary model of ecclesial space that facilitates discipleship—of a place centered around Jesus as depicted in the Gospels that abides within the biblical narrative; privileges the powerless and demonstrates love in action for neighbors, strangers, and enemies; makes clear the inherent social and political character of the gospel; shows the necessary interconnection of personal and social transformation; repents and takes responsibility for sin that harms fellow human beings; and prays for and participates in the coming kingdom of God. In doing so, I am not suggesting that it is a flawless depiction of Christian faithfulness, nor that churches must become exact replicas of this community. As one of the oldest and best-known intentional Christian communities in the United States, it warrants close analysis—an examination of its communal structure, power relations, leadership model, dominant personalities, strengths and weaknesses, influences and inconsistencies, and successes, failures, and blind spots.[5] That book may one day be written, perhaps by a seasoned leader in another intentional community or by a scholar who has spent adequate time in a number of similar settings. My intent is different. It is to write constructive theology out of the liturgical space that has been created by the Open Door Community, space intended to reduce distance across socioeconomic and racial lines, and, more specifically, to reduce distance between the housed and the homeless and between inmate and free. I am not so much analyzing the space as immersing myself in it in order to be formed by it and write out of this process of formation.

The Open Door Community is more of a dialogue partner than an object of study, as is true with the women in the prison theology program. My insights could not have happened without the Open Door (nor without the women), and this is central to my argument: church-communities like the Open Door are indispensable to discipleship formation. Still, the writing both grows out of and contributes to the theological reflection happening there and inside the prison. One of the most rewarding aspects of writing this book was the cyclical way in which the pages traveled to and from the prison and the Open Door. As I wrote about moments in the prison, I shared excerpts with a handful of the women when I visited them, which led to more discussion,

---

5. The Open Door Community is mentioned or analyzed briefly in a few publications. See Robert N. Bellah, Richard Madsen, William M. Sullivan, Ann Swidler, and Steven M. Tipton, *The Good Society* (New York: Random House, 1991), 30–32; Christine D. Pohl, *Making Room: Recovering Hospitality as a Christian Tradition* (Grand Rapids: Eerdmans, 1999), 74, 163, 194; Walter Brueggemann, *The Prophetic Imagination* (Minneapolis: Fortress Press, 2001), 122; Stanley P. Saunders and Charles L. Campbell, *The Word on the Street: Performing the Scriptures in the Urban Context* (Grand Rapids: Eerdmans, 2000), 6–10, 135–42, 156–76; Peter R. Gathje, "The Cost of Virtue: What Power in the Open Door Community Might Speak to Virtue Ethics," in *Ethnography as Christian Theology and Ethics*, ed. Aana Marie Vigen and Christian Scharen (New York: Continuum, 2011), 207–24; and Elizabeth Hinson-Hasty, *Dorothy Day for Armchair Theologians* (Louisville: Westminster John Knox, 2014), 195–99.

deeper theological reflection, and ongoing inquiry for us all. Likewise, some of the content incorporated in these pages first took the form of homilies at the Open Door the year I was a full-time participant there. Other sections were read in the worship service as polished drafts while I was in the process of writing. The effect was similar to that in the prison. As I learned from Open Door members, they learned from me. Together we helped each other think in new and nuanced ways about the call to discipleship.

My method is best described as "lived theology," which I define as theological reflection born from discipleship—from intentionally placing oneself in situations of social concern as one responds to Jesus's call to follow him there.[6] Lived theology privileges the incarnate word over a disembodied idea, and it guards against constructing a closed system that seals off theological thinking from the church and from those who suffer injustice. Instead it holds in dynamic conversation traditional theological discourse, the insights of marginalized people, and lessons learned from church communities engaged in transformative activity in the world. Lived theology is a turn from "the phraseological to the real," from theology beholden to the academy to theology responding to the needs of the world.[7] In this sense, quintessential lived theologians include Dietrich Bonhoeffer and Baptist pastor and civil rights leader Martin Luther King Jr., primary theological influences on my own thinking as well as the Open Door's.

## God's Beloved Community Come

I was drawn to the Open Door Community because it intentionally carries on the legacies of Bonhoeffer and King, particularly King's vision for beloved community. The members articulate this most

6. See also Jennifer M. McBride, "Public Discipleship, Constructive Theology, and Grassroots Activism," in *Lived Theology: New Perspectives on Method, Style, and Pedagogy*, ed. Charles Marsh, Peter Slade, and Sarah Azaransky (New York: Oxford University Press, 2016), 208–26.
7. Bonhoeffer, *Letters and Papers*, ed. John W. de Gruchy, trans. Isabel Best et al., vol. 8, *Dietrich Bonhoeffer Works* (Minneapolis: Fortress Press, 2010), 358. See also Charles Marsh, "Bonhoeffer on the Road to King: 'Turning from the Phraseological to the Real,'" in *Bonhoeffer and King: Their Legacies and Import for Christian Social Thought*, ed. Willis Jenkins and Jennifer M. McBride (Minneapolis: Fortress Press, 2010), 123–38.

explicitly through their weekly worship service as they pray an adapted version of the Lord's Prayer that emphasizes, in Bonhoeffer's words, the "this-worldliness" of Christian faith:

Our Beloved Friend, outside the domination system,
May your Holy Name be honored by the way we live our lives.
Your Beloved Community come. Guide us to:
walk your walk, talk your talk, sit your silence
inside the court room, on the streets, and in the jail houses,
as they are on the margins of resistance.
Give us this day everything we need.
Forgive us our wrongs, as we forgive those who have wronged us.
Do not bring us to hard testing, but keep us safe from the Evil One.
For Thine is the Beloved Community,
the power and the glory,
forever and ever. Amen.

As the prayer illustrates, the beloved community is another way of speaking of the kingdom of God, particularly as it is realized "on earth as it is in heaven." It is a concrete manifestation of God's kingdom—of God's intended social order—announced by John the Baptist and embodied in Jesus. The beloved community is comprised of right relationships that affirm the image of God in all people (Gen 1:27) and that manifest the hope of the reconciliation of all things (Col 1:20). As such, it is both a future eschatological promise and a present historic possibility, albeit one forged through struggle. With beloved community as the goal, King contends that oppression, exploitation, and scarcity do not have to be accepted norms in this life, and so Christians must hope not only for "the new Jerusalem" but also for "the new Atlanta," the new Ferguson, and the new Baltimore.[8] This hope for beloved community necessarily envelops all people, the privileged and the oppressed alike, and so it is distinct from but inclusive of the church. Its promise and possibility include, for King, restored relationships of justice: former slave owners and former slaves—"Pharaoh and Moses"—sitting together "at the table of

8. Martin Luther King Jr., *A Testament of Hope: The Essential Writings and Speeches of Martin Luther King, Jr.*, ed. James M. Washington (San Francisco: Harper & Row, 1986), 282.

brotherhood."[9] Although a divine gift rather than a human project, beloved community necessitates human participation and cooperation and encompasses life in all its dimensions—personal, relational, communal, and structural. It demands the kind of radical discipleship demonstrated by King and thousands of others as they embodied love of neighbors and love of enemies through nonviolent action. Through their struggle for economic and racial justice—for beloved community—the black church and the broader black community dramatized the Gospel narratives, particularly Jesus's life and teachings in the Sermon on the Mount.

The liturgy of the Open Door—its worship and work—is inspired by this dramatization of the Gospels and the full vision of beloved community. For King, this includes not only the demanding call for racial reconciliation between whites and blacks (the dream for which he is celebrated today) but also his unfolding and inconvenient insight, expressed most directly at the end of his life and yet to be embraced, that given the intricately intertwined nature of all injustice, American society needs restructuring.[10] King called for a change of heart, "a radical revolution of values," that would lead to a change of structures—specifically to American citizens questioning "the fairness and justice of many of our past and present policies" while confronting "the giant triplets of racism, materialism, and militarism."[11] Seeking to convict those who were privileged and to empower those who were poor through an interracial grassroots movement called "The Poor People's Campaign," King proclaimed exactly one year before he was murdered in Memphis, "The dispossessed of this nation—the poor, both white and Negro—live in a cruelly unjust society. They must organize a revolution against . . . injustice, not against the lives of . . . their fellow citizens, but against the structures through which the society is refusing to . . . lift the load of poverty."[12]

9. Ibid., 219.
10. See Vincent Harding, *Martin Luther King: The Inconvenient Hero* (Maryknoll, NY: Orbis Books, 2008), 1–22.
11. King, *Testament of Hope*, 240–41.
12. Martin Luther King Jr., *Trumpet of Conscience* (New York: Harper & Row, 1967), 59–60.

For King, as well as for the Open Door, the struggle for beloved community is forged with a healthy dose of Christian realism—intimate knowledge of the power of sin in social and political life. However inevitable, pervasive, and entrenched, sin is not the final word for these Christians, though, certainly not from an ultimate eschatological perspective. Instead, what is final is the goodness of creation and the redemptive power of the incarnate word, as expressed in King's famous line, "The arc of the universe is long but it bends toward justice."[13] Nor is sin the final word from the perspective of God's proleptic movement within this-worldly affairs, in other words, from the perspective of the call to discipleship that leads Christians to be a transformative presence within historical reality. Indeed, it is precisely the disciple's understanding of the seriousness of sin and an ever-increasing proximity to those who are most vulnerable to "powers and principalities" (Eph 6:12) that makes the struggle against sin all the more urgent.

The Open Door is a worshipping congregation that stakes its life on the promise and possibility of beloved community. As a fragile and localized expression of it, the participants order their lives around the this-worldly conviction that, because of the resurrection power of the living Jesus, life indeed may triumph over death, liberation over bondage, and redemption and reconciliation over sin, convictions that were deepened in me as I read the Bible in graduate school alongside such influential figures as Bonhoeffer, Mennonite theologian John Howard Yoder, and Latin American theologian Gustavo Gutiérrez.[14]

From Bonhoeffer, I learned that a primary significance of the incarnation is the way it presses Christians toward this-worldly concern, particularly how the Incarnate One leads us to participate in the sufferings "of God in the world." Through the incarnation, God

---

13. Martin Luther King Jr., *A Call to Conscience: The Landmark Speeches of Dr. Martin Luther King, Jr.*, ed. Clayborne Carson and Kris Shepard (New York: Grand Central, 2001), 131.

14. For a discussion of how appeals to Yoder are now problematic given his sexual abuse of women, see Karen V. Guth, *Christian Ethics at the Boundary: Feminism and Theologies of Public Life* (Minneapolis: Fortress Press, 2015), 113–52 and Karen V. Guth, "Doing Justice to the Complex Legacy of John Howard Yoder: Restorative Justice Resources in Witness and Feminist Ethics," *Journal of the Society of Christian Ethics* 35, no. 1 (Fall/Winter 2015).

immerses God's self in the joys and troubles of this life and calls Jesus's followers to do the same. "By this-worldliness," Bonhoeffer writes, "I mean living unreservedly in life's duties, problems, successes and failures, experiences and perplexities. In so doing we throw ourselves completely into the arms of God, taking seriously not our own sufferings, but those of God in the world—watching with Christ in Gethsemane. That, I think is faith; that is *metanoia*; and that is how one becomes a human being and a Christian."[15] From Bonhoeffer, I also learned the distinction between cheap grace, which exonerates the church from the demanding work of transformative activity in the world, and costly grace, which Bonhoeffer equates with discipleship and with the personal and social transformation that results from following Jesus. Referring to the Reformation gospel, Bonhoeffer writes, "The grace was costly because it did not excuse one from works. Instead, it endlessly sharpened the call to discipleship. But just wherein it was costly, that was wherein it was grace. . . . It is costly, because it calls to discipleship; it is grace, because it calls us to follow *Jesus Christ*. It is costly, because it costs people their lives; it is grace, because it thereby makes them live."[16]

From Yoder, I learned that "works," those demanding acts of obedience to Jesus's commands, are inherently political (inherently public and social) and thus any study and application of scripture needs to stay attuned to the social and political quality of Jesus's identity and mission. Underscoring this, the New Testament intentionally employs the political terminology of the Roman Empire yet assigns these words—like *gospel* (a publicly important proclamation sent by a runner), *ecclesia* (a political community), and *basileia* (empire/ kingdom)—alternative referents. Yoder contends that the New Testament texts "have a political witness" and point to an alternative social order that stands in tension with the violent and oppressive forces of any age.

From Gutiérrez, I learned that the central message of the Bible is

---

15. Bonhoeffer, *Letters and Papers* (Touchstone), 370.
16. Dietrich Bonhoeffer, *Discipleship*, ed. Geoffrey B. Kelly and John D. Godsey, trans. Barbara Green and Reinhard Krauss, vol. 4, *Dietrich Bonhoeffer Works* (Minneapolis: Fortress Press, 2003), 45, 49.

liberation from these forces, that is, liberation from sin in both its personal and social dimensions. Liberation theologies arise directly from the lived experiences and social situations of the oppressed and marginalized, encouraging a biblical hermeneutic of action reflection that necessitates that the marginalized community position its own story inside the biblical narrative. In doing so, the community holds lived experience and the scriptural text in dynamic conversation and thereby affirms the truth that the Bible contains a living word spoken for us (*pro nobis*) and to us by the living God. This is poignantly exemplified by those church communities engaged in the black freedom struggle from slavery through civil rights who understood the Hebrew story of liberation from Egyptian oppression as their own, and who, in turn, recognized Jesus as the second Moses, the final liberator. Thus, Christians best recognize scripture's liberative message when they read it, as Bonhoeffer says, with a "view from below." "It remains an experience of incomparable value," he writes to his colleagues in the Nazi-resistance movement, "that we have for once learned to see the great events of world history . . . from the perspective of the outcasts, the suspects, the maltreated, the powerless, the oppressed and reviled, in short from the perspective of the suffering."[17] The crucial point is that Christians like Bonhoeffer, like me, like the socially and economically privileged white founders of the Open Door have to learn this perspective. We have to be uprooted from a landscape that tempts us toward paternalism, judgment, security, and control and be placed on fertile ground where the truth of our common humanity, our solidarity in sin and redemption, may be known through an embodied and intimate existence with others. "If you have come here to help me, you are wasting your time," reads a poster prominently placed at the Open Door. "But if you have come because your liberation is bound up with mine, then let us work together."[18] This process of mutual liberation can only begin when one steps out of her previous existence and follows Jesus into a new situation.

17. Bonhoeffer, *Letters and Papers* (Fortress Press), 52.
18. Attributed to Lilla Watson, United Nations Decade for Women Conference: Equality, Development and Peace, Nairobi, Kenya, July 15–26, 1985.

## Discipleship and the New Situation

The primary claim of this book is that in order to be faithful to the gospel, Christians must become disciples of, not simply believers in, Jesus. This distinction between discipleship and belief animated Bonhoeffer's work in the Confessing Church's struggle against Nazism, and he explores it directly in the opening chapters of his most famous text, *Nachfolge*, originally translated in English as *The Cost of Discipleship*:

> Because we cannot deny that we no longer stand in true discipleship to Christ, [even] while being members of a true-believing church with a pure doctrine of grace, but no longer members of a church which follows Christ, we therefore simply have to try to understand grace and discipleship again in correct relationship to each other. We can no longer avoid this. Our church's predicament is proving more and more clearly to be a question of how we are to live as Christians today.[19]

Bonhoeffer observes that unintended consequences have arisen from the Protestant emphasis on grace over works. Christians can gallantly claim faith in Christ all the while ignoring the primary commands of Jesus to love enemies, make peace, have mercy, and do justice—commands that lead to concrete social and political actions. When these commands are ignored by the majority of believers, Christianity is no longer defined by discipleship, no longer defined by following the incarnate God in a literal, straightforward, and embodied way. Instead Christianity amounts to "personal trust" in God at best or morphs into ideology at worst—a disembodied system of belief that is too often at odds with the way of Jesus depicted in the Gospels.

Given this, Bonhoeffer's concern is how to reduce the distance between the experience of the first disciples and contemporary Christians. Unlike the disciples in the Gospel narratives, Christians today do not have to look Jesus of Nazareth in the eye and respond directly to the command at hand; we can profess belief in Christ without any real consequence to our established habits of being. In contrast, Bonhoeffer cites Mark 2:14—"As Jesus was walking along, he

---

19. Bonhoeffer, *Discipleship*, 55.

saw Levi son of Alphaeus sitting at the tax booth, and he said to him, 'Follow me.' And he got up and followed him." Bonhoeffer writes, "The call goes out. . . . The disciple's answer is not a spoken confession of faith in Jesus. Instead it is the obedient deed."[20] A spoken confession of faith, "an idea about Christ, a doctrinal system, a general recognition of grace or forgiveness of sins does not require discipleship," Bonhoeffer argues. It does not require, in others words, a relationship of costly obedience to the living Jesus but only relates to an idea it calls Christ. By holding onto an idea of Christ, the Christian may have some knowledge about God, may be filled with zeal and every good intention, and may even act on that enthusiasm with integrity and sincerity. Indeed, all of this may amount, Bonhoeffer says, to "trust in God, but not [to] discipleship."[21]

In contrast, discipleship necessitates concrete action. "Following Christ means taking certain steps," Bonhoeffer writes.

> The first step, which responds to the call, separates the followers from their previous existence. A call to discipleship thus immediately creates a new situation. Staying in the old situation and following Christ mutually exclude each other. At first, that was quite visibly the case. The tax collector had to leave his booth and Peter his nets to follow Jesus. According to our understanding, even back then things could have been quite different. Jesus could have given the tax collector new knowledge of God and left him in his old situation. If Jesus had not been God's Son become human, then that would have been possible. But because Jesus is the Christ, it has to be made clear from the beginning that his word is not a doctrine. Instead, it creates existence anew. The point was to really walk with Jesus.[22]

Here, still in the opening chapters of *The Cost of Discipleship* while discussing cheap and costly grace, Bonhoeffer seeks for his readers nothing less than conversion, the conversion of Christians from mere believers to embodied disciples, a conversion in which location matters, a conversion that arises from continually being *placed*. The call to discipleship creates a new situation, Bonhoeffer says, where the

20. Ibid., 57.
21. Ibid., 59.
22. Ibid., 61–62.

Christian must "learn to believe." "The first step puts the Christian into the situation of *being able* to believe," for it is only the new situation that can generate the possibility of a belief creditable to the gospel—"true faith"—that unites trust in God with discipleship.

## The Discipleship Origins of the Open Door: A New Situation That Reduces Distance

My "new situation" came a decade before I was introduced to the Open Door when I was an intern at an urban hospitality house in Washington, DC, that works with its impoverished neighbors to meet communal needs. That brief but decisive two-year stint propelled me into doctoral studies where I could reflect on Christian public witness and the mission of the church in light of what I had seen. After graduate school, while in the process of moving to Atlanta, I learned about the Open Door Community from German theologian Jürgen Moltmann, who shared with me that his friends at the Open Door exemplified what I was arguing about public witness in my book *The Church for the World*, which draws constructively on Bonhoeffer's thought. The primary concern of *The Church for the World* is how privileged Christians may offer a nontriumphal witness to the lordship of Christ in a pluralistic society, and it argues that churches do so through confession and repentance, by accepting responsibility for social sin in concrete ways. Although I had already begun to ask existential questions about my own privilege and faith in Washington, DC, and had begun to articulate some answers through formal study, I knew I still had a lot to learn. Furthermore, years of graduate school had made me feel distant from the communal work that first sparked my process of change. This process included unlearning aspects of my faith that were shaped by privileged churches, both the conservative evangelical churches of my adolescent and college years and the liberal mainline Protestant churches of my adult years. It also included learning anew a perspective and practice more faithful to the Gospel narratives. The Open Door's liturgy—its worship and work in the world—resonated with me and provided a framework that helped me continue to probe hard questions and articulate the answers I was intuiting. As I practiced and performed the gospel with the Open Door, I was able to more deeply internalize not only the lessons learned from that decisive experience in DC but also the insights of figures like Bonhoeffer and King, whose writings first showed me how to envision the gospel anew. What I brought to the Open Door was hunger for a community that could help me become a more faithful disciple.

The very origins of the Open Door are rooted in Bonhoeffer's call "to rigorously follow Christ."[23] The cofounders, Ed Loring and Murphy Davis, gradually heard the call to "unlimited discipleship" in the late 1970s while studying the Bible in a small urban congregation where Ed was serving as pastor.[24] Although in their doctoral training Ed and Murphy had been taught to approach the scriptures through scholarly methods like historical criticism, the driving question of the study at Clifton Presbyterian was more personal: What do these passages that narrate Jesus's constant contact with those who are outcast, oppressed, and in need mean for our lives? If salvation meant liberation from sin, which obstructs right relationship with God and fellow human beings, if it meant personal transformation through confession of sin and repentance in response to the coming kingdom embodied and inaugurated in Jesus ("Repent, for the kingdom of God is at hand!" John the Baptist proclaims at the start of his ministry), then, they concluded, "working out [their] salvation in fear and trembling" (Phil 2:12–13) centrally includes "a shared struggle with the poor and oppressed for justice" and *that* necessitates closer relationships with them.[25] The participants in the Bible study at Clifton were particularly formed by two passages, Matthew 25:31–46, which bases the judgment of the nations on their works of mercy: feeding the hungry, welcoming the stranger, clothing the naked, caring for the sick, and visiting the prisoner; and Isaiah 58, which ties acceptable worship to the work of justice:

23. Ibid., 53.
24. Ibid., 39.
25. Peter R. Gathje, *Sharing the Bread of Life: Hospitality and Resistance at the Open Door Community* (Atlanta: Open Door Community Press, 2006), 34.

Is this not the fast that I choose:
to loose the bonds of injustice,
to undo the thongs of the yoke,
to let the oppressed go free?
. . . . . . . . . . . . . . . . . . . . . . . . . . .
Is it not to share your bread with the hungry,
and bring the homeless poor into your house;
when you see the naked, to cover them?
. . . . . . . . . . . . . . . . . . . . . . . . . . .
Then your light shall break forth like the dawn,
and your healing shall spring up quickly.
. . . . . . . . . . . . . . . . . . . . . . . . . . .
If you remove . . .
the pointing finger, the speaking of evil,
if you offer your food to the hungry
and satisfy the needs of the afflicted
. . . . . . . . . . . . . . . . . . . . . . . . . . .
[then] the Lord will guide you continually,
and satisfy your needs in parched places,
and make your bones strong;
and you shall be like a watered garden,
like a spring of water, whose waters never fail.
. . . . . . . . . . . . . . . . . . . . . . . . . . .
You shall be called the repairer of the breach,
the restorer of streets to live in. (Isa 58:6–12)

Faithfulness to both passages necessitates entering into a new situation, reducing distance, or in the words of Isaiah, repairing the breach.

Seeking to implement the work of mercy and justice into the worshipping congregation at Clifton, the Bible study proposed that the church support Murphy's budding ministry to inmates, a calling sowed in college where she was first introduced to people in prison. Clifton provided office space for her work, and there she established the Southern Prison Ministry, which included coordinating visits for the many relatives of inmates who lived hours from the prisons and did not have the means to travel such a distance. Connecting Murphy's work to Clifton was a partial response to the call to discipleship heard during Bible study, but the occasional nature of the monthly visits left the participants searching for more.

In January 1979, Murphy and Ed traveled to New York City for a meeting on prison ministry, and while there, they visited one of the primary Catholic Worker houses of hospitality. At Maryhouse, Dorothy Day, cofounder of the movement, was living out her last year of ministry to the Bowery's hungry and homeless. When Ed and Murphy returned to Atlanta, they researched the state of homelessness in the city and discovered that, given the growing number of homeless people, the most immediate need was shelter—beyond what the Salvation Army and Union Mission already offered and, at times, what the city jail inadvertently provided. Clifton responded to this reality by opening a night shelter, preparing sanctuary for chronically homeless men in its worship space and thereby becoming the first church in Atlanta to offer free shelter. Adhering to the biblical truth of the Hebrew prophets that "the justice of the community must be measured by the treatment of the most vulnerable," Clifton began advocating for other churches to do the same, to offer hospitality in such a way that homeless people would not be objects of charity but would become friends.[26] This friendship is rooted in Jesus's friendship with "tax collectors and sinners" (Luke 7:34) and with his disciples (John 15:12–17), rooted in "God's friendship with us." Thus, the men who came were neither "charity cases" nor classifications of "deserving" and "undeserving poor," but were "people to whom shelter and food were due in justice."[27]

Lingering dissatisfaction with the distance felt between themselves and those who were poor—with the lack of authentic relationship and mutuality expressed in Ed's confession, "Our middle-class heritage has taught us to distrust the poor as people out to freeload, so we are in a constant faith struggle"—led to the founding of the Open Door, a community officially established when a covenant was signed on July 24, 1980. "As a servant community," the covenant read, "we are empowered by the Holy Spirit to do Christ's work in the world. We are particularly called to a ministry of hospitality and visitation. . . . Prison

26. Ibid., 55.
27. Ibid., 54, 56.

ministry, anti-death penalty advocacy, and night shelter ministry are the works we are called to do in Christ's name."[28] By drawing its name from John 10:1–10 (English Standard Version)—"I am the door," Jesus says. "Whoever enters by me will be saved, and will come in and go out and find pasture"—the Community acknowledged that those who are homeless and in prison need doors opened out to them so that they might be welcomed into the abundant life of beloved community. They also acknowledged through this biblical reference the sobering truth that as a church, as "the body of Christ" (1 Cor 12:27), they were called literally to be the physical manifestation of Christ in the world, the open door through which their friends would find pasture and be freed into community, friends that Matthew 25 had taught them were no other than Christ himself coming in the guise of a stranger. Thus the work of the Community would be nothing more and nothing less than participation in divine movement: Christ the stranger welcomed by Christ the open door, a mystical reality similar to what Paul describes in Romans 8 when he writes that the Spirit intercedes for us through sighs too deep for words. God speaks to God through our bodies and its sensations, such that we are caught up and become, without losing our humble distinctiveness as creatures, a part of the Trinity's circle of love.

The covenant partners, who had yet to find a space suitable for the mission, intended that the work of the Open Door be grafted into congregational life, "perhaps as a different type of membership in the church."[29] With lack of congregational support, though, there was little possibility for staying at Clifton and being faithful to the call. Ed and Murphy came to believe that the work they envisioned demanded a residential community where covenant partners "would sell their possessions and goods and distribute the proceeds to all, as any had need" (Acts 2:45). They sold their homes, liquidated their investments, and, with the help of the Atlanta Presbytery and individual donors, bought the old Women's Union Mission at 910 Ponce de Leon Avenue.

---

28. Ibid., 58.
29. Ibid., 59.

In December 1980, they moved into the neighborhood, situating themselves in midtown Atlanta, which is located a few miles from downtown, two areas heavily populated by homeless people seeking access to labor pools and basic services. Their work would expand into a soup kitchen; shared living with homeless friends and former inmates who would be invited into the community on an individual basis; showers, change of clothes, toiletries, mail service, and gathering space for those who remained on the streets; foot care and medical clinics; continued visits to prison and friendship with death-row inmates; vigils during state executions and other nonviolent strategic actions; and a newspaper that would connect them to friends in prison and supporters around the world.

Almost thirty years after its inception, I became a participant in the liturgical work of the Open Door. I write as one who chose, after much discernment, to live outside the community, in a sense on the boundary line of their communal discipline, since, at the time, developing a strong sense of agency was more important for personal and vocational growth than sacrificing some of that agency for residential community. The leadership team made this exception and permitted me to have a unique membership in its residential life beyond the average nonresidential volunteer. Together with the rare experience of being continually placed inside the prison for a consistent and extended period of time while directing the theology certificate program, the Community became a new situation that confronted me with the realities of homelessness, mass incarceration, and capital punishment and that led me deeper down the path of discipleship. Reflecting its namesake, the Open Door serves as the space that invites others into a new situation, that calls us who worship and volunteer there out of our previous existence into a place where discipleship can happen and where we can learn to believe, this time with a faith that has this-worldly redemptive power. That is to say, the Open Door is the new situation for many that demands we no longer remain distant from the human face of an unjust society.

This conversion from belief to discipleship, enabled by a new situation like the Open Door, is not simply a deepening of belief itself; it is not simply the transition from faith as mere intellectual assent to faith so strong and sure that one commits to, and centers her whole life on, trusting Jesus. That kind of robust belief is hastily labeled "discipleship" by some Christians. For instance, a few evangelical groups link it to an evangelism inspired by the concluding verses of Matthew's Gospel: "Go therefore and make disciples of all nations" (28:19).[30] Such an understanding of discipleship is incomplete, though, if it is abstracted from the social location necessary for the kind of transformation that accords with the kingdom Jesus inaugurates, embodies, and about which he teaches. If discipleship necessitates a new situation, this means that where we place our bodies matters. We learn through our bodies, our practice shapes our understanding, and so, like Jesus the homeless wanderer, the criminal on the cross, the members of the Open Door intentionally place their bodies with the guilty. "We are a community that stands with the guilty," says Ed, with those whom society despises and neglects, or in the words of Bonhoeffer, with "the outcast, the suspects . . . the reviled." For the Open Door, this includes the people we as a society find the most contemptible, those of whom we are most afraid: death-row inmates, many of whom are guilty of committing senseless or heinous acts, and people who are homeless, branded guilty by a society whose perspective is similar to that which denounced Jesus for befriending "tax collectors and sinners" (Luke 7:34) but whose offense is often little more than being poor and adopting practices that enable survival on the streets. As the following chapters will show, standing with the guilty should not be relegated to the Open Door's particular calling but must be central to discipleship today—the mark of a Christian—for no other practice will lead to a more truthful rendering of God, the good news, others, and ourselves.

The conversion from believer to disciple entails a change of position,

---

30. This is not to deny that many evangelicals are socially engaged. See, for example, Brian Steensland and Philip Goff, eds., *The New Evangelical Social Engagement* (New York: Oxford University Press, 2014). My point is simply that when Christians divorce discipleship from social location and from entering a new situation, it is incomplete.

namely from a privileged position that distances us from those whom society despises and neglects to a location that makes solidarity with them more possible. This conversion may happen only when we, in Ed's phrase, "reduce the distance" between ourselves and those who struggle under the dominant social order, when we step into a new situation and seek solidarity with others based on the life and teachings of Jesus. The conversion needed, then, is to nothing less than "radical" discipleship, that is, a discipleship that goes back to its roots and takes seriously Jesus as presented in the Gospels. The first disciples had no choice but to seriously attend to Jesus's way made manifest in his teachings and in a life that led to the cross and through the cross to abundant life in beloved community; otherwise, they could not have walked with him and thought of themselves as disciples. Thus, the way to reduce the distance between the first disciples and us—the way to literally walk with Jesus as they did—is to enter the Gospel narratives in real time through the liturgical calendar. By following Jesus through the narrative of the liturgical seasons, while simultaneously reducing distance through a new situation like the Open Door, we become formed as disciples who discover—not in the abstract but on the ground—what the content of the good news is, for us and for those now suffering under oppressive and unjust forces. In what follows, the gospel—the good news—will be explored through the lens, and performed within the theater, of homelessness and imprisonment, two realities that are of central concern to the witness of the Open Door and to the work of building beloved community.

# 2

---

# Advent

And Mary said,
"My soul magnifies the Lord,
and my spirit rejoices in God my Savior,
for he has looked with favor on the lowliness of his servant.
. . . . . . . . . . . . . . . . . . . . . . . . . . .
He has shown strength with his arm;
he has scattered the proud in the thoughts of their hearts.
He has brought down the powerful from their thrones,
and lifted up the lowly;
he has filled the hungry with good things,
and sent the rich away empty
. . . . . . . . . . . . . . . . . . . . . . . . . .
according to the promise he made to our ancestors."
—Luke 1:46–55

In those days John the Baptist appeared
in the wilderness of Judea, proclaiming,
"Repent, for the kingdom of heaven has come near."
—Matthew 3:1–2

We live, from a liturgical standpoint, in between. We are positioned in between what classical Christianity has called the first and second Advent, the coming of Christ into the world, initially as a vulnerable babe born in a manger because there was no room in the inn, whose life on the margins eventually leads to the cross, and then finally, at the end of time, who comes again in visible triumph over the powers of sin and death. We also live after the resurrection, the sign and promise of that ultimate victory, the new creation glimpsed in the here and now that will eventually gather into itself all things (Eph 1:10; Rev 21:5). Thus, we enter the movement from Advent to Pentecost always from the middle, with the knowledge of Christ crucified and risen constantly before us.

This means that no liturgical season is whole in and of itself. The boundary lines are fluid indeed as each points forward and backward, often in surprising ways, to central themes emphasized in the other, to themes like hope and repentance. As a prelude to a merry Christmas, for example, Advent is rarely viewed as a penitential season even though early Christianity and the traditional lectionary texts recognize that Christ's coming always leads to judgment—our judgment and redemption—for which we must prepare in hopeful and earnest expectation. Likewise, as the first season, Advent is rarely associated with eschatology, commonly defined as the doctrine of the last things (the second coming, final judgment, and consummation of the kingdom), yet as Jürgen Moltmann argues, because it concerns these realities, eschatology is essentially a doctrine of hope. Hope is no mere "epilogue" but "the key" in which Christian discipleship is set, "the glow" at "the dawn of an expected new day."[1] Because hope ignites active expectation, it belongs not at the end of liturgical reflection but at its beginning.

The dynamism inherent to this liturgical telling serves to inspire Christians toward continual seeking, toward a "faith seeking understanding" that perhaps challenges our embedded theologies, divesting us of static knowledge and reminding us that as narrative, the gospel cannot be possessed, it must be performed and discovered anew in each embodied retelling. The dynamic quality of the liturgical narrative mirrors a dynamic God on the move who, in the midst of the

---

1. Jürgen Moltmann, *Theology of Hope* (Minneapolis: Fortress Press, 1993), 16.

between, is always coming, always surprising, always disrupting what we thought we knew and understood, provided, as Jesus cautioned, we have the eyes to see and the ears to hear. Disciples then are people who respond to God's movement by courageously opening ourselves up to divine disruption, or, as Jesus says in the Beatitudes, by "hungering and thirsting" for the advent of God. We are to be a people who long.

As a season of expectant waiting, Advent trains Christians to be a people who yearn, but the vital question is: What are we longing for? What are we waiting for? Or better, how do we become people who long for the right things, those things that correspond with what God promises to bring?

As an adult, Advent has always been for me a time of longing, but the focus of this longing was my own personal need. Living through Advent at the Open Door, where the biblical texts are interpreted through the lens of homelessness or mass incarceration, expanded my longing and helped me see Advent more holistically, as a season with social and political significance. This chapter argues that the social and political character of Advent is made manifest through the great reversal Mary proclaims. For those of us who are privileged, this reversal involves the kind of repentance preached by John the Baptist, which inaugurates relational and social change. Relational change happens by building right relationships with those who are despised and oppressed and by taking responsibility for the social structures that cause them harm. Social change requires that we turn away from dominant attitudes about homelessness and mass incarceration, which overstate individual culpability, and recognize instead that these issues arise first and foremost from structural injustice—from decisions we have collectively made about how to order society. The chapter, therefore, concludes with a brief account of the structural nature of these realities and a call to overturn these social conditions that cause people harm.

Reading the Advent texts at the Open Door taught me that I will not know how to long for what is right unless I am alert, unless I acquire the eyes to see and the ears to hear, a development that comes only by walking through the Gospel narratives. In order to know where to direct our longing, we turn first to Mary. The promise of God that Mary proclaims is that God's coming brings about the "great reversal," an overturning of the established order, a disruption of unjust social arrangements and attitudes from which privileged people today effortlessly and often unwittingly benefit. Yet we who are privileged (perhaps because of our secure middle-class status in the wealthiest nation in history, our educational level, our gender and sexuality, or our white skin color) are ill equipped to think about our social location through the eyes of faith. We are ill equipped to think about the gospel—about Jesus's person and work—in social, political, and economic terms, or to think about sin as a structural, and not only a personal, reality. While we may know how to ask Jesus to come to us personally, to us and those dear to us, in order to meet our needs or heal our wounds, many of our churches have not formed us into people who know how to yearn for this promised kingdom—God's social order—in concrete ways "on earth as it is in heaven." This is exactly what the Gospel lectionary texts lead us to do, through Mary and her Magnificat, through John and his proclamation to repent.

## Mary and the Great Reversal

The Mary banner hangs in the Open Door's dining room and worship space on the first Sunday in Advent, occupying the cross's prominent position for the season. She is dark skinned, visibly pregnant, with her face turned toward Jerusalem, a city like most cities that manifests the dichotomies she sings about in her Magnificat: the place of the political, economic, and religious elites, the place of the powerless and destitute, the place where her yet-unborn son will die. "We welcome Mary into our hearts," says Nelia Kimborough, Open Door partner and resident artist, "and we pray that she will be one of our guides during this time of preparation."[2]

Although it may seem anachronistic to say, Mary is the first radical

2. Open Door Community Worship, author's audio recording, November 28, 2010.

disciple. As Catholic Mariology has long observed, she is the first person to say "yes" to Jesus. What makes her an especially important guide for us in our search for a discipleship that faithfully embodies the gospel is that she says yes with her body—she literally embodies the good news—and she risks guilt in doing so. She takes her place among the guilty, for she was pregnant and unmarried, a crime punishable by death. Her name means "rebellion," yet her rebellion stems not from the heroic zeal of a self-made revolutionary but from a pondering faith that, although "much perplexed" by what was unfolding before her, took seriously the reality of "a fulfillment" of God's promises in time. She rebels against the world as it is—she stands as a living contradiction to its unjust arrangements—simply by saying yes to God, yes to this historical possibility. Her yes includes not only verbal assent but also bodily participation in the movement of God, who, as her Magnificat proclaims, scatters the proud, brings down the powerful, lifts up the lowly, fills the hungry with good things, and sends the rich away empty "according to the promise."

Mary's Magnificat is a foundational text for Advent because it teaches us how to align our longings and strivings with the promises of God, and faithful alignment means yearning for "the powerful" to be "brought down" and "the lowly" to be "lifted up"—a leveling reminiscent of the "straight path" to be prepared for the Lord that John the Baptist proclaims in which "every valley will be filled and every mountain and hill will be made low" (Luke 3:4–5). The Magnificat describes the powerful and lowly in economic terms, associating them respectively with the "rich" and "hungry," yet economic realities and their inherent power relations—albeit integral to the Magnificat's message—do not exhaust its meaning. In a 1933 sermon on the text, almost a year into the Nazi reign, Bonhoeffer suggests that we discover the content of God's reversal by following the path of Christ's coming. "God is not ashamed of human lowliness but goes right into the middle of it," he declares; "God draws near . . . [to] the excluded, the powerless."

What people say is lost, God says is found; what people say is "condemned," God says is "saved." Where people say No! God says Yes! Where people turn their eyes away in indifference or arrogance, God gazes with a love that glows warmer there than anywhere else. Where people say something is despicable, God calls it blessed.[3]

The lowly in this rendering are people who are shut out of mainstream existence, condemned, and despised. They are, in Howard Thurman's famous phrase, "the disinherited,"[4] those who are up against a wall and see no way out, the people we dismiss or ignore, to whom we are cold and unresponsive, the people who are an affront to our values and moral sensibilities, the very people with whom the Open Door Community stands: those in prison and on death row, those who are homeless and hungry, most visible to us as beggars or even hustlers on the street, most threatening to us when their inebriation or mental illness bears striking resemblance to the demons Jesus cast out along his way. "There where our piety anxiously keeps its distance," Bonhoeffer says, "that is exactly where God loves to be."[5]

God's great reversal includes, then, an overturning of any dominating power that condemns, excludes, or oppresses. God's advent shatters any perspective, any conclusion drawn from distance that bolsters these powers, including, as we will see, an understanding of our own and others' innocence and guilt. God's advent overturns dominant social attitudes held by the religious and nonreligious alike—"he has scattered the proud in the thoughts of their hearts," Mary sings—and leads us to confront the ways in which we are complicit in systems of oppression and injustice, in structures like mass incarceration and homelessness. If this great reversal is not my longing, if I hesitate or downright refuse to construe Christ's coming in terms of systemic change and resistance to oppressive forces, Mary's Magnificat presses me to ask if I am among the satiated and satisfied, "the rich" who are "sent away empty" from this Advent season because

3. Dietrich Bonhoeffer, *London 1933-1935*, ed. Keith Clements, trans. Isabel Best, vol. 13, *Dietrich Bonhoeffer Works* (Minneapolis: Fortress Press, 2007), 344.
4. See Howard Thurman, *Jesus and the Disinherited* (Boston: Beacon Press, 1996).
5. Ibid., 343.

I am unable to hope for, and thus unable to receive, divine promise (Matt 7:7–8).

The Advent promise is addressed to people with concrete hopes that accord with God's great reversal. It is addressed to people like Kelly Gissendaner, one of the prison theology students who, seeking a manifestation of God's great reversal, the reversal of her sentence from death to life, shares the tangible hope of the psalmist, "I shall not die, but live, and declare the works of the Lord" (Ps 118:17), a verse that caught her attention in the testimony of a former death-row inmate whose sentence was overturned, a line with which she opens her final project, a ninety-day devotional entitled, "A Journey of Hope." In her 2011 graduation speech from the theology program, in the presence of prison staff and administrators, teachers, fellow students, family and friends, and her pen pal, our keynote speaker, Jürgen Moltmann, she describes how this hope is made concrete in her present, how, as Professor Moltmann writes in later correspondence, "God's future is not in chronological time but in the time of advent."[6] Kelly says,

> My task [in the biblical and theological courses] was to ask at every point what the teachings had to say about my social as well as my devotional life, my everyday private and public worship, my life here and now as well as my life in the "world to come." Only when I asked these questions could I fulfill the task of a good theologian—one who speaks and thinks about both the true God and real human beings in the real world.

> From the start of the theology class I felt this hunger. Never have I had a hunger like this. I became so hungry for theology, and what all the classes had to offer; you could call me a glutton. . . .

> There came a time when I thought the whole theology program would be pulled from me. You see, I am in a very unfortunate situation. . . . My reality is that I'm the only female on Georgia's death row; and while Warden Seabolt was at Metro State Prison, she gave me the opportunity to be a part of this wonderful program. Six months in, she left Metro to

6. Moltmann to Gissendaner, May 14, 2012. After studying Moltmann's theology in the Theology Foundations course, and knowing of his friendship with the Open Door Community and with me, Kelly reached out to Moltmann and began a friendship through letters. Their correspondence bore fruit for the whole theology certificate program when Moltmann sought to meet Kelly face to face. This opportunity allowed us to host him as the keynote speaker for our prison graduation that year. See also chapter 6.

a whole new administration. And my worst fears became my reality—I was pulled from the courses. I was taken from my theological community. Being pulled from the program devastated me as badly as if someone had just told me one of my appeals had been turned down.

Since I couldn't go to the theology class, the theology class came to me. The instructors came to me. Still, this was far from being ideal because now I had to have class and community through a gate. It was hard . . . but I pushed on. I pushed on because of that hunger. . . .

That gate at Metro was meant to keep everyone and everything separated from me. But that gate couldn't keep out the knowledge that I was so hungry for, nor friendship and community. And it sure couldn't keep out God.

The theology program has shown me that hope is still alive and that, despite a gate or a guillotine hovering over my head, I still possess the ability to prove that I am human. Labels on anyone can be notoriously misleading and unforgiving things. But no matter the label attached to me, I have the capacity and the unstoppable desire to accomplish something positive and have a lasting impact. . . .

. . . Even prison cannot erase my hope or conviction that the future is not settled for me, or anyone. . . . I have placed my hope in the God I now know, the God whose plans and promises are made known to me in the whole story of the life, death, and resurrection of Jesus Christ. . . .

The greatest journey I have ever taken . . . [is] through the theology program, which has affected all aspects of my life. . . . For a while now, and because I am on death row, I didn't have a plan for my life; but thanks to the theology program and the wonderful instructors, I now have a plan. Now I can do nothing but obtain all the knowledge I can through the Bible, theology, and great theologians like my friend Dr. Moltmann. . . .

. . . This journey will never end, and I've come to a point in my life where I've found out who I am, where I'm hoping to go, and what direction to take. In the theology program, I found people, my fellow students and instructors, who are on that same journey.

When we reduce distance between ourselves and those who hunger for liberation from imprisonment and sentences of death—when we reduce distance through friendship with fellow disciples and prison theologians like Kelly—we come to recognize the tangible consequence of the Advent proclamation.

Our temptation, though, is to sentimentalize Mary and spiritualize her Magnificat, to turn the "proud" and "lowly" into inner dispositions, to envision her, in the words of Bonhoeffer, as that "gentle, tender, dreamy Mary" so often portrayed in the portraits of our Western cultural imagination. This Mary does not make outward claims on us. Rather, the Christ incarnated in her womb comes into our hearts, this is all that matters, we say, and at the sight of Mary and her baby our hearts are gently warmed. Even if we recognize the gravitas of the situation, that the manger leads to the cross, we miss the sound of the prophetic woman and "her hard, strong, relentless hymn" if we relegate Advent to an inner affair of individual believers. Preaching on the Advent text, "Behold, I stand at the door and knock" (Rev 3:20), and linking it to Matthew 25:31–46 (two definitive texts for the Open Door's identity and mission), Bonhoeffer warns against divorcing Christ's coming from external circumstances and an engaged and costly response:

> Christ is standing at the door, knocking . . . "for I was hungry." . . . Jesus is at the door, knocking, in reality, asking you for help in the figure of the beggar, in the figure of the degenerate soul in shabby clothes. . . . Christ walks the earth . . . as your neighbor, as the person through whom Christ summons you, addresses you, makes claims on you. That is the most serious and most blessed part of the Advent message. . . .
>
> It may seem odd to see Christ in a countenance so close to us, but he did indeed say it. Those who avoid the serious reality of the Advent message cannot speak about Christ coming into their hearts. Those who do not learn from Christ's own coming that we are all brothers [and sisters] through Christ, through God, have understood nothing of the meaning of that coming.[7]

Our recognition of Christ's coming must be, like Mary's, rooted in bodily participation in "the beginning of a complete reversal, a new ordering of all things on earth."[8]

7. Dietrich Bonhoeffer, *Barcelona, Berlin, New York: 1928-1931*, ed. Clifford Green, trans. Douglas W. Stott, vol. 10, *Dietrich Bonhoeffer Works* (Minneapolis: Fortress Press, 2008), 545.

Bonhoeffer calls Mary's prophetic song "the most passionate, the wildest, and one might also say the most revolutionary Advent hymn that has ever been sung," one that is at odds with the idyllic and tamed tone of many of our carols.[9] Still, at times, we hear echoes of Mary's wild, revolutionary spirit break through our worship, for example in the nineteenth-century European hymn "O Holy Night," when churches throughout the Western world proclaim, "Truly He taught us to love one another / His law is love and His gospel is peace. / Chains shall He break for the slave is our brother; / And in His name all oppression shall cease." We hear this same wild, revolutionary spirit at the Open Door when we sing the spiritual "Mary Had a Baby" and listen for its double meaning, which correlates the salvation Jesus brings with liberation from slavery and racism, as the song connotes the Underground Railroad and more broadly the black freedom struggle itself: "Mary had a baby (yes, Lord) / Mary had a baby (Yes. My. Lord.) / Mary had a baby (YES! Lord) / The people keep a-comin' but the train done gone." Even amidst its playful tune, the Spiritual serves as a poignant reminder of the serious, world-shaping message of Mary's Magnificat: the coming of God ignites a reversal. As Jesus will later describe in his inaugural public address, this reversal is made manifest when the poor receive good news, prisoners are released, the blind recover sight, and the oppressed go free (Luke 4:18).

Although we have focused so far on the path the privileged must take to be made low, participation in God's reversal belongs just as much, as Mary's performance makes clear, to "the lowly" empowered by a revolutionary God. Mary's yes is an instant manifestation of God's great reversal, not only because she is "a lowly servant," as Murphy preaches—"a Nobody from Nowheresville . . . Mary from Nazareth in Galilee. . . . That's sort of like saying the angel came to . . . Tamika Smith in Hahira, Georgia,"[10]—but also because she is a woman whose

8. Bonhoeffer, London, 344.
9. Ibid., 342.
10. Open Door Community Worship, author's audio recording, November 28, 2010. A version is also printed in Hospitality 29, no. 9 (November–December 2010): 8–9. (Issues of Hospitality from February 2003 to the present may be found at http://opendoorcommunity.org/resources/hospitality. Accessed July 30, 2016.) Here Murphy is painting a different picture of Mary than is

simple obedience disrupts patriarchal power. The two scenes that open Luke's Gospel, the promise that Elizabeth will conceive a son named John and that Mary will conceive Jesus, comprise a story in which "the nobodies of ancient culture—women—play the primary role."[11] Elizabeth and Mary are protagonists not simply as child bearers, the common role of women in patriarchal societies, but also as theologians, prophets, and cocreators of the kingdom of God. Mary shows herself to be an "astute theologian" when she, as Murphy says, "model[s] the intentional practices of a disciple" asking with a faith seeking understanding, "How can this be?" (Luke 1:34), "What is God doing here? And what is God asking us to do?" In contrast to Zechariah, the priestly husband who is struck mute on account of his disbelief, Elizabeth recognizes with Mary that "nothing is impossible with God." Deeming Elizabeth a prophet, the text says that upon Mary's entrance she "was filled with the Holy Spirit and exclaimed with a loud cry" that here and now there is a fulfillment of the promises of God. Both women discover that they are participants in this fulfillment. Empowered by the feminine *Ruach*—"the holy, creative Spirit of God" that "brooded over the waters of the earth, separating land from water, darkness from light" and that now "moves over the waters of the womb" of each woman—Mary becomes the agent of the new creation and Elizabeth, the agent of the Spirit who prepares the way. As Ched Myers, biblical scholar, activist, and close friend of the Open Door, observes, "When the angel of the Lord visits, the first thing that happens is the silencing of the male clergy and the springing forth of the voice and songs of women!"[12] God's advent orders life anew.

If we are to reduce the distance between our twenty-first-century expressions of faith and these first disciples, if we are to enter the Gospel narratives in order to learn to believe, we must ask where we find ourselves in the overturning of powers about which Mary sings. "If we want to be a part of this event of Advent . . . we cannot just

often depicted. Catholic feminist theologians, for example, criticize the church's image of Mary as submissive to patriarchal power.
11. Ibid.
12. Ibid.

sit there like a theater audience and enjoy all the lovely pictures," Bonhoeffer says in that 1933 sermon. "We ourselves [must] be caught up in this action, the reversal of all things . . . [and] become actors on this stage."[13] In order to become agents, though, we must be clear about our social location in this unfolding drama. When our position and circumstance numbers us with the privileged, the powerful or rich, we would do well to participate willingly in this great reversal by following the path of Jesus's advent—reducing distance between ourselves and those who are oppressed and marginalized. When we are the ones hard pressed, be it on account of intentional solidarity or some dimension of our own identity at odds with the prevailing order, we would do well to tune our ears to the primary message of the Coming One, proclaimed to Mary and sown into the base of her Open Door banner: be not afraid. By casting ourselves honestly in this unfolding drama, we take seriously Mary, her song of praise, and the God to whom she sings.

## John and the Proclamation to Repent

The overturning of the social order about which Mary sings requires that those of us who are privileged heed John's call to repent—to make way for the advent of God's kingdom embodied in Jesus Christ. The connection between Mary and John is established in the Gospel of Luke early in the story, after Mary receives the angel's news and travels with haste to see Elizabeth. As soon as Elizabeth heard the sound of Mary's greeting, "the child in [her] womb," already filled with the Holy Spirit, "leaped for joy" (Luke 1:15, 44). Mary and John not only share the opening act of this great drama, they also share the same spirit-filled proclamation about the kingdom. The coming of God's social order in Jesus ignites a reversal, Mary sings, and participation in this new order, John announces, necessitates repentance in accordance with the kingdom established and made known in Jesus. Jesus is completely identified with this new social order. "The kingdom of heaven has come near," John proclaims about Jesus and Jesus proclaims about

13. Bonhoeffer, *London 1933–1935*, 344.

himself after John's arrest (Matt 3:2; 4:17). "Bear fruit worthy of repentance," John continues in Luke 3:8, fruit born, for example, from abiding by Jesus's Sermon on the Mount, teachings that echo John's wilderness preaching. "Whoever has two coats must share with anyone who has none; and whoever has food must do likewise," John says in response to the crowd's inquiry about the nature of these repentant acts (Luke 3:11). Jesus commands his disciples to preach the same message, and he offers a similar depiction of what this entails, one characterized by a number of tangible reversals that have serious social significance for the recipients: "As you go, proclaim the good news. 'The kingdom of heaven has come near.' Cure the sick, raise the dead, cleanse the lepers, cast out demons" (Matt 10:7–8). Yet when John is in prison, he begins to wonder if this great reversal is taking effect and if Jesus is "the one who is to come, or are we to wait for another?" He sends his disciples to find Jesus and ask him, to which Jesus replies, "Go and tell John what you hear and see: the blind receive their sight, the lame walk, the lepers are cleansed, the deaf hear, the dead are raised, and the poor have good news brought to them" (Matt 11:2–6). The kingdom of God is near, John proclaimed, but, as his prison restlessness reveals and as Jesus affirms, it must be made manifest here and now. In an Open Door Bible study on this text, after a Tuesday-morning soup kitchen, Nelia asks us to add to the reply, to share what we heard and saw that day that was a sign of good news:

> "I saw pallets on the floor for twenty-five men we invited in to stay the night."
> "I saw the cold and shivering come in and be warm and the hungry come in and be fed."
> "I saw thick, almost stew-like portions of soup being served. I saw abundance."
> "I saw a closet full of shoes ready to be given away that actually smelled good!"

"All of these," Nelia concludes, "are only tiny, tiny signs of the good news, but it is what we can do as we work toward beloved community. It is how we declare that 'God always keeps God's promises' and 'judges in favor of the oppressed.'"[14]

With John the Baptist as a central Advent figure in our lectionary texts, the season of Advent calls us to repent, but John proclaims repentance in an unfamiliar tune. Through their chorus, "Repent, for the kingdom of God is at hand," John and Jesus grant repentance a social and political character. Although we commonly think of repentance in relation to individual morality—"Get right with God," warns revivalist religion—nothing in the Gospel texts connects repentance with individual sin absent a broader social context. In no place does it refer to an individual's exclusive relationship with God; rather repentance in the Synoptic Gospels and Acts concerns human relations with one another. Describing in detail this "radically political character of Advent," twentieth-century activist and theologian William Stringfellow writes,

> The repentance of which John the Baptist preaches is no private or individualistic effort, but . . . is related to the reconciliation of the whole of creation. . . . The eschatological reference is quite concrete. John the Baptist is warning the rulers of this world, and the principalities and powers as well as the common people, of the impending judgment of the world . . . signaled in the coming of Christ.

> There seems to be evidence in the Luke account about John the Baptist that indicates that some of the people, notably the ecclesiastical officials, did not comprehend his preaching or if they did, they did not heed it. . . . Yet it is equally edifying that the political authorities, represented as Herod the tetrarch, *do understand* the political scope of John's admonition . . . enough to imprison John and, subsequently, subject him to terrible interrogation, torture, and decapitation (a typical fate for political prisoners now, as then). That, in such circumstances, Jesus makes John's preaching his own and instructs his disciples accordingly, foreshadows his own arrest, trial, humiliation, and crucifixion, and for that matter, the Acts of the Apostles.[15]

John's advent message calls "ecclesiastical officials" and lay religious folk to make their social and political thoughts and actions accord

14. Open Door Community Bible Study, author's audio recording, November 30, 2010. Nelia paraphrases Psalm 146 as adapted by Murphy Davis and printed in *Hospitality* 29, no. 8 (September–October 2010).
15. William Stringfellow, *A Keeper of the Word: Selected Writings of William Stringfellow*, ed. Bill Wylie Kellermann (Grand Rapids: Eerdmans, 1994), 386.

with the kingdom of God, which is inaugurated and defined by Jesus's person and work. John's proclamation is integral for understanding the whole of the Gospel narratives since the gospel is primarily concerned with this coming kingdom. Because John's preaching of repentance is a call to align one's thoughts and actions with the new social order made known through the life-act and teachings of Jesus, the fruit of repentance results in a change in the way people think about and view others, especially the despised and marginalized. As the Open Door observes, this is signaled by the fact that John calls people out to the wilderness—to the margins of society—to respond to the call to repent. Being baptized by John places disciples at the margins, and, as a continual outworking of baptism, repentance keeps disciples there. The impetus behind the repentance John proclaims, then, is political and public concern for social flourishing rather than egocentric and private concern for one's own moral status before God. As a faithful response to God's advent, it is, as Bonhoeffer writes from prison, "not thinking first of one's own needs, questions, sins, and fears" but following the path of Jesus Christ, the human being who exists for others.[16]

Like Stringfellow, Bonhoeffer recognizes that those of us who are religious have a hard time comprehending and heeding John's message, perhaps because we inhabit cheap grace and understand ourselves already as forgiven sinners but not as those in need of constant reawakening. Perhaps because we are unaware that repentance plays a crucial role in the drama of redemption and, as such, is fundamentally not a condemning word from which to cower but a word of hope to wholeheartedly embrace. For Bonhoeffer, God's continual coming brings continual judgment, but it is a judgment rooted in redeeming love for us and for the world. Disciples who wish to live by costly grace alone must prepare for God's continual coming by being ready to hear and receive the hard word of God's transforming love. In a 1940 Advent meditation on Isaiah 9, Bonhoeffer says,

---

16. Bonhoeffer, *Letters and Papers* (Fortress Press), 480.

[God's] judgment does not spare the community of the faithful—no, it is precisely here that he exercises his strictest judgment, and the church community proves itself to be his in that it does not withdraw from this judgment but submits to it. Only where Jesus judges sin can he bestow new righteousness. His kingdom is to be a kingdom of righteousness, not of self-righteousness but of divine righteousness, which can be established only by means of the judgment of sin. The strength of this kingdom will be that it rests on justice. . . . A kingdom of peace and righteousness, humanity's unfulfilled desire, has dawned with the birth of the divine child. We are called into this kingdom.[17]

The context of Isaiah 9 suggests that, for Bonhoeffer, preparation includes openness to the painful reality that the church may be among the oppressors of whom the prophet speaks:

> The people who walked in darkness
> have seen a great light;
> those who lived in a land of deep darkness,
> on them light has shined.
> . . . . . . . . . . . . .
> For the yoke of their burden . . .
> the rod of the oppressor,
> you have broken
> . . . . . . . . . . . . .
> for unto us a child is born.

It includes openness to the painful reality that the distance I have kept from people who live in the deep darkness of an abandoned building or a prison cell has made me an unwitting maintainer of an unjust status quo.

Central to Bonhoeffer's understanding of the church community, though, is that it is the body that actively accepts God's judgment, in his words, that accepts guilt and takes responsibility for sin, suffering, and injustice through repentant activity in public life. Bonhoeffer even goes so far as to equate discipleship with repentance: Repentance is continual movement along "the path that Jesus walks" and continual transformation fueled by "living fully" in life's complexities, taking

17. Dietrich Bonhoeffer, *Conspiracy and Imprisonment: 1940-1945*, ed. Mark S. Brocker, trans. Lisa E. Dahill, vol. 16, *Dietrich Bonhoeffer Works* (Minneapolis: Fortress Press, 2006), 616.

seriously "the sufferings of God in the world." "This is *metanoia*," he says, "and this is how one becomes a human being, a Christian."[18] For Bonhoeffer, as well as for the Open Door, the suffering of God in the world are the sufferings of those in need, the sufferings of those our society excludes and condemns, like the homeless beggar or the convicted criminal; for God suffers in the world through Jesus in the stranger's guise. As the definitive activity of the Christian, repentance arises from privileged disciples acknowledging their complicity in, and accepting responsibility for, societal structures, forces, and attitudes that bar these people from the abundant life of beloved community. As they inhabit repentance, privileged disciples find entrance into beloved community as well and are given a vocation of incomparable worth. Through creative and courageous repentance in public life, they participate in the great transformation proclaimed by John. By accepting God's judgment and taking responsibility for the conditions that harm fellow human beings, they participate in God's concrete redemption of this world.

## The Interconnection of Personal and Social Transformation

When Christians respond to John's call to repent and make a straight path for God's new social order, we also make way for personal transformation otherwise unavailable to us. Advent reveals the intrinsic relationship between social and personal transformation, and this Advent truth animates three of the Open Door's most trusted guides—Bonhoeffer, Dorothy Day, and King—each of whom place personal responsibility for others at the center of discipleship. For Bonhoeffer, personal and social transformation are interwoven since repentance includes taking responsibility for societal sin and injustice. Bonhoeffer roots this responsibility precisely in Jesus's own person and work, namely in Jesus's "vicarious representative action" for the world. Jesus is the representative of humanity and, as such, he takes responsibility for others, most vividly on the cross, where he directs

---

18. Bonhoeffer, *Letters and Papers* (Fortress Press), 480, 486. See also Jennifer M. McBride, *The Church for the World: A Theology of Public Witness* (New York: Oxford University Press, 2011), 63–65.

God's judgment away from others and toward himself as he bears humanity's sin. As followers of Jesus and as the body of Christ, the discipleship community is also "required to act on behalf of others," since, as Bonhoeffer writes from prison, "the church exists for others."[19] Bonhoeffer's theology helps us see, then, that the Advent proclamation "Repent!" is at once a command for responsible action. The repentance preached by John happens when disciples take responsibility for others. Responsible action should not be misconstrued as charity work as we have come to understand charity, a voluntary addition to a life of faith that makes us feel like we have done some extra good in the world. Rather, a life rooted in responsible action is the only faithful and logical response to John's urgent Advent command: Repent, because the great reversal is at hand! Repent and create community with those whom we have outcast! Repent, because the great transformation has already begun.

Just as Bonhoeffer connects responsible action to repentance and argues it is the discipleship community's definitive mission, Dorothy Day and Peter Maurin also place responsibility at the center of Catholic Worker hospitality. Their core conviction that we must assume personal responsibility for others (that we are our brother and sister's keeper) arises from personalism, a philosophy rooted in the affirmation of the intrinsic value of every human being made in the image of God. Just as responsibility rooted in repentance is animated by an acute understanding of one's own sin in relation to others and does not excuse oneself from responsible action by pointing instead to the sin and responsibility of other human beings, responsibility rooted in personalism also avoids turning other people's sinfulness into an excuse for our own inaction. Christian personalism defines other human beings not first as fallen but as created (which is, of course, the biblically appropriate order), not first as sinful but as valued with inherent worth by a loving Creator. Theological thinking that does the opposite—that prioritizes human fallenness over created

---

19. Dietrich Bonhoeffer, *Ethics*, ed. Clifford J. Green, trans. Reinhard Krauss et al., vol. 6, *Dietrich Bonhoeffer Works* (Minneapolis: Fortress Press, 2005), 257–59; Bonhoeffer, *Letters and Papers* (Touchstone), 382. See also McBride, *Church for the World*, 81–86, 126–29.

worth by reasoning, for example, that either the fall has erased God's image completely (Luther) or distorted it to such an extent that it is hidden (Calvin)—has serious ethical implications. When we do not consciously affirm the intrinsic value of other human beings, it is easier to neglect their needs and justify dehumanizing acts against them, especially if we deem them guilty and ourselves relatively innocent.

The philosophy of Christian personalism embraced by the Catholic Worker was introduced to the movement by Peter Maurin, who drew from the writings of French philosopher Emmanuel Mounier (1905–1950). Mounier calls personalism "a philosophy of engagement" and argues that Christians have a responsibility to play an active role in history even as they believe in an ultimate reality beyond history.[20] Sharing Bonhoeffer's analysis of sin's social character, Mounier writes, "Modern narcissism has reduced sin to an individual preoccupation. It has placed stress on the tarnishing of one's image of oneself," but human beings are not isolated individuals. "Personal man [sic] is not desolate," he says. "He is a man surrounded, on the move, under summons" and so must be ready to respond.[21] For Day and Maurin, personalism was a third way beyond capitalism's rugged individualism on the one hand and communism's numbing collectivism on the other. Although it prioritizes personal relationships and transformed hearts, personalism is distinct from an individualistic orientation toward the world. Whereas the bourgeois individualist lavishes in her own accumulation and comfort while demanding that suffering human beings be self-sufficient (pull themselves up by their bootstraps, as the saying goes), the personalist "has a social doctrine of the common good," and gives of herself personally like Jesus commands his followers to do in the Sermon on the Mount and through the works of mercy found in Matthew 25.[22]

While Day and Maurin incorporate French personalism into their

---

20. Emmanuel Mounier, *Be Not Afraid: A Denunciation of Despair*, trans. Cynthia Rowland (New York: Sheed & Ward, 1962), 135, quoted in Mark Zwick and Louise Zwick, *The Catholic Worker Movement: Intellectual and Spiritual Origins* (New York: Paulist Press, 2005), 98.
21. Mounier, *Be Not Afraid*, 132, 150, quoted in Zwick and Zwick, *Catholic Worker Movement*, 104, 110.
22. Zwick and Zwick, *Catholic Worker Movement*, 113.

reading of the Gospel narratives, King draws on a similar school of thought, Boston personalism, to shape his civil rights ministry. The philosophy he embraced in seminary and more fully as a doctoral student at Boston University reinforced what Rufus Burrow calls his "homespun personalism," those familial and ecclesial convictions about God's justice and human worth that permeated the black church tradition in which he was raised. King frames his entire ministry, from Montgomery to Memphis, around personalist principles that he learned in the academy and at home, specifically four interrelated biblical truths about God, human beings, and community: (1) God is personal and loving, (2) human beings have inherent dignity because they are made in the image of this God, (3) the nature of human beings is communal and social, and (4) injustice and social evil must be resisted by creating conditions for community that align with the kingdom of God.[23] As a leader of an oppressed people, King understood that affirming the inherent dignity of people includes oneself, and so members of marginalized groups must be empowered like Mary to be agents in the great reversal by standing up for themselves and insisting that they be respected as human beings "created in freedom, for freedom."[24] For King, this means concretely affirming the sacredness of people by eradicating the conditions that demean their worth.[25]

King's treatment of the story of the Good Samaritan (Luke 10:25–37), which spans multiple sermons and speeches, demonstrates this conviction: disciples must hold simultaneous concern for individual people and the social structures they inhabit. At the sanitation strike on the eve of his assassination, in poignantly prophetic words that speak to his own decision to come to Memphis, King highlights the need for costly personal engagement. He says of the man who fell among thieves and was left by the roadside that maybe the Levite didn't stop because he was on his way "to organize a 'Jericho Road

---

23. See Rufus Burrow Jr., *God and Human Dignity: The Personalism, Theology, and Ethics of Martin Luther King, Jr.* (Notre Dame: University of Notre Dame Press, 2006), 80.
24. Ibid., 83.
25. Ibid., 69–70.

Improvement Association'" and he "felt it was better to deal with the problem from the causal root, rather than to get bogged down with an individual effort." Maybe the Levite was afraid of getting caught up in a messy and dangerous situation. "And so the first question the Levite asked was, "'If I stop to help this man, what will happen to me?' But then the Good Samaritan came by. And he reversed the question: 'If I do not stop to help this man, what will happen to him? That's the question.'"[26] A year before, while drawing on the same biblical passage, King demonstrated the interconnection of personal and structural realities, showing how deep-rooted personal engagement cannot help but lead to unsettling questions about the dominant social order. "On the one hand we are called to play the Good Samaritan on life's roadside," King says, but "one day we must come to see that the whole Jericho road must be transformed so that men and women will not be constantly beaten and robbed as they make their journey on life's highway. True compassion is more than flinging a coin at a beggar; it is not haphazard and superficial. It comes to see that the edifice which produces beggars needs restructuring."[27] Given the intertwined nature of all injustice—the interconnectedness, for example, of poverty, racism, mass incarceration, and homelessness—King calls for a radical restructuring of our society and, interestingly, he casts this need for societal transformation in terms of personal conversion, in terms of Nicodemus, who had to be "born again." Like Nicodemus, King proclaims that our nation's whole structure must change. "America," he says, "you must be born again!"[28]

Admittedly, it is hard for most American Christians—especially those of us who have grown up in white churches—to wrap our minds around King's imagery above. It is hard for most of us to think in terms of collective guilt and collective redemption, even as the Hebrew prophets characteristically spoke in these terms, and even as every element of Christian faith is, arguably, communal in character (from original sin, to Jesus as human representative, to the church

26. King, *Testament of Hope*, 284–85.
27. Ibid., 241.
28. Ibid., 251.

community, to the kingdom of God). In *Blacks and Whites in Christian America*, sociologists Jason E. Shelton and Michael O. Emerson demonstrate this difficulty by showing that white and black Christians understand Christian faith through two fundamentally different perspectives, which are shaped by each group's relationship to the history of oppression in this country. White Christians, who are beneficiaries of racial and economic injustice, tend to hold an individualistic orientation that defines personal merit (individual choices, work ethic, and character) as the most significant determinant of personal success, while black Christians, who are survivors and victims of oppression, tend to hold a structural orientation that emphasizes social factors, like the way society's institutions, policies, and laws provide some people with systematic advantages and some people with systematic disadvantages. As Shelton and Emerson show, the vast majority of Americans hold an individualistic worldview. It is the nation's "dominant ideology" that makes it hard for Christians who benefit from social, economic, and political structures to hold ourselves accountable for the injustices that plague our society.[29] Our extreme individualism makes it difficult, in other words, for most American Christians to understand repentance and responsibility in the way Bonhoeffer, Day, and King urge us to do. When we deny our complicity, though, we deny our responsibility to respond with concrete action. We deny the need for real change, perhaps because we know it will surely exact a personal cost.

Just as Mary's Magnificat witnesses to the character of God's great reversal, announcing its unfolding in our midst and thus challenging any status quo that opposes it, so too is John the Baptist's proclamation to repent a call for change in social attitudes and arrangements and in the structures that maintain them. Mary's Magnificat and John's proclamation, then, are a harmonious call for nothing less than the establishment of beloved community. When we ask Jesus to come into our lives at Advent, what we await, according to the biblical witness, is

29. Jason E. Shelton and Michael O. Emerson, *Blacks and Whites in Christian America: How Racial Discrimination Shapes Religious Convictions* (New York: New York University Press, 2012), 172–75.

change in society and in ourselves. When we ask Jesus to come, God's advent asks us to prepare the way—to yearn and work—for tangible structural and relational change.

## The Great Transformation of Jericho Road: Advent and Prison

As I leave the prison every Friday afternoon, a litany plays on a loop in my mind, a first attempt to process the details of the women's incarceration I was privy to that day. It is a lament for our collective apathy and an expression of helplessness over the magnitude of the crisis: *What have we done? What have we done? Dear God, what have we done?* At first it is just a murmur, background noise to the more immediate experience of fullness and joy—the lingering laughter from a playful good-bye, the echo of the rich insights of class discussion, the ease and comfort of being among friends and the organic growth of those friendships over time. Like a distant drum, like a ticking clock, the litany's steady beat follows me the rest of the night. Some nights, I sit alone in my apartment allowing myself to be absorbed into its sound. I sit still. I cry. I pray. I owe it to them, I think, to feel the full weight, to let the pain sink deep into my bones, to take a good look at all I have observed inside the prison and let it become an undeniable part of me. Other nights, I meet up with family or friends. I move on to the rhythmic beat; the women remain. Over wine or margaritas, my dinner companions ask about my day, and I feel the situation out. Too much talk of prisons can lead to uncomfortable silence and an abrupt change of subject, I've found, yet I am fortunate. Most of my relationships in Atlanta have been forged through common work, activism or scholarship on topics of shared concern, and so I am likely to find a sympathetic ear. Some nights in particular, a friend makes room for lengthy reflection. I am allowed to grope for adequate and truthful words, and as I hear them spoken, I choke back tears. What I feel is grief. What I feel is rage. *What have we done—dear God what have we done?*

"If only there were evil people somewhere insidiously committing evil deeds, and it were necessary only to separate them from the rest of us and destroy them," writes Aleksandr Solzhenitsyn, a decorated hero in Stalin's Red Army who later became a prisoner in one of the regime's labor camps. "But the line dividing good and evil cuts through the heart of every human being. And who is willing to destroy a piece of his own heart?" With a description that envelops people in prison as well as people who are free, he continues,

> During the life of any heart this line keeps changing place; sometimes it is squeezed one way by exuberant evil and sometimes it shifts to allow enough space for good to flourish. One and the same human being is, at various ages, under various circumstances, a totally different human being. At times he is close to being a devil, at times to sainthood. But his name doesn't change, and to that name we ascribe the whole lot, good and evil.[30]

As Solzhenitsyn's life powerfully portrays, human beings may be both oppressor and victim, people who have sinned against others and people who have been sinned against at different points and in varying social relations. We may readily affirm this truth if it is cast in the language of individual and interpersonal sins—we sin and are sinned against. But there is something about the designations "victim" and "oppressor" that we resist, that seem too extreme, especially if the former (victim of social harm) is applied to convicted criminals and the latter (maintainer of an oppressive status quo) is applied to ourselves. Even if we affirm the Apostle Paul's words, "all have sinned and fall short of the glory of God," the temptation is strong to divide the world into dualisms, the innocent and the guilty, believers and unbelievers, good people and "evil people somewhere insidiously committing evil deeds." Our prepackaged and straightforward conversion narratives are partly to blame, for they leave little room for Solzhenitsyn's insight (made after his own conversion to Christianity) that we may find ourselves on the side of grave evil even given faith in Christ. What is missing is an understanding of the structural reality of sin that holds in its grasp "believers" and "unbelievers" alike. For we participate in forces of oppression when our everyday living allows those social

---

30. Aleksandr Solzhenitsyn, *The Gulag Archipelago* (New York: HarperPerennial, 1991), 1:168.

conditions to thrive that, as Solzhenitsyn says above, divide and destroy human beings. The evidence that the line in my heart keeps shifting is the extent to which I actively care.

These forces of oppression act as a press, suffocating those who bear their weight. As feminist theorist Marilyn Frye writes, "Presses are used to mold things or flatten them or reduce them in bulk. . . . Something pressed is something caught between or among forces and barriers which are so related to each other that jointly they restrain, restrict or prevent the thing's mobility." These forces and barriers are not occasional and therefore avoidable but are related systematically; they "exist in complex tension with every other, penalizing or prohibiting all of the available options." Oppression, in other words, is the experience "of being caged in."[31]

Frye's description of oppression bears striking resemblance to imprisonment—restrain, immobilize, penalize, cage in—although this is not to say that removing someone from society for a time who has done great harm to others or themselves is inherently oppressive. Indeed, some of the women I have come to know in prison say that their lives needed to be interrupted. The vital question, though, is whether the conditions under which the intervention takes place are empowering, respectful, and healing. Some unwelcomed restraints are imposed for our benefit, like traffic regulations, to use a minor example; they do not reduce well-being but allow it to flourish more fully. Other barriers diminish and cause irrevocable damage to an entire group of people, and since "we are caught up in an inescapable network of mutuality," as King famously said, they harm society as a whole. The factors that have led to the phenomenon we call mass incarceration and the dehumanizing conditions that accompany the warehousing of an extraordinary number of human beings are such barriers. Taken together, the injustice is twofold: the enormous growth of imprisonment over the last forty years is based on laws and policies that have targeted a specific group of people, and the destructive

31. Marilyn Frye, "Oppression," in *Privilege: A Reader*, ed. Michael S. Kimmel and Abby L. Ferber (Boulder, CO: Westview Press, 2003), 14–16.

conditions of prison violate the inherent worth of human beings. As an oppressive system, mass incarceration is a structural sin for which God's advent demands disciples accept guilt and responsibility and work to overturn.

### Mass Incarceration and the War on Drugs

Legal scholar Michelle Alexander and public interest lawyer Bryan Stevenson have shown separately and in extensive detail that mass incarceration is the primary form of institutionalized racism today and that it exacts harm not only on people of color but also on poor whites who are affected by policies that were created with racial minorities in mind. Mass incarceration is, in Stevenson's words, one of the "four institutions in American history that have shaped our approach to race and justice but remain poorly understood." Depicting the progression from slavery to lynching and the "reign of terror" following Reconstruction, to the convict leasing system, to Jim Crow segregation, to the "War on Drugs" and mass incarceration, he writes, "The extreme overrepresentation of people of color, the disproportionate sentencing of racial minorities, the targeted prosecution of drug crimes in poor communities, the criminalization of new immigrants and undocumented people, the collateral consequences of voter disenfranchisement, and the barriers to re-entry can only be fully understood through the lens of our racial history."[32]

Likewise, in her widely acclaimed study of the War on Drugs and the consequent growth of imprisonment over the last forty years, Alexander argues that mass incarceration is the new Jim Crow, a form of social control over people of color and the poor that confines them to a parallel universe of second-class citizenship both in prison and after release. Alexander further argues that the enormity of the crisis demands a social movement comparable to the civil rights struggle for racial and economic justice in the mid-twentieth century. On the

---

32. Bryan Stevenson, *Just Mercy: A Story of Justice and Redemption* (New York: Spiegel & Grau, 2015), 301. See pages 298–301 for a brief explanation of "the four institutions in American history that have shaped our approach to race and justice."

surface, her claim may appear outlandish, but it is one that the Open Door Community has been making for decades, as shown by their play on words that designates the criminal justice system, "the criminal control system." Upon the 2010 release of *The New Jim Crow*, Murphy excitedly shared that Alexander backs up with extensive legal and statistical analysis the basic conclusions the Open Door had come to after decades of listening to the testimonies of inmates they either befriended in prison or shared residential community with after prison, that is, after becoming acquainted with autobiographical and case details like those of my friend Natalie.

I met Natalie shortly after she came to state prison at the age of fifty-six, after a lifetime of drug addiction that sought to bury the pain of childhood sexual abuse. She was convicted of felony murder. The friend she popped pills with died of an overdose after Natalie had returned home one night, and the State argued, without providing conclusive evidence, that out of all the drugs her friend consumed that day, it was the OxyContin pill given to her by Natalie that killed her. Natalie was committing a felony, taking illegal drugs, when her friend died. Natalie's sixtieth birthday is a painful reminder of the tragic irony of her conviction. Her life needed interruption, and she is grateful to be drug free and clean. Now full of life and humor, full of theological insight she never knew she had, full of love for her eighty-two-year-old mother, sister, daughter, and grandchildren, she has awakened from the haze of addiction into the haze of prison, where she will likely live out the rest of the time she has as a physically strong and mentally healthy person. As she turns sixty, she cannot help but think of turning seventy, her first chance to come up for parole, fourteen years into her sentence. Yet even this is unlikely because the State wants at least twenty-one to thirty years for a murder conviction—decades of time wasted, time lost, time that she desperately wants to spend with her grandchildren.

The details of her case—targeted and exclusive blame, harsh and lengthy sentencing—are not anomalies for the people lacking economic means or the people of color who fill our prisons. With drug convictions accounting for the majority of the fivefold increase, the United States has the highest rate of incarceration in the world, expanding from fewer than 350,000 individuals in 1972 to over 2.3 million today, with a shocking 7 million Americans (1 in every 31 adults) under the system's control, whether behind bars, on probation, or on parole. Those under the control of the system are disproportionately black and poor, even though people of all races and ethnicities use and sell drugs at similar rates. For the primary targets of the drug war have been inner-city populations, not the white middle class. "People of color are ... no more likely to be guilty of drug crimes and many other offenses than whites," but as Alexander demonstrates in great detail throughout her book, "racial disparities" are present "at every stage in the criminal justice process," from roundup to conviction to attempted reentry into society.[33] As a historical look at crime and punishment shows, sentences are far more severe, and alternatives to incarceration far more rare, once behaviors become associated with populations of color. Alternatives like rehabilitation programs, probation, and community service are more readily available for crimes like drunk driving, associated with the white middle class, which allow the defendants to remain functional people in society. This "speaks volumes," Alexander argues, about "who is viewed as disposable—someone to be purged from the body politic—and who is not."[34] Seeking, like Solzhenitsyn above, to paint a more complex and truthful picture of innocence and guilt, Alexander writes of the primary targets in the War on Drugs, "It is far more convenient to imagine that a majority of young African American men in urban areas freely chose a life of crime than to accept the real possibility that their lives were structured in such a way that virtually guaranteed their early admission into a system from which they can never escape."[35]

During the War on Drugs, funding for law enforcement all but

33. Michelle Alexander, *The New Jim Crow: Mass Incarceration in the Age of Colorblindness* (New York: The New Press, 2010), 17.
34. Ibid., 201.
35. Ibid., 179.

replaced funding for drug treatment, prevention, and education, thereby shifting drug addiction and abuse from a medical condition—a public health concern—to a matter of "law and order," a seemingly race-neutral slogan that nevertheless has its roots in the Jim Crow South where it served as a battle cry against desegregation. Every politician, no matter the political ilk, has had to demand "law and order" and prove that they are "tough on crime" to get elected.[36] Referenced by Republican president Richard Nixon in the late 1960s and formally announced by Ronald Reagan in 1982, the drug war was escalated by Democratic president Bill Clinton a decade later, with Clinton's tough-on-crime policies resulting in the largest number of federal and state prisoners in American history.[37] Alexander summarizes,

> The launching of the War on Drugs and the initial construction of the new system required the expenditure of tremendous political initiative and resources. Media campaigns were waged; politicians blasted "soft" judges and enacted harsh sentencing laws; poor people of color were vilified. The system now, however, requires very little maintenance or justification. . . . This extraordinary circumstance—unheard of in the rest of the world—is treated here in America as a basic fact of life, as normal as separate water fountains were just a half century ago.[38]

"This is the new normal," Alexander writes, the status quo against which Mary's Magnificat sings.

The War on Drugs was an integral component of "a broader ideological, political, and economic shift" in the 1980s away from purported concern for individual offenders and toward the development of what is now known as the "prison-industrial complex."[39] Ideologically, retribution became the dominant framework

---

36. In recent months, politicians have begun to speak in terms of prison reform alongside messages of law and order. It remains to be seen how this rhetoric will translate into change.
37. *Harper's Magazine* reporter Dan Baum recently published a frank quote from President Nixon's policy advisor, John Ehrlichman, who admitted in 1994 that the Nixon administration invented the War on Drugs "to disrupt" black communities. See Dan Baum, "Legalize It All: How to Win the War on Drugs," *Harper's Magazine*, April 14, 2016, http://tinyurl.com/jbvgdru.
38. Alexander, *New Jim Crow*, 176.
39. Megan Sweeney, *Reading Is My Window: Books and the Art of Reading in Women's Prisons* (Chapel Hill: University of North Carolina Press, 2010), 40.

justifying punishment, all but replacing previous theories centered on rehabilitation and deterrence. Retributive justice—defined as "repayment in kind" or "giving back to someone what he or she deserves"—centers on the idea that punishment is inherently just. Crime upsets the moral order, so punishment is required to restore the moral balance. Rooted in the principle of proportionality, the retributive theory is meant to ensure that the punishment fits the crime, but in practice, retribution has too easily morphed into revenge. In the 1980s, retribution led to draconian practices of harsh and lengthy sentencing not only for drug-related crimes but also for a variety of nonviolent and violent offenses. Grounded in the notion that punishment qua punishment is justified and thereby good, retributive ideology has led to an ever-increasing deprivation of the resources in prison that could foster some degree of agency, self-respect, healing, and growth—like education, recreation, therapy, nutritious food, and dignified work.

In contrast, the main strength of rehabilitation and deterrence theories was their acknowledgment that punishment is not a good thing in and of itself, since it is the deliberate infliction of pain. These utilitarian theories were based on the idea that punishment may serve the greater good, though, and although naive in their assessment, they operated under the assumption that the benefits outweighed the harm. As Christopher Marshall argues in *Beyond Retribution: A New Testament Vision for Justice, Crime, and Punishment,* the strength of the rehabilitation framework was precisely that it sought reform. It had a corrective goal as it recognized that the offender is a part of the broader community, that her identity is not defined by the crime, and that she can grow and reintegrate into society. Still, the rehabilitation and deterrence theories have significant weaknesses that disqualify them as frameworks that could transform the criminal justice system today. The most basic problem is that neither of them work in practice, not before mass incarceration and certainly not after it. Instead of deterring violent and criminal behavior, prison actually fosters it. As Marshall argues, true rehabilitation cannot happen in a harsh and dehumanizing environment, since the goals of improving and injuring are at odds with one another. Transformation requires personal cooperation and dedication, and it is hard to cooperate with a system when most of one's energy is spent surviving it. As a society, we are confused about the purpose of punishment, Marshall argues, thus prison officials are told "to deter, hurt, and rehabilitate all at the same time."[40]

Politically, the clarion call of "law and order" and the promise to be "tough on crime" made public safety—not the growth and needs of convicted people—the purpose of punishment, as articulated explicitly in the 1987 guidelines of the United States Sentencing Commission. Economically (and perhaps most importantly), the caging of human beings has become exceedingly profitable for a range of companies and beneficial for rural communities throughout the nation. In *Reading Is My Window: Books and the Art of Reading in Prisons,* Megan Sweeney writes,

> In the 1980s, this shift toward highly draconian penal practices resulted in a sharp increase in the prison population, a frenzied drive to build more prisons, and a massive investment of capital in the punishment industry. The prison building boom provided huge infusions of state money to economically depressed regions, and rural towns began competing to attract new prisons. . . . Prisons have become a cornerstone of economic development in impoverished rural areas because they offer year-round employment with benefits, and they "are recession proof, usually expanding in size during hard times." Building more prisons and housing more prisoners has been equally lucrative for architecture and construction firms, investment banks, companies that supply products and services to prisons, companies that employ nonunionized prison laborers, and corporations that operate private prison systems. The development of the prison industrial complex—this web of constituents invested in the expansion and maintenance of the punishment industry—thus reinforced the political and economic centrality of prisons in the United States.[41]

God's advent implores disciples to work to overturn the new normal of imprisonment, and this will be a great reversal indeed since there

---

40. Christopher D. Marshall, *Beyond Retribution: A New Testament Vision for Justice, Crime, and Punishment* (Grand Rapids: Eerdmans, 2001), 131.
41. Sweeney, *Reading Is My Window,* 40.

is enormous economic incentive to expand, not dismantle, the mass incarceration of human beings. As state budgets become increasingly tight, the trend is to move toward private prisons, which increase profit by decreasing already rare resources for inmates. The architecture alone of private prisons reveals this goal: visitation, library, and gym space is cut to make room for more cells to cage an ever-increasing number of human beings "who can be held captive for profit."[42] These political and economic motivations for imprisonment should make claims about mass incarceration as the new Jim Crow (as Alexander argues) or as a continuation of slavery (as prison abolitionists argue) seem less far-fetched. It is now big business, a profitable industry, to cage human beings whose well-being we boldly admit is of lesser importance than our own sense of safety (be it perceived or real) and who are by definition a vulnerable population under the total control of a depersonalized state and thus a people easily victimized and already dehumanized as "property of the state."

*Advent's Call: Wake Up!*

Amidst such horror, the greatest barrier to dismantling mass incarceration is public consensus, which drives the ideological, political, and economic forces described above. The greatest barrier is the will of the people, Christians and non-Christians alike, who reduce convicted criminals to their crime and hastily assume they are in a category all their own, more like monsters than complex human beings like us, at times "close to being the devil and at times close to sainthood," as Solzhenitsyn writes. The greatest barrier is that most of us do not see those in prison as human beings who bear God's image. We do not *see*. We do not think about their humanity, nor about the conditions that degrade or promote this humanity. Yet the Bible speaks about blinding ourselves to others with great seriousness, as demonstrated by King in a speech delivered during the Memphis sanitation workers' strike. Using Jesus's parable of Lazarus and Dives

42. Alexander, *New Jim Crow*, 218.

and applying it to dominant society, King says, "You are here tonight to demand that Memphis will do something about the conditions our brothers face. . . . You are here to demand that Memphis will see the poor. You know Jesus reminded us in a magnificent parable one day that a man went to hell because he didn't see the poor. . . . Dives went to hell because he allowed Lazarus to become invisible. . . . America, too, is going to hell" if we do not open our eyes to the evils we foster and maintain.[43] In our blindness, the Advent message resounds: Wake up! Be alert!

In her remarkable study of women's reading practices in prison, Megan Sweeney shows how profoundly important it is for us to witness—to be awakened to—the lives of those in prison. What strikes me most about the book is how the insights and experiences of the ninety-four women incarcerated in North Carolina, Ohio, and Pennsylvania directly parallel those of the forty or more women I have come to know in Georgia, and how Sweeney's observations mirror my own. "Although I believe that imprisonment constitutes a 'wastefulness of life' and a form of 'social revenge' that damages prisoners and the wider society," she writes, "my research has inspired me to witness to the myriad ways in which the women claim their humanity, practice their freedom, and transform themselves while in the grip of 'a death-generating institution.'"[44] The women I know are courageous, creative, and persistent in their pursuits "to better" themselves, as they say, and to create meaning out of their past and present despite the dearth of resources to help them and the enormous barriers that all but prevent them from doing so. Statistics show that the great majority of women in prison were victims of physical, sexual, and/or emotional abuse before committing their crime, and some of their crimes entail, in turn, victimizing others. "As women prisoners are keenly aware," writes Sweeney, "the U.S. justice system leaves little room for accommodating complex and partial notions of agency,

43. Martin Luther King Jr., "American Federation of State, County and Municipal Employees: Memphis, Tennessee, March 18, 1968," in "All Labor Has Dignity," ed. Michael K. Honey (Boston: Beacon Press, 2011), 172–73.
44. Sweeney, Reading Is My Window, 3.

responsibility, and guilt."[45] Our justice system, in other words, does not allow truth-filled accounts that hold in tension the complexity of being both victims and agents, much less provide resources to help women face their pain and heal from prior abuse. Once in prison, there are few resources, like therapy, that help the women name and unravel the structural, psychological, emotional, and interpersonal issues that led to their crime. There are few resources period, and even fewer resources like counseling or "groups" that do not promote the dominant individualistic ideology of exclusive blame, which negates structural analyses of the conditions the women have endured both outside and inside prison.

Ironically, while the prison system presumes individual culpability and exclusive blame, the infantilizing conditions of the prison—including the fact that every aspect of an inmate's life is monitored, controlled, and forced into conformity—more often than not strip the women of opportunities for self-determination, opportunities that are integral to our humanity and necessary for growth in moral agency. Women are stripped of the capacity to make decisions about their own bodies, for example; they are robbed of what ethicist Christine Gudorf calls "bodyright."[46] They learn that it is often futile and even counterproductive to reach out to prison staff (be it medical personnel or counselors who work for the State) for help with depression, grief at the loss of a loved one, and other emotional pain, because the likely outcome is either numbing meds or isolation in solitary confinement where they are watched "under the camera." This happens even when an inmate clearly states that she is not struggling with suicidal thoughts and that she simply needs community—people to listen and offer support—not further isolation.[47]

Moreover, the prison mirrors many of the abusive situations in which women found themselves before incarceration. While some officers make a point to be respectful, the women are subject to the

45. Ibid., 105.
46. Christine E. Gudorf, *Body, Sex, and Pleasure: Reconstructing Christian Sexual Ethics* (Cleveland: Pilgrim Press, 1995), 161.
47. Sweeney, *Reading Is My Window*, 86.

whims of those who have complete authority and power over them. One woman shares how her ten-year-old son was crying uncontrollably at a visitation, and when she reached out to comfort him with a touch, the guard ordered her to sit on her hands, which sent the son into further hysterics. Another tells of being granted permission to make a phone call on a Friday morning, only to be denied by an officer. When she showed him the memo from the warden's office, she was accused of forgery even though the memo was on government letterhead that would be impossible to obtain. Another woman shares that the inmates are allotted a certain number of tampons per month, but she has a heavy flow; when she asks the officers for more, she is denied and has to go without. Yet another speaks of the unavoidability of receiving a disciplinary report (D.R.), which goes on her permanent record and affects parole decisions. Forced at the time of pill call to take her medication, which induces severe drowsiness, she will receive a D.R. if she falls asleep during her evening group, but she will also receive a D.R. if she is caught hiding the pill in her pocket so that she may wait and take it before bed. While some of these situations may be corrected by filing a grievance, some have enduring effects, like the trauma the visiting son experienced. The larger point, though, is that the daily indignities and injustices happen so often in prisons across the country that they characterize incarceration in the United States. They not only depict Frye's description of oppression above but also, as oppressed groups have long observed, reveal the whole situation as a farce—prisons as theaters of the absurd within which women and men are ordered to make something of themselves. While some absurd and dehumanizing realities arise from officer whims, others are embedded in prison policy, and over time, the women I know are no longer shocked by their basic denial of certain rights, like not being served lunch Fridays through Sundays in Georgia prisons. If they have families who can place money in their accounts, they can buy a honey bun or noodle cup from the store to tide them over. If they are indigent, they may find creative ways to get food through the inmate barter system or they may have to go without. As Sweeney writes,

"In the prison environment, where prisoners are totally dependent on others for their basic physical needs, and where the constant threat of physical and emotional violence replicates experiences of domestic violence, many women struggle to maintain some sense of control over their lives."[48]

While it is vital that we attend to the particularities of women's experiences in prison, it is also crucial that we listen to the experiences of men who suffer under similarly debilitating conditions, especially given that our perception of men in prison are shaped by numerous television shows that sensationalize and demonize prisoners for dramatic effect. In an article published in Open Door's *Hospitality* newspaper in February 2000, a male friend of the Community who is incarcerated in Georgia describes the prison system as "soul stealers," and recounts many incidents that the women in Georgia and in Sweeney's book also undergo. Published anonymously for his protection, he writes about "an institution that as a by-product of its day-to-day operations steals thousands of souls" as "humiliation seeps in . . . layer by layer" and strips away dignity. Walking the reader through his own journey of incarceration, he recounts his first hours in the prison when "most, if not all," of his valuables were "damaged, destroyed, or confiscated," as he was "told repeatedly" that he "does not merit owning anything of value" because he is "a useless piece of crap," a message expressed in a variety of ways throughout his incarceration. As he enters the compound, this newly incarcerated man observes "several guards . . . screaming at the people in line . . . haranguing the men to enter the building, to keep against the wall, to keep their mouths shut and their eyes straight ahead." He continues,

> As you walk down the hallway, your spirits plummet. In noticing the prisoners already confined, one observation stands out. Most people avoid eye contact and keep their heads lowered abjectly. Whether through humiliation or a broken spirit, their dull gazes stay focused elsewhere. With quiet resolve, you shore up your spirits and wonder what has reduced these men to this state.

48. Ibid., 193.

Similarly, one friend, Terri, told me that upon release she had a difficult time making eye contact with others, a habit that formed during her six years of incarceration where she was repeatedly told not to look the officers in the eye. She worked hard to overcome her prison formation when practicing for job interviews. "In doing time in prison," the author of "Soul Stealers" writes, "you will learn that many people . . . bow down to the humiliating demands of overbearing prison guards." Sometimes a prisoner stands up for himself and "challenges the dehumanizing brutality of the guards," but there is a cost. "This prisoner is always harassed" and "winds up in and out of the isolation unit," writes the Georgia inmate. Even for the men who try to keep to themselves and avoid conflict, disciplinary reports are handed out with ease, according to the author. Like the woman above caught in an unavoidable situation, he writes about how common it is for different officers to give conflicting orders, "so regardless of what you do, you will fail to follow someone's instructions. . . . When one of the officers walks by and sees you do something different from what they instructed, you will receive a D.R. for failure to follow instructions. If you try to explain the conflicting orders, you will be given an additional D.R. for insubordination." More generally, many officers enforce different sets of rules as a matter of course—"the rules change from day to day, from prison guard to prison guard"—creating particularly stressful and upsetting conditions for the many inmates who yearn for some sense of stability in their lives. "You are fighting a system aimed at your destruction," the author summarizes, "so you are fighting for your very life and soul."[49]

The oppressive forces characterizing life in prison follow men and women as they seek to reenter society as responsible and functional citizens. Central to Alexander's argument about mass incarceration as the new Jim Crow is that "once labeled a felon, the badge of inferiority" dispensed in prison "remains with you for the rest of your life, relegating you to a permanent second-class status."[50] While many of

49. Peter R. Gathje, ed., *A Work of Hospitality: The Open Door Reader* (Atlanta: Open Door Community Press, 2002), 133–43.
50. Alexander, *New Jim Crow*, 139.

the women I know internalize the retributive idea that incarceration is about paying their debt to society, Alexander shows that "one's debt to society is never paid" in the sense that it is virtually impossible for ex-offenders to integrate into the mainstream, both socially and economically.[51]

The first obstacle is housing—most immediately, figuring out where to sleep that first night, a reality with which I became personally acquainted while serving on house duty one night at the Open Door. There was a knock around midnight, and on the other side of the door stood Jeff Autry, a resourceful man who, having nowhere else to go, took the bus from Jackson State Prison to a downtown Atlanta station, found a map of the unfamiliar city and walked four miles to the Open Door in hopes that he could find a home. Jeff received the *Hospitality* newspaper in prison and corresponded with Murphy, whom he had never met. He gladly spent that first night in our front yard with a sleeping bag, cardboard, and a blanket. The next day he volunteered in the soup kitchen. We added a bed in one of the rooms, and he moved into the house, where he has lived as a member of the residential community ever since. While some people in prison have families or support systems that they can return to, most, like Jeff, do not. As Alexander says, "More than half a million people are released from prison each year, and for many, finding a home appears next to impossible, not just in the short run, but for the rest of their lives."[52]

For those with or without housing, a further barrier to reentry is finding work; nearly every application asks the applicant to "check the box" if they have been convicted of a felony, and those who do rarely receive an interview. In a context of survival, the decision whether or not to check the box is a serious ethical dilemma. When the subject has come up in our theology program, the women overwhelmingly say they want to "live honestly" and "trust in God's provision." God's provision, in this case though, necessitates employers who do not reduce ex-offenders to their crime and thus are willing to hire them to

---

51. Ibid. Alexander is quoting Jeremy Travis, *But They All Come Back: Facing the Challenges of Prisoner Reentry* (Washington, DC: Urban Institute Press, 2002), 73.
52. Alexander, *New Jim Crow*, 145.

do dignified work that pays a living wage. Even the few people who do find decent jobs still struggle, however, to "survive in the mainstream, legal economy" since they are "saddled with large debts" that must be paid or else they go back to prison. Newly released prisoners have to make monthly payments to probation departments and courts and must pay the cost of numerous fees that were charged to them before the arrest for things like pretrial detention, public defender applications, and jail booking—fees that have all been created within the last twenty years of mass incarceration.[53] The greatest barrier to social integration though, which underlies all others, is the shame and stigma associated with the label "felon." Shame and stigma bring isolation and alienation—the utter lack of the communal support that we all desperately need.

*Holding One Another Accountable*

None of this means that we do not need to hold each other accountable for what we have done to others. Holding each other accountable is how we honor our dignity and agency as human beings and bring some healing to victims of crime. This is why the new paradigm of restorative justice, which seeks to repair situations and heal all those affected by a crime, emphasizes the need to create conditions where offenders are given the psychological and emotional strength to face what they have done and take responsibility for it. While the conditions of prison are characterized by "stigmatizing" or "disintegrative" shame, which condemns the behavior and the person, the restorative framework is characterized by "re-integrative shame," which "denounces the offense but not the offender" in order for the offender to take steps to make right and gain self-respect and acceptance in the community.[54] Restorative justice includes suffering and pain—the pain of facing what one has done—but it is a necessary pain that leads to healing, repair, and renewal.

53. Ibid., 151.
54. Howard Zehr, "Restorative Justice," in *Capital Punishment: A Reader*, ed. Glen H. Stassen (Cleveland: Pilgrim Press, 1998), 27.

As we hold individual offenders accountable for their actions, we must hold ourselves accountable, too, for "locking up the human evidence of our social failures."[55] Speaking of the "exaggerated individualism" of the retributive mindset, Marshall writes,

> The retributivist emphasis on personal responsibility and choice is valuable and important; individuals do *choose* to commit crimes. But choices are constrained by environmental circumstances, and it is naïve, if not dishonest, to speak of crime solely in terms of personal free will. People who would remain law-abiding in certain social climates will turn to crime under other social conditions. Poverty, unemployment, racial inequality, social prejudice, and drug and alcohol abuse all have a role in fostering crime. A significant portion of criminal offenders have been offended against as children before they became offenders. *It is crucial, therefore, to inquire into the societal causes of crime and [our] collective responsibility for it.*[56]

Disciples who participate in Mary's great reversal and John's call to repent will want to understand the social causes of crime and the systematic injustices of the prison system so that we may foster instead the institutional structures needed for prevention, healing, and growth.

## The Great Transformation of Jericho Road:
## Advent and Homelessness

King's depiction of Jericho road, where he urges his readers to take collective responsibility for structural injustice while attending to individual need, offers imagery directly relevant to homelessness. "On the one hand we are called to play the Good Samaritan on life's roadside," King says, but "one day we must come to see that the whole of Jericho road must be transformed. . . . True compassion . . . comes to see that the edifice which produces beggars needs restructuring."[57]

In *Disrupting Homelessness: Alternative Christian Approaches*, Laura Stivers shows how rarely Christians direct their compassion toward

55. Sweeney, *Reading Is My Window*, 254.
56. Marshall, *Beyond Retribution*, 117–18.
57. King, *Testament of Hope*, 241.

structural change. She argues that most Christians—even those engaged in mercy ministries like shelters and soup kitchens—assume that the causes of homelessness are individual faults and behaviors; therefore, Christian solutions to homelessness tend to focus on moralistic aims to change the individual. Homelessness, however, is "clearly linked to structural factors, namely a lack of affordable housing, poverty, and oppression."[58] To illustrate this, Stivers turns to an analogy of musical chairs, often used by experts in the field to show the relationship between structural causes and individual characteristics, where the chairs represent affordable housing units. Because there are more poor households than affordable units, when the music stops some people will inevitably be left homeless. Those who do not secure affordable housing are the people who are most vulnerable in our society because of "individual factors or social exclusion."[59] These personal factors are not, as too many of us readily assume, the source of homelessness. Rather, they are contributing causes. As researchers at the Urban Institute write,

> Over the years, most people have come to realize that both structural and individual factors play a role in producing homelessness. The structural factors set the stage, without which fewer people would be homeless. They help to answer the question, "Why more homelessness *now?*" ... Then the individual factors help to identify "*Who?*"—which particular people subject to the worst combinations of structural factors are most likely to lose their housing. However, as the structural conditions worsen, even people without personal vulnerabilities other than poverty may experience crises that precipitate a homeless episode.[60]

The basic structural causes of homelessness are lack of affordable housing and extreme poverty. Poverty is itself a structural reality based on changes in the economy, lack of employment opportunities, lack of jobs with adequate pay and benefits, and corporate power that

---

58. Laura Stivers, *Disrupting Homelessness: Alternative Christian Responses* (Minneapolis: Fortress Press, 2011), 41.
59. Ibid., 33.
60. Martha Burt, Laudan Y. Aron, Edgar Lee, and Jesse Valente, *Helping America's Homeless: Emergency Shelter or Affordable Housing?* (Washington, DC: Urban Institute Press, 2001), 5, quoted in Stivers, *Disrupting Homelessness*, 34.

profits from exploiting workers by keeping labor costs too low. Within the context of poverty, contributing causes of homelessness may include personal factors like disability or sudden illness, addiction, mental disorders, youth aging out of foster care, reentry from prison, and domestic violence, with discrimination based on race, gender, and sexual orientation also increasing one's vulnerability. Without the context of poverty, none of these factors alone are causes of homelessness; for example, mental illness and addiction disorders are prevalent across socioeconomic lines and people with means suffering from these rarely become homeless. "Instead of asking what people do to cause their homelessness," Stivers argues that privileged Christians should engage in self-critique and ask "why our society has allowed and in many ways structurally supported poverty and homelessness."[61] Stivers shows that without such critical analysis, even individual Christians and church communities who are engaged in mercy work "can often unwittingly reinforce some of the stigmas and structures that keep poverty and inequality in place."[62]

The prevalent ideology that keeps homelessness in place is that people are homeless because of a personal fault or failing, the common notions being that people are either lazy, morally deviant, or choose to be homeless. The assumption is then that individuals may escape homelessness if they make different choices by being trained in the middle-class values of discipline, hard work, and independence. These assumptions may be overturned—"we will be less likely to view their choices as irrational," Stivers argues, and less likely to assume that these people do not want to work or are not already working hard to survive—if we get to know people who are homeless and listen to their insights about the structural barriers they face.[63] Stivers also argues that racism plays a role in dominant ideologies and that the individualistic framing of homelessness becomes especially problematic when privileged white Christians see the solution as changing people of color rather than challenging the structural roots

61. Stivers, *Disrupting Homelessness*, 12.
62. Ibid., 22.
63. Ibid., 110.

of homelessness. "The result is that 'we' who have the power (mostly white) aim to change 'them' (overwhelmingly minority)" instead of recognizing that we live in a society "that still gives greater advantages to whites."[64] By ignoring structural injustice and focusing on individual behavior, "society gets off scot-free from having to address poverty and oppression."[65]

Our dominant ideologies are often based on shallow observations of the homeless people most visible to us since they live on city streets—the chronically homeless, which is the population the Open Door Community primarily serves. These are the people our society renders guilty of their predicament and labels the "undeserving" poor. Whereas "transitionally homeless" families or individuals often become homeless because of a crisis like eviction, foreclosure, unemployment, or divorce and spend a short time in a shelter before transitioning to more secure housing, and whereas "episodically homeless" individuals cycle in and out of homelessness for various lengths of time, "chronically homeless" individuals live on the streets or in shelters for persistent periods of time or the rest of their lives. About 15 percent of the 3.5 million people who experience homelessness in a given year are chronically homeless.[66] As a group, these people endure high rates of mental and physical health problems that living on the streets and in crowded shelters only makes worse. They are also the primary targets of punitive city ordinances, begun in the 1990s, that criminalize homelessness by banning "urban camping," panhandling, and "loitering" in public space. Through these "quality of life ordinances," as they are called, police rid the streets of homeless people by locking them in jail. In the last three decades, city jails and city shelters have become the primary means of addressing homelessness. In other words, our society has been more willing to use tax dollars for shelters, jails, and prisons than for secure and permanent housing.

The most direct solution to homelessness is, of course, housing. One

64. Ibid., 112.
65. Ibid., 110.
66. Ibid., 30–31.

approach, Housing First, is gaining popularity because of its proven success in the United States and Canada. The premise is straightforward and simple: first housing, then services. As the National Alliance to End Homelessness reports, research shows that the way to solve chronic homelessness is through "permanent supportive housing," which is housing that includes supportive services. Rather than viewing support services as the means to "fix" individuals so that they may then obtain housing, a Housing First model identifies permanent housing without conditions as the necessary foundation for addressing individual need. The Housing First model is, perhaps surprisingly, "a cost-effective intervention" and an effective long-term strategy because chronically homeless people living in permanent and supportive housing are less likely to use expensive public services like city shelters and emergency rooms and are less likely to end up in jail. For example, one study in Seattle, Washington, found that a program that provides supportive permanent housing to formerly homeless people "with extensive health problems" saved almost "$30,000 per tenant per year in publicly-funded services, all while achieving better housing and health outcomes for the tenants."[67] As the National Alliance to End Homelessness argues, transitional housing also needs to be a priority for preventing at-risk individuals, like people leaving prison or psychiatric facilities, from becoming homeless.

As privileged Christians gain clarity about the structural and interconnected nature of mass incarceration and homelessness (through accessible and rich resources like Stivers's and Alexander's texts), we may better understand the kind of reversal the coming of God ignites. Participation in the coming kingdom demands a repentance that inaugurates social and relational change—the transformation of structures and our own hearts, including our perception and will. This happens, the next chapter contends, when we

---

67. "Chronic Homelessness—Overview," National Alliance to End Homelessness, http://tinyurl.com/hsf49vb (accessed February 28, 2016).

build right relationships with those who are oppressed as we reduce distance through practices of peace.

# 3

---

# Christmas

The people who walked in darkness
have seen a great light.
Those who live in the land of deep darkness
on them light has shined.
You have increased their joy;
you have given them great gladness.
And they rejoice before you
as with joy at the harvest,
as people exalt when sharing the goods that sustain their lives.
For the yoke of the burden,
the bar across their shoulders,
the rod of their oppressor,
you have broken. . . .
For unto us a child is born!
. . . the prince of peace.
—Isaiah 9:2–7 (Open Door Community adapted version)

Herod gave orders to kill all the boys in Bethlehem
and its neighborhood who were two years old and younger. . . .
"A sound is heard from Ramah,
the sound of bitter weeping.
Rachel is crying for her children;
She refuses to be comforted, for they are dead."
—Matthew 2:16–18 (Good News Bible)

## Reducing Distance through Practices of Peace

On Christmas Eve, the small, ragtag residential community gathers in the dining room of the Open Door under the light of candles generously spread across windowsills and tables set for a feast. "The people who walked in darkness have seen a great light," Open Door partner Calvin Kimborough proclaims as he reads the opening scripture of Isaiah 9. "Those who live in a land of deep darkness"—a land of prison cells and cat holes hidden in the shadows of city streets—"on them light has shined. . . . For unto us a child is born! Unto us a child is given!" Circled around familiar tables where daily they "share the goods that sustain their lives," the Community rejoices this particular night "as with joy at the harvest" as it listens to shepherds and angels, to Gospel texts and carols, announce the birth of Jesus. "We come now to this night of nights for which we have waited," says Murphy as she opens her Christmas Eve meditation; "we have heard the excitement, the knock at the door, the jubilant cries from the heavens that Jesus Christ is born, that God has made a home among us. And so, on this night, our waiting is done."

"And yet . . ." she continues,

> We know that there are still dark places in our world. We know this new life in Jesus is tinged with tragedy, for the birth of this life and the presence of the one who brings solidarity, justice, and hope also ignites the rage of powers and principalities, those forces and mechanisms of war, poverty, homelessness, loneliness, enmity, estrangement, and hunger. So while we celebrate the end of this season of waiting, we begin another vigil; we look for the fulfillment of the promises of the kin-dom of God.[1]

The transition from Advent to Christmas is thus from longing to longing. In Advent, we learn to long for the right things through Mary's Magnificat and John's proclamation of God's coming social order. We learn that when we ask Jesus to come, God asks us to prepare the way, to yearn and work for tangible structural and relational change. For we are called to prepare the way not only for the birth of this

---

1. Open Door Community Christmas Eve Service, author's audio recording, December 24, 2010.

person—Jesus, Immanuel, God with us—but for the kingdom he embodies and ignites. We are called to prepare the way, in other words, for Jesus's person and work, which cannot be separated from one another. And as we will see, with the arrival of Jesus this night—the one whose very identity is peace—we learn how to work for structural and relational change: by living his way of nonviolent love.

What arrives in this transition from Advent to Christmas is not what we had hoped. Indeed, it is more than many of us wish to receive. Those of us who thrive under the present social order are content to celebrate the arrival of this person, God's presence with us as we struggle today and tomorrow with individual sin and need, but we do not necessarily wish to participate in his incarnate and cruciform work. To be sure, most Christmas sermons, even those that point to the cross, end with Murphy's pregnant pause: "And so, on this night, our waiting is done." We hear this good news and rightly breathe a sigh of relief: our God has come. God has "seen the misery of the world" and has "come personally to help," writes Bonhoeffer.[2] But the same Gospel text that announces the arrival of Jesus reveals the journey ahead. The birth of Jesus thrusts us into social and political struggle. It "ignites the rage," as Murphy says, of powers and principalities, of Herod, whose political power is threatened by the reign of this Jewish Prince of Peace, the one whose authority "shall grow continually as the circle of Beloved Community is established and upheld with justice and solidarity" (Isa 9:7 [Open Door Community adapted version]). If we wish to be faithful to the truth revealed in the birth narrative of Jesus, we cannot ignore Herod's slaughter of Bethlehem's children and "the sound of bitter weeping," of Rachel crying and refusing to be comforted. The birth narrative reflects both God's determination that peace reign on earth ("the zeal of the faithful one will do this" [Isa 9:7]) and the hard reality that the peace of God never arrives without incident. The biblical text reveals what contemporary practitioners of nonviolent resistance know well: the arrival of the peacemaker stirs up and exposes the violence at the core of an unjust social order. Integral

2. Bonhoeffer, *Barcelona, Berlin, New York*, 588.

to the work of peacemaking, then, is identifying and engaging that which resists its reign.

Herod's rule is a specific manifestation of the powers and principalities that the Apostle Paul discusses in Galatians, Ephesians, Colossians, Romans, and 1 Corinthians. According to Paul, the powers are the fallen rulers, authorities, and forces at work in the world, against which followers of Jesus are called to struggle (Eph 6:12). These powers were created through Christ to be good; they were intended for human flourishing. But they are sinful insofar as they have betrayed their vocation, and they are in the process of being redeemed through the peace of Christ's cross (Col 1:15–20). While Herod's rule is a manifestation of "the powers at their demonic extreme"—domination perpetuated through systematic direct violence—Dutch scholar Hendrik Berkhof argues that Paul's notion refers more broadly to all social, economic, cultural, and political systems that are both necessary for human life and the source of varying degrees of oppression and injustice.[3] In his groundbreaking study, Berkhof shows that while Paul's terminology is not his own making—it was present, for example, in Jewish apocalyptic writings—Paul gives the language of powers and principalities new meaning. Instead of assigning them a purely spiritual referent, he defines them as "structures of earthly existence," various realities that "condition earthly life," and, in a fallen world, create conditions of domination.[4] The powers are meant to be instruments of God's love that enable the flourishing of creation, but when distorted, they become tools of domination that manifest in realities as diverse as human tradition and public opinion, morality and religious regulation, and political ordering—all the various structures that serve as scaffolding and provide stability to life. Biblical scholar Walter Wink expands Berkhof's study and describes these institutions, structures, and systems as suprahuman in that they cannot be reduced

3. Walter Wink, *The Powers That Be* (New York: Galilee Doubleday, 1999), 6.
4. Hendrik Berkhof, *Christ and the Powers* (Scottdale, PA: Herald Press, 1977), 16–19, 23–24. Berkhof introduced this often-ignored yet vital aspect of Paul's thought into twentieth-century modern theology where it was taken up by theologians particularly attuned to the social and political implications of scripture, like Karl Barth, John Howard Yoder, Jacques Ellul, William Stringfellow, and Walter Wink.

to the individuals that comprise them and they possess a certain kind of transcendent nature, "an inner spirit, corporate culture, or collective personality."[5] Because of their encompassing character, Paul insists that "the struggle is not against flesh and blood" but against the oppressive forces themselves that envelop human beings. Paul and other biblical writers identify this transcendent dimension with words drawn from their ancient worldview (angels, demons, principalities, gods, and elements) that point, Wink argues, to the "spirituality at the center of the political, economic, and cultural institutions of their day."[6] According to the biblical texts, the powers have both an outer, visible structure and an inner, spiritual reality, and the latter cannot be separated from the former. In other words, the powers grow out of human institutions and social systems and so, in this way, are embodied. They are "creatures" like us, fallen and needing to be redeemed.[7]

Thus, when we overlook the central role the powers and principalities play in Matthew's birth narrative, we not only depoliticize the text, we restrict the reach of the Gospel's pronouncement of peace on earth. The good news is that the transformative work of the incarnate God envelops not only individual human beings but also the structural forces "that surround us on every side" and that we otherwise cannot escape. Wink argues that while "God does not endorse any particular power at any given time," much less "systems that have been overcome by evil," the powers, as such, are within the purview of God's sovereign reign, at once affirmed, judged, and reconciled through the incarnate, crucified, and risen Prince of Peace. Wink writes, "God at one and the same time *upholds* a given political or economic system, since some such system is required" for human flourishing, "*condemns* that system insofar as it is destructive," and "*presses for its transformation* into a more humane order."[8] The transformation of destructive powers happens, Paul says

---

5. Wink, *Powers That Be*, 4, 24.
6. Ibid., 24. Wink is vague about whether or not the powers have metaphysical being apart from the institutions and structures they inhabit.
7. Ibid., 5.

and the Gospels demonstrate, through the incarnate God who makes peace by way of the cross, in other words, by the alterative route of nonviolent engagement.

The Christmas narrative inaugurates nonviolent resistance against the forces and mechanisms of death, violence, and oppression; its proclamation of peace is a confrontation with these powers. When we relegate heaven's jubilant cry, "Peace on Earth!" to a pious dream or the inner life, we close our ears to "the sound of bitter weeping," the pain of those who bear the brunt of the "powers and principalities," as well as to God's promise of an engaging and abundant life. What arrives in this transition from Advent to Christmas is abundance, more than many of us would like to receive, because it is an invitation to participate in Jesus's person and work, to participate in the incarnation of peace—the Word become flesh—and to follow his peacemaking way. What arrives in this transition is a call to discipleship, and discipleship is no arrival at all.

Discipleship, as we have seen, is inherently social and political because it entails following Jesus into the world as he embodies and proclaims the kingdom of God. Because the social and political significance of Christmas is rooted simultaneously in the reality of the incarnation and the birth narrative of Jesus, the liturgical season of Christmas requires embodied resistance to the powers. It demands that we who are systematically advantaged draw near to people who suffer acute forms of structural violence (what Paul calls "powers and principalities") and demonstrates that the way we draw near is through practices of peace that take a variety of forms. At the Open Door, these practices take shape in one of two main ways: they resist structural violence as they meet human need or they interrupt direct violence as community members place their bodies on the line in situations of social concern.

8. Ibid., 32.

## Entrance into the Birth Narrative of Peace

At the Open Door, the sober reality that God's arrival does not end expectant waiting but inaugurates it anew is exemplified by the fact that Christmas day comes and goes, but homeless and incarcerated people remain. The Community marks the transition from Advent to Christmas by continued meals to their homeless friends and continued visits in prison. Indeed, the mere reality of a Christmas meal for the homeless should be fodder enough for renewed thinking about the birth of Jesus and our hasty conclusions about its meaning. Ed gestures at this as he reminds the many volunteers gathered for the Christmas meal—some regulars and some occasional—that even as we serve in the context of this high holiday in which roasted turkey, green beans, and sweet potatoes replace the usual soup, "We want to be careful not to separate the joy of feeding people from the anguish of hunger," not to separate, in other words, the joy of volunteering this day from the realities of poverty, enmity, and estrangement that make this meal necessary.[9] Hospitality to the Open Door's friends from the streets is no mere ethical act, a good deed to help spread Christmas cheer. It is entrance into the birth narrative of peace and nonviolent resistance to the powers of death and hunger that oppose its reign.

The Community inhabits the story of Jesus's birth in a variety of ways, but perhaps the most unique to the season is the delivery of Christmas packages to Georgia's death-row inmates and "permanents" at Jackson State Prison. As the wise men set out to bring gifts to the baby Jesus, the Open Door embarks on a journey toward this same Jesus who now sits in prison. "The child who lies in the manger became an adult," says Murphy, an adult who lived among the poor, ate with the despised and excluded, was arrested, tried, and convicted by religious and state courts, and for his crimes was executed. "He became a prisoner so that we would know that no category of person is beyond the love, care, and mercy of God. And he came back from the other side

---

9. Ed Loring, opening remarks at the Open Door Community Christmas Meal Circle at which the author was present, December 27, 2010.

of death, torture, and execution to let us know that destructive powers and our own judgments are never the last word."[10] The last word is the life, love, and liberation of God.

The liturgy of the Christmas boxes begins at the Eucharist table, the source of all the Open Door's peacemaking activities. "We are welcomed to this table," says Nelia in her call to worship, "which tonight is made out of cardboard boxes, each full of the gifts that are going to Jackson." She continues,

> We often in this community say that our Eucharist table extends to the meals we serve our homeless friends during the week, but this particular week, the table expands down into the 358 packages represented here as they go forth to the prison. So we give thanks for this table that is spread on these stacks of boxes, for this bread and this juice that later in the service will become for us the great gift of God, the pouring out of God into his son Jesus. And we give thanks that by partaking in these, we are made whole and given strength for the journey.[11]

The journey includes, as Ed reminds us in the call to the table, the regular visits community members make to individuals on death row and the monthly Hardwick trips where families without means are driven to Milledgeville, Georgia, for fellowship and a meal at the Presbyterian church before visiting their loved ones in prison. "So, it is with a special sense of commitment," Ed says, "that we come to *this* day for *this* Eucharist. These packages and their edible contents continue to flow out from this table in the Eucharistic love that we share with each other, which gives us strength and energy to tear down prison walls—to relate, love, and be loved by those who are in prison."[12]

When we befriend and relate to those on death row, we hear the pain of people who daily endure the brunt of the "powers and principalities." We hear from people like Kelly Gissendaner, who bears what she calls "fearful encounters," the pervasive presence and monstrous weight of the powers of death that surround her. As invitation into the prayers of the people this night, the Community

10. Open Door Community Worship, author's audio recording, December 19, 2010.
11. Ibid.
12. Ibid.

listens to her voice through mine, hovering over the cardboard boxes upholding the Eucharist meal, celebrated this week—and every week—in remembrance of the one who became the prisoner and is still found among prisoners. In an imaginative reflection on Matthew 6:9–13, where Jesus teaches the disciples to pray for God's earthly kingdom, Kelly personifies her fears in the form of visitors at the prison. "I peeked into the room," she writes. "It was quite crowded. Many people were checking their watches as if they were expecting someone. I took a deep breath before opening the door. I'm the one they're expecting." It was a diverse group, "but I recognized them immediately. They were my worst fears." One by one, Kelly inquires into their identities.

"I'm your fear of being abandoned," says one man as he adjusts his tie; "You never know who might walk out of your life."

"I'm your fear of dying," says a well-dressed woman in a proud tone of voice. "I've been with you ever since you were placed on death row." She gestures to another woman sitting behind her, "She reports to me. She's your fear of suffering."

"I work really hard and put in long hours. I think I deserve a raise." I had to agree with her. Since my federal appeals had started, she'd been paying me a visit first thing in the morning and last thing at night. I certainly couldn't accuse her of slacking off.

"I'm one of your main fears," says a man with his hand held high, looming tall over the rest. "I underpin all the others. Without me the rest would be nothing." He paused and then delivered the punch line, "I'm your fear that the promises of Christ are false. I'm your fear that when you die you will confront total nothingness." A hush fell over the room. Everyone looked at me, but I was too stunned to reply. I couldn't deny what he'd said. Didn't Christ say over and over, "Fear not," and "Don't let your heart be troubled?" Wasn't he always saying, "Peace be with you," nothing can separate you from the love of Christ, no ruler or power or anything else in all creation?

Kelly then noticed a man "with big soulful eyes" sitting by himself in a corner. "Which fear are you?" she asked.

"I'm not a fear," he said quietly. "I sneaked into the meeting out of curiosity. I represent hundreds of others who aren't here right now. I stand for all the prayers still being said for you by your friends, church communities, family, fellow inmates, and theology course teachers."

He reached out his hand and Kelly grasped it firmly.

As his fingers intertwined with mine, I felt my anxiety starting to ebb. But then suddenly there was an ugly sound of snarling and growling. Looking up I saw the fears rising from their seats. Horrified, I realized they were heading straight for us. Mouth dry, heart pounding, I did the only thing I knew how to do. I tightened my grip on the gentle guy's hand and closed my eyes. Then I began to pray aloud: "Our Father who art in heaven, hallowed be thy name. Thy kingdom come, they will be done on earth . . ."[13]

If we are to remember those who are in prison, we must know something about their lives. We must listen as they name the oppressive forces that permeate their days, a process the Apostle Paul calls "discerning the spirits" (1 Cor 12:8–10). Yet as we identify destructive powers and struggle against them, "we become discouraged," says Murphy, "for it seems that we can do so little for our friends. We write letters, we make visits, we sit in court and encourage the lawyers, we vigil on the capitol steps and join forces with all who work to lift death sentences in Georgia. Yet the best efforts of the best people don't bring an end to the executions."[14]

Although it may seem ridiculously small when set against forces so great, the Christmas packages are a faithful response to the birth of peace. In the gifting of packages filled with cookies, mixed nuts, a bar of soap and a fluffy towel, a writing tablet, a warm hat, fresh socks, a hand-decorated card, and a glossy picture of the community, "we continue the movement of eucharistic love already unleashed," Ed says, "in the theology program at the Atlanta women's prison, in family reunions at the Hardwick prison complexes, and in death-row visits at Jackson State Prison."[15] With eucharistic joy, the Community continues this movement, joining the wise men that came from the East searching for Jesus:

13. Kelly Gissendaner, handwritten piece given to author, March 2010.
14. Ibid.
15. Ibid.

When the wise folk saw the star, how happy they were, the joy was theirs! It went ahead of them until it stopped over the place where the child was. They went in and when they saw the child with his mother Mary, they knelt down and worshipped him. They brought out their gifts—their prisoner packages, their boxes—which were full of gold, frankincense, and myrrh, and they presented them to him. Then they returned to their country by another road, since God had warned them in a dream, and calls us in this moment: Do not return to Herod. Go by another road. (Matt 2:9–12 [Open Door Community adapted version])

"It is that alternative road of nonviolent love that leads us to this table," says Ed, "to this bread and juice, these gifts that we will take to the prison on Tuesday. These boxes participate in this story, in the wise ones' joy of wanting to give gifts, in the desire to give oneself away through the medium of a package."[16]

Murphy calls these packages "gestures of solidarity," concrete attempts to draw near to a multitude of people who spend "Christmas in a cage."[17] They are simply "gestures" because most in the Community cannot begin to comprehend what it feels like to live under a State-sponsored death sentence, much less exist in a cage. Moreover, they are stand-ins for a face-to-face visit, that more immediate and direct expression of the Christmas proclamation that God has drawn near through God's very body. Because of its liturgical immediacy, some members of the Community journey to the prison on Christmas morn, an especially powerful time for visitation since embodied encounters demonstrate so well God's incarnate love. God has reduced the distance between God and humanity through the incarnation—through bodily participation in this-worldly suffering—and so disciples are called to reduce distance through embodied attempts at solidarity with those who suffer the most under destructive powers.

Still, even in the absence of direct human contact, the packages are, Murphy says, "cracks in which the light may shine through," those proclamations of peace that Kelly strains to hear continually—fear not, don't let your heart be troubled, no ruler or power can separate you

---

16. Ibid.
17. Murphy Davis, "Another Christmas in a Cage: Beauty in the Cracks and Between the Lined," *Hospitality* 31, no. 10 (November–December 2012): 1.

from the love of Christ—proclamations that carry special weight when spoken from communities actively engaged in dismantling destructive powers. The packages not only serve as cracks in the system, they are themselves light—if only "the flickering flame of a small candle in a very dark night"—as they express solidarity and meet basic need.[18] So the Community gathers in their upstairs hallway where the gifts are stored to remember by name over one hundred men and one woman on death row, read letters of gratitude from inmates like Clay—"y'all bring light to such a dark world"—and finally form a chain, an ongoing prayer of blessing for each person who will receive a package, as hand after hand is laid on each box that winds down the staircase, out the front door, onto the sidewalk, and into the vans.[19]

In poignant correspondence, the recipients articulate the power of that flickering flame and the nature of the dark night: "For most confined [to prison], Christmas is the low point of a dark spiritual tunnel," writes Tony Amadeo. "For those of us who live in a concrete cage, the Christmas season is a time of soul-wrenching sadness. We recriminate ourselves over bad decisions and tragic mistakes. Our days are filled with thoughts of failed dreams and lost hope. [At night] we lie awake questioning ourselves . . . and questioning God."[20] But the Christmas packages "provide a temporary reprieve from [this] perennial dark shadow," writes Marcus Wellons. Describing the humanizing impact of giving and receiving gifts, he says,

> My first Christmas here on death row was 1993. I was amazed by the spirit and the way guys embraced and celebrated the season. . . . Family and friends could send a 30 pound Christmas box. We had supplies for crocheting so that we could give gifts. . . .
>
> Now fast forward to the present. Little by little all those privileges were arbitrarily stripped away, causing a tremendous painful paradigm shift for us and our loved ones. To no longer hear my mother's loving voice ask, "Son, did you like the box I sent?" Robbing her of all the personal care, love, and pride put into it was difficult for both of us to accept.

18. Ibid., 8.
19. Open Door Community Liturgy of the Boxes, author's audio recording, December 20, 2010.
20. Tony Amadeo, "The Meaning of Christmas Is Love," *Hospitality* 31, no. 10 (November–December 2012): 9.

Now we must order our boxes from one centralized, super-expensive, state-approved vendor in Missouri, if our families can afford it. This severely hampers the warm flame of sharing. . . .

Fighting off the onslaught of feelings of oppression and depression is a constant battle. Nevertheless, even in our dungeon-like world, a cold, dark place of concrete, steel, gray bars and fences where we are locked down 23 hours everyday, there are moments of happiness. . . .

But the sporadic joy inevitably gives way to sadness. Loneliness. Christmas songs sometimes evoke nostalgia: missing family and friends, thinking about our miserable condition. When it gets thick here, there sometimes is a deathly silence, reminiscent I regret to say, of an execution night. . . .

. . . Later we go to the gate with our pillowcases to receive our gift box from the Open Door Community, filled with everything we need. Revival! . . . Once again the place is brimming with joy, life, and . . . activity.[21]

"Prison is intended to be a miserable place, and its architects have succeeded," writes Jack Alderman, "but there have also been instances of failure. When Christmas is not just another day, we, the caged, triumph."[22]

The lectionary text of Isaiah proclaims that "the people who walk in darkness have seen a great light," the birth of the Prince of Peace. The incarcerated men above testify to the power of that light when it is embodied in the acts of the discipleship community. The prophet announces that the authority of the Prince of Peace grows continually, in the words of the Open Door, "as the circle of beloved community is established and upheld with justice and solidarity." In other words, the reign of peace is made real in this world when the discipleship community grows in solidarity with those who are despised and oppressed. The circle of beloved community expands not only as the Open Door draws near to those in prison but also as it creates space for oppressed groups to grow in concern for one another. Many death-row inmates who read the Open Door's *Hospitality* newspaper participate in

---

21. Marcus Wellons, "Christmas Under the Shadow," *Hospitality* 31, no. 10 (November–December 2012): 8.
22. Jack Alderman, "Not Just Another Day After All," *Hospitality* 31, no. 10 (November–December 2012): 9.

that "warm flame of sharing" that Marcus mentions above by sending to the Community the little money they have in order to support the Open Door's homeless ministries. This generous act, reminiscent of the story Jesus tells of the widow giving away her last two coins, reveals that reducing distance happens between oppressed groups as well, who are active disciples and agents of nonviolent love (Mark 12:41–44).

## The Incarnation of Peace

We may be tempted to see the triumph of the Christmas box over the power of death and estrangement as merely symbolic, but the men spending Christmas in a cage describe its concrete impact. Even as "gestures" toward solidarity, the triumph of the gift is rooted in the concreteness of the incarnation, that decisive and determinative act of God's solidarity with real human beings. The primary significance of Christmas is the incarnation, the fact that "God in the conception and birth of Jesus has taken on humanity in bodily fashion," says Bonhoeffer.[23] God has reduced distance by experiencing "in his own body the essence of the real" and "spoke out of the knowledge of the real like no other human being on earth."[24] Thus, God not only draws near through the incarnation, God teaches us how to live embodied lives. As disciples participate in Jesus's incarnate love and follow his peacemaking way, they find his hard sayings—like commands in the Sermon on the Mount to make peace, love enemies, and creatively resist evil—trustworthy and true for social and political life, because they arise out of a realistic knowledge of this-worldly existence. Whereas dominant streams of Christian tradition have argued for centuries that Jesus's teachings are politically unrealistic, and thus apply to inner attitudes and interpersonal relationships alone, a growing number of modern theologians, like Bonhoeffer and King, align instead with the earliest disciples. For them, the teachings disclose Jesus's deep and abiding realism and are his realistic prescriptions for engaging dehumanizing and death-dealing powers.

23. Bonhoeffer, *Ethics*, 6, 84.
24. Ibid., 263.

As "the proclamation of the incarnate love of God," the Sermon on the Mount shows disciples how to embody a love strong enough to engage, and sometimes, even, triumph over, these powers.[25]

The incarnation draws us into an intricate web of peacemaking activity that weaves together small and seemingly insignificant acts with large and overwhelming prospects. Peacemaking is central to an embodied discipleship that seeks structural and relational change, and it comes in various interrelated forms, from the daily practices of hospitality and solidarity performed above by the Open Door to the larger campaigns for social change gaining visibility and legitimacy in the twenty-first century as responsible and practical modes of resistance.[26] Regardless of which form it takes, discipleship necessitates a basic conviction and nonnegotiable commitment to the practice of peace; it is the only way to foster beloved community and make the good news of peace on earth concrete.

Bonhoeffer and King both view peacemaking as a way of life, a daily practice and formation based on reducing distance between human beings, as well as a call to specific action against the powers—a struggle that often involves creative, nonviolent protest. For Bonhoeffer, the disciple's commitment to peace is distinct from a rule-based or passive pacifism, which refuses to engage violence and has been readily dismissed as too idealistic by the majority of Western Christians. Instead of a principle of pacifism, Bonhoeffer speaks of a holistic ethic of peace that participates in Jesus's person and work and envelops all of life. An ethic of peace grounded in discipleship thus encompasses so much more than the outdated and dualistic debates over pacifism and violence suggest. Since discipleship is not about following abstract principles but about following the living God, the discipleship community participates in the reign of the Prince of Peace by taking the form of Christ in the world—the shape of Jesus in public life—a presence defined by existence for others, incarnate love. Like the incarnate God, the discipleship community immerses itself into the

---

25. Ibid., 242.
26. See Gene Sharp, *Waging Nonviolent Struggle: 20th Century Practice and 21st Century Potential* (Boston: Porter Sargent Publishers, 2005).

messiness of fallen existence and concerns itself, as King says, with "the economic conditions that strangle" and "the social conditions that cripple" human beings.[27] Thus, a commitment to peace based on the person and work of Jesus is at once more open and more demanding than a rule-based ethic, because it calls Christians to practice peace continually and work out Jesus's incarnate love while deeply enmeshed in the complexity of specific spaces of social concern. Sharing Bonhoeffer's conviction that the power of peace is rooted not in ideology but practice, King proclaims in his "Pilgrimage to Nonviolence" that he is no armchair or "doctrinaire pacifist." The experience of the Montgomery bus boycott at the start of the civil rights movement "did more to clarify my thinking in regard to the question of nonviolence than all the books that I had read," King says. "As the days unfolded, I became more and more convinced of the power of nonviolence. . . . Many issues I had not cleared up intellectually concerning nonviolence were now resolved within the sphere of practical action."[28] As King's testimony contends, disciples only come to know the power of peace by way of embodied practice.

This incarnate ethic of peace is rooted in an active and practical love for the "enemy-neighbor," the term King uses to convey that incarnate love "makes no distinction between enemy and neighbor" as it creates community and "goes to any length to restore community."[29] Grounded in the reality of human interdependence, King defines this love as "understanding, redemptive good will" for all human beings.[30] What love understands is that every human being has common needs and vulnerabilities, as the testimonies of death-row inmates show, needs that are material, social, and cultural like food, housing, and health care; education, dignified work, and a fair wage; affirmation of one's worth and a sense of belonging; security from harm and predictability in relationships; and participation in personal and political decision making processes.[31] Loving enemy-neighbors

27. Martin Luther King Jr., *Strength to Love* (Philadelphia: Fortress Press, 1981), 149.
28. Ibid., 150.
29. King, *Testament of Hope*, 19.
30. Ibid., 46.

requires meeting human needs, and given the range of needs, this must be done on multiple levels: interpersonally, through localized expressions of church community, and through larger social structures. When we love the enemy-neighbor by meeting human need, we in turn make peace, for, as we will see, most violence results from injustice and unmet need.

When institutions, policies, and systems are not meeting human need, the discipleship community is called to press for their transformation, or in the words of Paul, to struggle against these powers. What Paul identifies as "powers and principalities," contemporary peace scholars call "structural violence," defined as the injury that happens "when systems, institutions, or policies meet some people's needs and rights at the expense of others."[32] Whereas privileged people tend to assume that a lack of visible violence or conflict constitutes peace (since their lives often remain unaffected and maintain the status quo), King shows that this absence of conflict is really a "negative peace" because it obscures the violence hidden within unjust structures. In contrast, "true peace," the peace that Jesus brings, is, as King famously says, "not the absence of tension but the presence of justice." King writes,

> I think this is what Jesus meant when he said, "I come not to bring peace but a sword." . . . Now Jesus didn't mean he came to start a war. . . . What Jesus was saying in substance was this, that I come not to bring an old negative peace, which makes for stagnant passivity and deadening complacency, I come to bring something different, and whenever I come, a conflict is precipitated, between the old and the new, whenever I come a struggle takes place between justice and injustice, between the forces of light and the forces of darkness. I come not to bring a negative peace but a positive peace, which *is* . . . justice, which *is* the kingdom of God.[33]

The incarnation of peace is the presence of God's justice. It is

31. Lisa Schirch, *The Little Book of Strategic Peacebuilding* (Intercourse, PA: Good Books, 2004), 13–15.
32. Ibid., 22.
33. King, *Testament of Hope*, 51. Italics mine.

nonviolent love working to establish the just conditions that manifest Jesus's reign in every dimension of life—personal, relational, communal, and structural.

This notion that justice is the essence of peace is the basic starting point for contemporary peace studies. Their inherent interconnection is also the foundation for understanding biblical justice. In the Old Testament, the Hebrew word for peace, *Shalom*, signifies this interconnection as it refers to the presence of wholeness, harmony, health, and flourishing. God's justice makes things right, restores things to their rightful and intended condition. In the New Testament, the term "righteousness" connotes the same. Indeed, righteousness means justice since it involves "doing, being, declaring, or bringing about what is right."[34] Righteousness does not concern personal, moral, or religious piety in a narrow sense, as many Christians tend to assume, but involves making things right for the sake of the flourishing of creation. The antithesis to whole and healthy community is violence, which peace scholars agree is most often a response to things not being right—an attempt to achieve justice and undo real or perceived injustice. Thus, social justice is quite tangibly the essence of peace as it secures against violence in many forms. In contrast, structural violence is damaging and vicious in and of itself—"the deadliest form of violence is poverty," Gandhi observed.[35] It is also the primary producer of more obvious forms of behavioral violence, those destructive acts that occur on individual, communal, national, and international levels, from suicide and substance abuse to domestic violence and other forms of crime to civil war and terrorism. Peacemakers work to overcome violence in all its forms, relationally by reducing distance between human beings while cultivating community, and systemically by working to transform the unjust structures themselves.

In *Violence: A National Epidemic*, Harvard psychiatrist James Gilligan examines the multifaceted work of peace in his psychoanalytic study. Gilligan works with the most violent male offenders in prison and

34. Chris Marshall, *The Little Book of Biblical Justice* (Intercourse, PA: Good Books, 2005), 11.
35. James Gilligan, *Violence: A National Epidemic* (New York: Vintage Books, 1996), 191.

argues that as a society, we have the capacity to both understand their violence and prevent it. This capacity lies in the willingness to challenge the moral/legal framework that simplistically divides individuals into the innocent and guilty and then punishes the guilty, and to instead attend to the empirical relationship between violence and lack of love. He writes, "What we need to see—if we are to understand violence and prevent it—is that human agency or action is not only individual; it is also, unavoidably, familial, societal, institutional. Each of us is inextricably bound to others—in relationship. Understanding that point is essential to understanding the origins of violent acts, and the strategies that might be helpful in preventing them."[36] He reminds his readers that the attempt to understand the violent behavior of offenders is not to excuse it but to offer realistic proposals for its prevention.

Gilligan worked for over fifteen years in the Massachusetts State Prison system with men serving life sentences, people we commonly think of as cold-blooded killers, and he saw a pattern emerge, namely that these men endured such extreme victimization as children in the form of "physical violence, neglect, abandonment, rejection, sexual exploitation and violation" that they were left with a complete deficit of love.[37] Violence is "the ultimate means of communicating the absence of love," he says, and without the experience of being loved, "the self cannot survive."[38] This absence or deficiency of self-love in turn results in shame. "The soul needs love as vitally and urgently as the lungs need oxygen," he says, so children who do not receive sufficient love from others do not have the appropriate reserves of self-love needed to survive "the inevitable rejections and humiliations" that all human beings endure.[39] When the buildup of shame and the intensity of humiliation become too much, these men resort to violence, which replaces shame with an experience of pride. Exemplifying the reality that violence is a response to real or perceived

36. Ibid., 7.
37. Ibid., 45.
38. Ibid., 47.
39. Ibid., 51, 47.

injustice, Gilligan says that he has "yet to see a serious act of violence that was not provoked by the experience of feeling shamed . . . and that did not represent the attempt to prevent or undo shame" or "save face."[40] He argues that for violent men, experiences of shame are "the primary or ultimate cause" of intentional violence toward others or self, and that shame is the "necessary" but not "sufficient" cause of violence.[41] Before shame turns violent, several other preconditions must be met: the men perceive themselves as lacking nonviolent means to gain pride, of having no "socially rewarded economic or cultural achievements" like education or job prestige; they feel vulnerable to a loss of self or total disintegration of male identity; and they lack the emotional capacities to be moved by the feelings of others.[42] Like extreme cold, shame is at first very painful, but too much of it can lead to a deadening of feeling, an inability to feel altogether. Thus, the men that Gilligan works with describe themselves as numb, empty, "the living dead."[43] Finding such a state excruciating, many of these men try to counteract it through further violence directed outward and inward. In prison, many of them harm themselves in hopes of creating any physical sensation, even a painful one.

Given the innumerable ways that the prison humiliates, disintegrates identity, and deprives inmates of opportunities for accomplishment, imprisonment only furthers violence as it increases shame. "Punishment is a *form* of violence in its own right," Gilligan argues, since its explicit intent is to inflict pain, and in a retributive system, prisons do so for no other purpose than the sake of suffering.[44] Given its relationship to shame, the punishment of prison is also a cause of violence; "nothing stimulates crime as powerfully and as effectively as punishment does."[45] Indeed, prison actively deprives people of the basic needs mentioned above, like dignified work for a fair wage, affirmation of personal worth, predictability in

40. Ibid., 110.
41. Ibid.
42. Ibid., 112.
43. Ibid., 31.
44. Ibid., 184.
45. Ibid., 187.

relationships, security from harm, and decision-making power. The more punitive our society has become, the higher our rate of violence, a phenomenon demonstrated, for example, by the otherwise peculiar fact that after a state execution, homicide rates outside the prison increase. As King says, "Through violence you can murder a murderer but you can't murder murder. . . . Darkness cannot put out darkness. Only light can do that."[46] In contrast to spaces of shame, what is needed for both healing and prevention are conditions that "enable love to grow" and that foster a healthy sense of pride—of self-esteem, self-respect, and self-love.[47] Although Gilligan believes that there are a few men he worked with who are so damaged and dangerous to others that there is "no alternative but to quarantine them for the foreseeable future," his research shows that humanizing conditions and experiences of concrete love and care would have transformative power for the vast majority of these male offenders,[48] like Kevin, a man I met shortly after his release from prison. Kevin's transformation began when a medical worker, in a rare display of compassion, gently placed his hand on Kevin's shoulder and held it there for a time as Kevin was tied to a gurney in solitary confinement after an episode of extreme violence. Recognizing himself in the men Gilligan writes about, Kevin says that it was the first moment in his life that someone showed him love and conveyed his worth. This simple act of love was powerful enough to spark new life and determination.

Gilligan argues that the violent conditions that produce shame are not only familial but also social. Even if individuals survive family violence with a capacity to feel intact, they are still vulnerable to the "power of systemic shaming" that results from structural violence like poverty.[49] Disparities of income and wealth between the rich and the poor are the best predictors of homicide rates in any geographical region, and in light of this, Gilligan calls for more equitable policies

---

46. King, *Testament of Hope*, 249.
47. Gilligan, *Violence*, 236.
48. Ibid., 184. In recent years, there have been a number of articles about Scandinavian prisons as more humane models of incarceration. See, for example, Doran Larson, "Why Scandinavian Prisons Are Superior," *The Atlantic*, September 24, 2013, http://tinyurl.com/hf8ggqh.
49. Gilligan, *Violence*, 197.

that close the economic gap and reduce shame. It is not poverty per se, the lack of material things in and of themselves, that causes shame but rather the gap, one's relative deprivation to others—"living in a hovel next to a palace."[50] Shame results when one's life lacks witness, when one is wholly overlooked and rendered invisible. Violence then becomes a vehicle to make oneself visible when people lack an intact community or culture that bears witness to their personal worth. Shame also results from fear of dependency, argues Gilligan, particularly in countries like the United States that are critical of social welfare and particularly for men who embrace our cultural construction of masculinity, which portrays professed need as a weakness, be it material need like food or housing or relational need like love and care. "We are afraid of dependency in the country," argues Gilligan, and so "we as a nation do less for our own citizens than any other democracy on earth; less health care, child care, housing, support for families, and so on" and then we shame and blame "those whose needs are exposed."[51] He concludes, "We have the level of criminal violence we do because we have arranged our social and economic life in certain ways rather than others. . . . If we continue to tolerate the conditions that have made us the most violent of industrial societies," it is because we have decided that it is easier to condemn criminal violence than to work to prevent it.[52] Prevention addresses all the diverse "powers and principalities" that seek to dominate and constrain human flourishing, be they economic realities like poverty, public opinions that shame entire demographics, or cultural constructions of gender identity.

Likewise, prison abolitionist Angela Davis observes that the prison performs significant "ideological work" that "relieves us of the responsibility of seriously engaging with the problems of our society."[53] Locking people up requires less effort and radical social

50. Ibid., 201.
51. Ibid., 237.
52. Ibid., 22. Gilligan is citing Elliot Currie, *Confronting Crime: An American Challenge* (New York: Pantheon, 1985), 19.
53. Angela Y. Davis, *Are Prisons Obsolete?* (New York: Seven Stories Press, 2003), 16.

analysis than acknowledging the link between behavioral and structural violence, a link that would require us to face the severity of the injustice in our society and take seriously King's conviction that America needs a "radical revolution of values" that fundamentally alters dominant perspectives and the will of the people. The work is radical because it asks us to thoroughly examine the structural roots embedded deeply in our nation's soil. While doing so, Angela Davis invites us to explore "new terrains of justice where the prison no longer serves as our major anchor."[54] She directs our imaginations instead toward "a constellation of alternative strategies and institutions," arguing that the solution to imprisonment lies not in replacing the prison with some alternate and isolated institution but in addressing the many social injustices that foster crime.[55] This constructive work envelops a variety of social structures, from a school system that "encourages the joy of learning," to a health system "that provides physical and mental care to all," to a justice system "based on reparation and reconciliation" in which "punishment itself is not a central concern."[56] It includes a commitment to decriminalization applied, for example, to drug addiction, homelessness, and undocumented workers. It includes envisioning and creating humanizing conditions inside and outside the prison as we strive toward decarceration.

Against this backdrop, the realistic nature of Jesus's commands is revealed. Gospel realism is based, as King says, in the uniquely transformative power of love, relationally and structurally. Relationally, "love is the only force capable of transforming an enemy" or perceived enemy "into a friend."[57] Structurally, love is realistic at its core because it interrupts the "chain reaction" of evil and violence that perpetuates harm. "Returning hate for hate multiplies hate, adding deeper darkness to a night already devoid of stars," King says. "Darkness cannot drive out darkness; only light can do that. Hate

---

54. Ibid., 21.
55. Ibid., 107.
56. Ibid., 107–13.
57. King, *Strength to Love*, 54.

cannot drive out hate; only love can do that. Hate multiplies hate, violence multiplies violence, and toughness multiples toughness in a descending spiral of destruction."[58] King concludes that Jesus's command to love the enemy-neighbor is "an ultimately inescapable admonition" given the manner in which evil unfolds.[59]

## The Role of Bodies in the Work of Peace

Be it the relatively small act of delivering Christmas packages to people in prison or the more complex work of nonviolent campaigns for social change that address the systems above, the incarnation teaches disciples that peacemaking requires active, bodily engagement in this world. This means the willingness to reduce distance between safety and insecurity, between ourselves and those whom we would otherwise fear, be they powerful authorities or poor strangers living on the streets. For Herod's rule has the power to unleash violence simultaneously through unjust structures and the people made to endure them.

In a Tuesday-morning Bible study, Nelia leads the community in a reflection on the moments of fear and the moments of faith that may arise for us and for those we serve as we reduce distance. She invites us before our time of hospitality to reflect on our own fears and to be alert to the faith and fear of the men and women who gather in the front yard, eat in the dining room, receive clothing and toiletries in the sorting room, and encounter one another in the hallway. Moments later, Nelia finds herself in a situation, rare at the Open Door, where she has to courageously face the real possibility of violence on her person as she intentionally places her body in between two homeless men in order to receive the aggression, harsh words, and even the spit of one man who was new to the front yard. Nelia positions her body in between this man and our mentally ill friend Roger in order to protect him from harm, diffuse the situation, and get the violent man off the property.

58. Ibid., 53.
59. Ibid.

Afterwards, in our lunchtime reflection, she asks us to examine honestly if we as a community would have maintained our commitment to nonviolence had the man hit Nelia, a question particularly addressed to the men in the room who have internalized cultural messages that define southern masculinity in terms of female protection. The conversation reinforces not only this community's commitment to nonviolence but also the necessary role of our bodies in following Jesus's nonviolent way. Nelia's nonviolent tactic was to bank on the likelihood that the aggressive man would think twice before hitting a gray-haired woman, but had he hit her, Nelia makes it clear to us, the only response permitted in the yard would have been further nonviolent action. Then during Wednesday's lunch and discussion, Ed reflects on the call of scripture, a favorite of Dorothy Day's that is repeated often in this house, "to present our bodies as living sacrifices" (Rom 12:1), what Ed calls "a biblical method of social analysis."[60] In order to understand social issues, Ed contends, disciples must first place their bodies in the midst of the struggle.

Ed and Nelia each remind us that when we come to the Open Door, we enter into the possibility that what happened to Nelia may happen to us. The gift of this place is that it invites us into a space in which the possibility of violence is real and at hand. It is a gift because the gospel of peace cannot be proclaimed and the nonviolent way cannot be formed within us, unless, as Ed tells us, we place our bodies "in the arena of violence." For the peace that Jesus brings is not, in the words of King, "obnoxious negative peace," the peace of "escapism" that "fails to confront the real issues of life" and therefore bolsters the status quo.[61] Rather, God's peace is that presence of justice fostered through agape love, which seeks to create community. King says, "The cross is the eternal expression of the length to which God will go in order to restore broken community. The resurrection is a symbol of God's triumph over all the forces that seek to block community. The

60. Ed Loring, "Serving the Humiliated Christ: Public Toilets," *Hospitality* 2, no. 3 (December 1983): 3.
61. King, *Testament of Hope*, 295; Martin Luther King Jr., "When Peace Becomes Obnoxious," in *The Papers of Martin Luther King, Jr.*, ed. Clayborne Carson, vol. 3 (Berkeley: University of California Press, 1997), 208.

Holy Spirit is the continuing community creating reality that moves through history."[62] For the Open Door, the daily arena of violence where beloved community is sought is that of the streets, "the rage that comes with having nothing to do and nowhere to go," as Ed says, the violence that comes from the drive to survive in a hostile world full of oppressive forces like hunger and homelessness, jails and prisons, and addiction to drugs and alcohol.[63] The violence of the "powers and principalities" finds expression, then, not only through the actions of powerful elites like Herod but also through the people suffering under them. Engaging the powers entails loving people that are caught beneath their weight, but to do this, Day reminds us, "we must get close" to "those we fear."[64] When the community draws near enough to receive the rage, frustration, and suffering of those in the yard, it participates in the incarnation of peace.

Participation in the incarnation demands distance be reduced, and disciples are called to reduce distance in a particular way. The incarnation speaks directly to the centrality of bodies in Christian faith, to the necessity of bodily presence and bodily formation in the work of peace. I was drawn to the Open Door in part because of their emphasis on the role of bodies in discipleship, the role of bodies, that is, in personal and social transformation. Before I became a full-time volunteer, I told a male friend that I wanted to learn how to use my body as an instrument of nonviolence, how to intervene in situations of violence. His response was protective, like some of the men in the Tuesday lunch with Nelia, and it was fearful: "Well I don't want you to learn that," he said defensively. But like the founders of the Open Door, my vision of a Christian faith with this-worldly relevance had been shaped by the civil rights movement, by the role of bodies in a movement that brought about concrete social and political change, a movement that taught me what the church could be and what obedience to the nonviolent Jesus could accomplish. In graduate school, I had the honor of meeting and sharing meals with the late

62. King, *Testament of Hope*, 20.
63. Ed Loring, Open Door Community Meeting at which author was present, June 20, 2011.
64. Jim Forest, *All Is Grace: A Biography of Dorothy Day* (Maryknoll, NY: Orbis Books, 2011), 251.

Victoria Gray Adams of the Mississippi Freedom Democratic Party, whose racially marked body at the 1964 Democratic National Convention challenged the all-white regular Mississippi delegation; with Ed King, the white chaplain at Tougaloo College who, alongside a group of black students, would place his body on the steps of white churches on Sunday mornings only to get door after door slammed in his face; and with Bob Moses, director of the 1964 Mississippi Freedom Summer Project and voter registration drive that brought over a thousand grassroots volunteers into the state, three of whom were viciously murdered by the Ku Klux Klan. Shaped by the courageous witness of these and others, my desire has been to be formed into a person and be a part of a community that enacts costly discipleship. I do not want to be spat upon as Nelia was, or hit, but I do want to be a person who places herself in difficult situations for the sake of Jesus and his nonviolent redemption of this world. I want the formation of my body to be such that, be it small or extreme situations, I am ready to respond in faithfulness and courage—a response that may be formed within me through something as small as a knock at the door.

Those of us who fulfill the leadership role of house duty at the Open Door are trained to answer the doorbell every time it rings. The bell rings, we go to the door, and we welcome a friend or stranger. When I first started doing house duty, especially evening duty, I wondered who might be on the other side of the door when I answered it: Would it be a familiar face? Would it be someone asking for something, or *demanding* something, that I could not give? What if the person was drunk and aggressive and there was no one inside to help should a situation get out of hand? These would be quick, passing thoughts, almost unconscious, but they were there nonetheless—entrenched fears that betrayed the reality of numerous friendly and respectful encounters I experienced daily with men and women from the streets. Relatively soon, though, I became comfortable with the process because I got lots of practice in a short amount of time—the doorbell kept ringing! It rang so often that it became second nature—a habit—to hear the bell, jump up in response, and head to the door with ease.

As I would get to the foyer, I would pause, no longer to take a breath before I opened the door as in those first weeks, but to make sure that my attention was fully focused on the person standing on the other side. Responding to the doorbell became effortless. It was immediate, "single-minded obedience" to use Bonhoeffer's wonderful phrase. Through the habit of responding to the bell, I became confident in my ability to address the various questions and needs, be it sandwiches, blankets, mail check, or surprisingly often, simply a cup of cold water.

I've been struck by how often a person at the door simply needs a cup of water. I go inside, fill a plastic mug, take it to the door, they drink it down, and with a big smile of relief say, "Thank you so much." During the soup kitchen one morning, our friend Stephen said to me, "You have no idea what something as simple as a cup of water or a clean T-shirt means to those of us who are out here on the streets." Even the tiniest of acts, "even a cup of cold water," Jesus says to his disciples against the backdrop of a hostile political climate, can unleash transformative power (Matt 10:42). Oftentimes the cup of water is combined with other needs, like a blanket, book bag, or pair of shoes. Sometimes the cup of water has been a cup of coffee, two peanut butter and jelly sandwiches, and bedding for our mentally ill friend Timothy, who for some time was sober, drug free, and clearheaded enough to arrive at an appointed time and make a pallet for himself on the public restroom floor. I came to look forward to his knock. Invariably, Timothy and I would have some semblance of a conversation that would leave me belly laughing out loud.

The point is that as I moved my body time after time toward that door and responded to the need, often with the tiniest of acts—just a cup of water, a sandwich, a blanket, a piece of mail—I underwent formation. There is a process of habituation (the cultivation of a *habitus* as Aristotle called it) that has been taking place in me—taking place in all of us at the Open Door—that, over time, shapes how we live and act in the world and how we respond to new and unfolding situations. Through the simple act of responding to the doorbell time and time again, welcoming the stranger and attending to need becomes second nature for us, a part of our very being. We become formed in such a way that we no longer have to think twice, nor do we know how to not respond. We become like the French community of Le Chambon, whose members, when asked why they chose to shelter Jews during the Holocaust at risk to themselves, responded that it was not a choice.[65] They already had been formed as a people who protect the vulnerable. Likewise, through the simple act of answering the door and giving a cup of cold water, we become a people who can no longer do otherwise. Through the daily acts of welcome and embrace, we become formed into agents of justice and peace. The advantage we get from using our bodies in this way is personal and social transformation. And the end is abundant life.

The further advantage of cultivating a *habitus*—of undergoing this kind of formation—is that we become better prepared to improvise, better prepared to handle more complex situations like the one Nelia found herself in during Tuesday's soup kitchen. For me, the more complex situation comes when Beth, a burly woman from the streets who is at least twice my size, breaks into the house in the middle of a rainy night by cutting a large square piece out of the front porch screen. I am on overnight house duty, so David Christian, a resident at the Open Door who hears the commotion, comes to get me. He knocks on the door of the Rosa Parks room and says, "Uh, Jenny, there's a woman in the house." We head downstairs and search for the woman, who had last been seen in the living room, but she is not there, nor in the dining room.

As I open the door to the side porch, I am confronted by Beth, who is frantically moving about and shouting, "There are people dying out there! They are dying! They are dying of pneumonia! *They are wet and dying!*" Still unclear how she has gotten into the house, I say, "Ma'am, you cannot be here right now; the house is closed." She responds to my gesture ushering her in from the enclosed porch, and as we stand in the corner of the dining room she continues to shout, "*There are*

---

65. See Philip Hallie, *Lest Innocent Blood Be Shed: The Story of the Village of Le Chambon and How Goodness Happened There* (New York: HarperPerennial, 1994).

*ple dying out there!*" I move my hand toward the back of her shoulder, repeating over and over in a calm but direct voice, "You cannot be here right now," and as she sees my hand almost upon her, she throws her arm back, a clear message that she is not to be touched.

I have no idea how David and I are going to get Beth out of the house. The whole situation is quite surreal, and I am still half asleep, but in that moment an amazing thing happens. I notice that the positions of both my body and David's are open to Beth, an intruder. My body is open without my consciously willing it to be, because it has already learned to be open through the practice of welcoming the stranger at the door. My shoulders are back and my arms outstretched, almost like one celebrating the Eucharist. And as David and I take small, slow steps toward the hallway, Beth responds, still shouting but responding to our bodies and movements as if the three of us are in a dance. We dance our way slowly to the front door. I push it open and Beth shuffles out, still shouting, "*They are dying!*" as the door slams on its own weight.

Becoming formed into practices of peace does not mean that we can act perfectly in the situations that present themselves. It does not mean that we never again struggle with fear, aggression, and violent impulses, or that we may avoid the tragic dimensions of life, as the example with Beth conveys. That story ends with a door slamming in the face of an intruder who sure did sound like a prophet: "They are dying out there!" she continually shouted. But it does mean that when we place our bodies in a position to be formed, we are habituated into certain acts that usher in the reign of God, the beloved community, and how beautiful it is that some of those acts are as simple as opening a door to a stranger or providing a cup of cold water to one in need. Most importantly, the incarnation of peace teaches that personal and social transformation does not come about merely by way of good intentions or even a pure heart. We have to place our bodies in situations of struggle. We have to be formed continually through the practice of nonviolent love.

# 4

------

# Ordinary Time

Then Jesus went to Nazareth, where he had been brought up,
and on the Sabbath he went as usual to the synagogue.
He stood up to read the Scriptures
and was handed the book of the prophet Isaiah.
He unrolled the scroll and found the place where it is written,

"The Spirit of the Lord is upon me,
because I have been chosen to bring good news to the poor.
God has sent me to proclaim liberty to the captives
and recovery of sight to the blind,
to set free the oppressed
and announce that the time has come when
the Lord will save the people."

Jesus rolled up the scroll, gave it back to the attendant, and sat down.
All the people in the synagogue had their eyes fixed on him,
as he said to them,

"This passage of Scripture has come true today,
as you heard it being read."
—Luke 4:16–21 (Good News Bible, adapted)

## Perform Redemption Now

In his first public address in his hometown of Nazareth, Jesus makes clear the content of the gospel to be proclaimed: good news for the poor, liberty to prisoners, and freedom for the oppressed. Significantly, he directs the hope of fulfillment not to the future but to the present: "The time has come." This scripture "has come true today, as you heard it being read." Ordinary time is thus a time of fulfillment, "a decisive time . . . that demands action," as Murphy says, a time that demands intentional structuring so that disciples may "make good use of every opportunity" we have to lean into the reign of God.[1]

In their yearly planning retreat at Dayspring Farm, Murphy reflects "on the discipline of being intentional about the use of our time" as she reminds the Community why they structure their common life around lectionary readings and the liturgical calendar. "Living in resistance to . . . what Paul calls the powers and principalities and what Dr. King delineated as the giant triplets of racism, materialism, and militarism" necessitates that disciples "structure and define our time differently" than society at large. She continues,

> We who claim the faith of Jesus are living in the time of fulfillment, even as we wait for the ultimate fulfillment. . . . Anything that is not good news for the poor is not of the gospel. Any time that the captives are not being set free and the blind are not recovering their sight, we are promoting rather than resisting the "evil days" (Eph 5:15).

> If we just drift from one day to the next and "go with the flow," we give our passive and silent assent to the realities of war, oppression, violence, crushing poverty, mass imprisonment, executions, the destruction of the earth. It is easy enough to move through our days asleep at the wheel. But count on this: the powers and principalities—the forces of death and oppression—are not asleep at the wheel. . . . That is why so many Scriptures (like the first Sundays of Advent) shout at us: WAKE UP! . . . Be attentive. . . . Discern the signs of the time. And pray without ceasing.[2]

Time is a gift, and so we are "to use the days we have to do good

---

1. Murphy Davis, "It's About Time," *Hospitality* 28, no. 9 (October 2009): 9–10.
2. Ibid.

work," says Murphy, "to act, to engage, to 'make the most' of the time we have." Disciples are called "to redeem the day—redeem time . . . to do with our time what God has done for us," she says, "'perform' redemption—act it out!"[3]

The possibility of performing redemption may sound simultaneously exhilarating and exhausting. Perhaps instead of the message "act out redemption," what we need to hear are the words from the psalmist, "be still and know that I am God," a reminder of a peace that may be experienced through intimate knowledge of the presence of God in life's ordinary moments. In a community organized, practically speaking, around work—the works of mercy and the work of justice for the oppressed—the calming presence of God must be found not only in rare moments of solitude but also in the inexhaustible chores of daily life. Performing redemption, as Murphy says above, includes the practice of praying without ceasing, not only because the work must be done through the power of God, but also because the practice of continuous prayer cultivates some sense of stillness, however fragile and fleeting it may seem.

At the Open Door, solitude and stillness are sometimes sought, and often found, as one discovers God in the basement. Ed refers to the "spirituality of the basement," the presence of God in the place that stores everyday needs, God's presence in the ordinary stuff of refrigerators packed with ham and cheese sandwiches given out daily, of shelves stacked with beans, bags of rice, and cleaning supplies, and of closets full of travel-size toiletries and yet-to-be-sorted donated clothes. It is in the basement in the early days of shared life with the Community that I hear a voice whisper, "Be still, be still, my love" as I wash and dry the clothes of homeless men and women to the rhythm of the timed machines. As I am folding the clothes at a slow and measured pace, with care and intention, the folding itself is prayer, prayer for others who will wear these clothes, prayer for myself, who desperately needs God to be as intimate as a worn garment. There, in these moments, I hear words of stillness and peace, of calmness and the

3. Ibid.

nearness of God. In these moments in the basement, I am overwhelmed with a profound sense of what Brother Lawrence, a seventeenth-century layperson in a Carmelite monastery in Paris, called "practicing the presence of God." There is a peace and stillness that may be formed in us through the everyday duties and chores of common life together, a peace that confirms the significance of the work down to the most mundane and unpleasant detail and that reminds us of God's presence and redemption even and especially in the details. We may indeed hear, even in the never-ending tasks that meet us day after day, "Peace, peace. I am God." If we seek to perform redemption, this is a mantra we must hear over and over again because the work of redemption includes immersing ourselves in difficult and painful realities.

The discipleship community is called to engage hard realities as it enacts good news for the poor and liberty for the oppressed in its everyday life. This is the social and political significance of ordinary time; it is Jesus's very mission, summed up in his first public address. Disciples practice God's reign and make it known to others as they perform the redemption that, according to Jesus, "has come true today." The discipleship community does this most consistently, this chapter argues, by infusing ordinary acts with sacramental power.

### The Work of Encountering Reality in the Raw

My third day on the Open Door's weekly schedule, I am assigned Wednesday laundry. As the soup kitchen bustles upstairs in controlled chaos, I wait below for Annie, a resident volunteer, to walk me through the process. She explains that the clothes dropped down the chute will be coming from forty or so men who are taking showers that day, discarding their old clothes and getting new ones from the clothing closet. She leads me to the big plastic bucket that we fill with water and Clorox, where we separate out and soak the underwear that is badly soiled, and she asks if I will contribute to the art project of a former resident volunteer. Lulu is collecting the underwear still badly stained after being bleached and washed, which can no longer be used in the clothes closet, for a piece she has entitled "Holy Shit."

After Annie leaves and with the playfulness of Lulu's title receding into the back of my mind, I focus on filling the Clorox bucket and making sure I know how to properly use the large industrial machines. So I am slightly taken aback when *swoosh*, the first load of clothes tumbles down into the basement carrying with it the smells and debris from the streets. I separate the soiled and stained underwear of strangers whose names I do not yet know, and will only slowly come to learn, and am struck by the profundity of it all. It is gross and beautiful at the same time, an example of what Southern novelist Flannery O'Connor called "the grotesque"—that place where raw reality and God's grace are so intricately intertwined that you cannot separate one from the other. God's grace manifests itself in the raw, the crude, and the uncouth—so much so that uncomfortable realities become grace filled and thick with the presence of God. This unity of the gross and the beautiful is holy. Lulu is right—there is no better description of the soiled and stained underwear worn by these strangers and friends.

The next week, Johnny, another resident volunteer, walks me through the process of cleaning the public restroom in the basement. The last thing he shows me is the little stoop outside the alley door, which Community members regularly clean. As he opens that side door and peers out, Johnny comments that it is good today that there is no poop to clean, for sometimes a homeless friend will go to the bathroom there when the public restroom is closed. Once again I encounter "holy shit," and am pressed to consider further: What makes it holy? Or, put another way, what makes the work of encountering reality in the raw holy?

As I have glimpsed human vulnerability to structural violence and degradation through my friendships with people in prison and on the streets, I have become convinced that integral to Christian faith is the courage to squarely face dehumanizing realities. Disciples may face these realities out of an unflinching commitment to life, a stubborn refusal to wish nothing less for others and for ourselves than total human flourishing.

Christians have two reasons for affirming the dignity and working for the flourishing of human beings: the logic of creation and the logic of the incarnation. God has first granted human beings dignity by creating all of us in the image of God and further substantiated that dignity by choosing to become one of us even after the fall, by becoming Jesus, the real human being who was also vulnerable to life on the streets, vulnerable, perhaps too, to soiled and stained underwear. In a letter from prison, Bonhoeffer says it poignantly and piercingly: "The truth is, if the earth was deemed worthy to bear the human being Jesus Christ"—if this life, this reality, was good enough for Jesus—"then and only then does our life as human beings have meaning."[4]

Our work of encountering reality in the raw is holy because this is precisely what Jesus did. He, in the words of Bonhoeffer, drank "the earthly cup to the dregs." He drank in every bit of what it means to be human in this world, and in doing so, gave meaning and significance to every experience and every expression of our human fragility. At the Open Door, we too drink the earthly cup to the dregs as we sort laundry and clean grimy restrooms, as we gently scrub blistered feet in the foot clinic and mop up afterwards, as we stand on the steps of the capitol and vigil for men being put to death by the state at that very moment. As disciples, we need not ignore but rather turn toward, face, and welcome into our lives harsh and raw realities. This is the ordinary work of redemption, and it happens in basements and bathrooms, in the overlapping private and public spheres of our lives.

Public restrooms are politically contested spaces, historically and today. They are places of raw existence and basic human need, where our common humanity is hard to ignore. Perhaps this is why they become central sites of exclusion, places where so much effort is spent trying to cover over this obvious reality. Whether in the Jim Crow South of the twentieth century or in urban centers across the United States today, as sites of exclusion, they are sites where redemption begs to be performed. They are holy ground.

The Open Door built its basement bathroom as a way to act out

---

4. Bonhoeffer, *Letters and Papers* (Fortress Press), 515.

redemption during an ongoing campaign for public toilets in downtown Atlanta. Against the opposition of Central Atlanta Progress, a private, nonprofit organization tasked with insuring business and tourist interests, the Open Door and fellow advocates have fought inhospitable public policies for decades by trying to educate and engage city and business leaders on the primary causes of homelessness and the needs of homeless people; by speaking at public hearings, asking the city to stop arresting homeless people for public urination until they provide restrooms throughout downtown Atlanta; and by performing creative acts of nonviolent resistance that dramatize the urgency of the matter: Ed sitting on a toilet in the mayor's office, reading scripture loudly, and proclaiming his campaign motto, "Pee for free with dignity!" As they agitate the city for broader structural change, the basement restroom serves as an act of personalism, a way to perform redemption now and take responsibility for their friends' needs amidst piecemeal campaign achievements. Yet even public toilets on their own property have proven to be controversial, as seen through their neighbors' persistent complaints in the mid-1980s about the backyard porta potties surrounded by thick brush, which preceded basement construction. The hard-won, modest victories of the campaign in downtown Atlanta and in their own backyard—just one or two public toilets—reveal how readily our society sees homeless people as contaminants, people who are unfit to share basic bodily needs with us. And they reveal how reticent we are to recognize that ordinary needs of real human beings are holy and that facing and embracing common need makes us holy. In a 1983 *Hospitality* article at the start of the campaign, Ed writes, "Many of the homeless among us are denied the privacy we find essential and take for granted. Now, working to provide public restroom facilities may not seem like a particularly religious thing to do." It might not seem like a holy act. "But that's where we could be surprised. For in the end Jesus may well declare, 'I was exposed and humiliated and you gave me the dignity of privacy.'"[5]

---

5. Ed Loring, "Serving the Humiliated Christ," *Hospitality* 2, no. 3 (Dec. 1983): 1. Ed is quoting Paul

At the overcrowded women's prison, toilet use is rarely private. A commode protrudes from the wall of a two-person room that is inhabited by six, exposing the women to alternating strangers, foes, and the occasional ally with whom they navigate this small space. Privacy is more likely found in visitation and program facilities where toilets have their own rooms, designated either "inmate" or "staff." The latter is distinguished by the persistent presence of soap and toilet paper, a plant or inspirational poster, and a lock on the door. In the central inmate restroom of the programs building, a sign prominently placed over the sink reads in all caps, "MRSA, AKA: STAPHYLOCOCCUS IS HIGHLY **CONTAGIOUS**!!!! PLEASE WASH YOUR HANDS AFTER USING THE BATHROOM!" But the soap dispenser is almost always empty.

My last official day as program director of the theology certificate, the women present me with a book of handmade artistic notes and spontaneously break into speeches and stories of our years together, the kind of personal and public discourse mixed with laughter and tears that happens at weddings and graduations. Sierra, who is known for both her boisterous personality—her determination to cultivate joy in these harsh surroundings—and also her serious and piercing insights, breaks down in sobs. Through them, she only says this: "You used the inmate bathroom." I had always passed it off as a momentary decision based on practicality. It was "no big deal," and officers seemed to never be around to unlock the staff restroom during those quick classroom breaks. But Sierra knows her civil rights history—beloved community triumphing over segregation and "whites only" signs—and she rightly receives this gesture as my attempt to perform redemption, to act out liberation for the captives "today" through the simple refusal to differentiate between "inmate" and "free" on such holy ground.

Eckel of First Presbyterian Church, Atlanta, Georgia. For details about the campaign, see Gathje, *Sharing the Bread*, 192–94.

## The Sacramental Power of Ordinary Acts:
## Vending Machine Eucharist and Baptism by Shower

"Don't forget the quarters," Kelly writes to me once I have moved away and am planning what will become one of many return visits. Although most of our one-on-one time will continue under the auspices of the theology program, every once in a while, for various bureaucratic reasons, we will set up a "special visit" instead. Our meeting space had already changed from her cell, where we discussed theology on opposite sides of an iron cage, to a small room located off the large visitation area, accessible through two mechanically locked doors. Special visits give Kelly and me the opportunity to share a meal—whatever we can cobble together from the vending machines that line the back of the visitation room—something that program volunteers are prohibited from doing.

Rolls of quarters take on sacramental value at the Open Door precisely because they are the means through which Community members break bread with the men they visit on Jackson's death row. For years, I have heard of these daylong visits and the power of the shared meal as an extension of the Community's Sunday Eucharist. On an almost weekly basis, Community members reflect during the prayers of the people on the details of the visit they made the day before, so it is only natural that I would hear Kelly's quarter reminder as an invitation to eucharistic celebration.

Perhaps only inside a Georgia state prison do Big Az Bubba Twin Cheeseburgers become the real presence of Christ, but that is exactly what Kelly sends me off to buy, along with a bag of Cheetos, a twenty-ounce bottle of Diet Coke, and animal cracker cookies—sixteen quarters for the burgers, four for the chips, eight for the Coke, and six more for the cookies. I open the burger's plastic wrap, stick it in a microwave that must have been the first model of its kind, turn the timer knob, and watch it sputter and shake. With an armful of food, I am buzzed back through the metal doors, the elements tumbling onto the short, stool-like table between us. With smiles and a few chuckles,

Kelly and I acknowledge the grotesquely holy act in which we are about to participate.

Empowered with authority conferred on me by the Open Door, I, a layperson, fumble through the pages of scripture until I come upon the appropriate Gospel text. "When it was evening, Jesus took his place with the twelve. While they were eating, he took a loaf of bread, and after blessing it he broke it, gave it to the disciples and said, 'Take, eat; this is my body." I pause and hold the Big Az burgers up to the heavens. Replacing the burgers with the Diet Coke, I continue, "Then he took the cup, and after giving thanks he gave it to them, saying, 'Drink from it all of you, for this is my blood of the covenant, which is poured out for many for the forgiveness of sins.""[6]

We eat, drink, and catch up on each other's lives, enveloped by this word of forgiveness. The little visitation room has already become sacred space for Kelly and me by virtue of the hours we share there together. Our companionship is already eucharistic: "Where two or three are gathered in my name, I am there among them," says Jesus.[7] The benefit of this conscious celebration, though, is an increase in faith, since faith comes from hearing the word proclaimed *pro nobis*—for us. In that one unifying word of forgiveness, the sins of this death-row inmate and my own are bound together in the flesh of the incarnate God—in the crude materiality of a Big Az burger, crudely named and crudely performed in the barren space of an isolated visitation room. There in that burger and Coke, Jesus makes himself immediate to us.

The Eucharist is one form of Jesus's continued incarnation—an incarnation, as we have seen, that makes the ordinary holy, indeed that makes holy even the rawest realities of human existence. Along with the church community itself (what Paul calls "the body of Christ"), the Eucharist serves as Jesus's contemporary bodily presence in the world, a material presence through which God is simultaneously exalted and humiliated. Luther refers paradoxically to God's presence in human

6. Matt 26:20–28.
7. Matt 18:20.

flesh, human community, and raw materiality as God "hidden" in places one wouldn't expect. God is hidden in the sense that God's visibility in the world, God's self-revelation, is startling and offensive to religious sensibilities. The hidden God chooses to be revealed not through characteristics associated with divinity, as we might predict, but through humiliation and weakness: first, through Jesus, who drinks the earthly cup to the dregs as he experiences vulnerability as an enfleshed creature, and then through the Eucharist, the natural elements of the created and fallen earth. God desires to remain near and concrete through the contemporary humiliation of a Big Az burger, a choice that displays God's radical freedom over the world—freedom to reveal God's self in whatever way best speaks of God's love for real human beings—as well as a willingness to sustain vulnerability in the world, to bind God's self to the ordinary stuff of material reality and human production.

The Big Az burger is a crude sacramental presence not only in name but also in lack; for it is the product of a food industry arguably more concerned with profit value than nutritional value. At the Open Door, the fresh homemade loaf made weekly by Community members Nathan and Zac is a ready reminder that through the Eucharist, God gives Christ's body as nourishment, as strength for the journey. The nutritious and flavorful loaf is a clear proclamation that God desires the flourishing of human beings. In contrast, the Big Az burger in and of itself damages Kelly's diabetic body, a condition that developed over the last decade while ingesting cheap, highly processed prison food. At the same time, though, the vending machine burger serves as a special meal through which she may, in sensuality and pleasure, "taste and see that the Lord is good," good to the taste and nourishing for body and soul.[8] In the sacrament, the Lutheran Bonhoeffer argues, Christ *breaks through fallen creation* at a defined point. He is the new creature. He is the restored creation of our bodily and spiritual existence." Because "he is in bread and wine"—in cheeseburgers and Diet Coke—"they are really nourishment for a new being."[9]

8. Ps 34:8.

When the Eucharist is celebrated in extremis, in this case, in confinement under a totalizing system of dehumanizing scarcity, ordinary American food—what could be called without much exaggeration a diet of death—becomes the mediating presence of life. It becomes, in Open Door parlance, "the bread of life and the cup of liberation." As will be shown below, in this extreme situation where the ordinary is in fact sub-ordinary—artificial in the most totalizing way—it would be wrong to equate the forced ordinariness of prison life with ordinary life "on the outside." Instead, what is ordinary outside prison walls—this quintessential American diet of a burger, chips, and Coke—becomes extraordinary for Kelly on the inside. It becomes a joyful, even liberating, occurrence that releases her from the stagnant normalcy of prison food, which lacks not only nutrition but also taste, food that has sparked hunger strikes in politically active prisons around the country as male inmates demand the fresh food we all need for physical and mental well-being, fresh food that announces God's desire for total human flourishing and God's promise to make it so through continual new creation.

The power of our shared meal in prison hinges on its eschatological dimension—on that promise and on its fulfillment. The shared meal is God's vision of justice made real in eucharistic celebration. Its practice in prison institutes a word of forgiveness into a system of law and order and challenges societal assumptions that those who commit horrible crimes can never really be redeemed. The forgiveness announced through the Eucharist is not what Bonhoeffer calls "cheap grace," self-deception, and "cover up for one's sin" by which the offender refuses to face and take responsibility for the harm she has done, for the wounds she has caused that may never fully be healed. Rather, the Eucharist creates space for beloved community, the possibility of hard-won reconciliation, as exemplified by Kelly's reconciliation with her three children, whose father was murdered on account of her plan. The forgiveness announced in the Eucharist does not deny the damage Kelly regrets and mourns; rather, grace inserts itself precisely there.

9. Bonhoeffer, *Christ the Center* (New York: HarperCollins, 1978), 57–58. Italics mine.

More fundamentally, the shared eucharistic meal makes claims about the nature of reality itself. Through this ritual celebration, practitioners are given the gift of faith to see Christ's presence—the presence of the reign of God—everywhere, a reign, that as this feast makes clear, is not otherworldly but this-worldly and politically concrete. Through the eucharistic celebration, the kingdom of God presses in and reveals that if the Eucharist is real—if it is valid and authentic—the death penalty is not. Through eucharistic vision, punishment by death is exposed as a lie, for only the most erratic thinking can hold together the politics of this feast with the politics of state execution. Practicing the Eucharist serves then as "a discipline of resistance" to powers of death and oppression. The celebration "redeems time" as it announces, "things are not as they must be." A new world has come, and the reality of its being here, in this sacramental feast, creates the pressure Jesus displays in his Luke 4 public address. "The time has come!" the Eucharist shouts, for captives to be released. Practitioners of the feast play a central role in making this new world concrete, "in building the new world in the shell of the old."[10]

While the Eucharist is itself a political act, increased solidarity is the continued "political expression of the eucharistic vision," says Murphy.[11] The visitation room where Kelly and I meet becomes overtly political space through the celebration of the Eucharist, as the solidarity Paul proclaims in Galatians 3:28—in Christ there is neither inmate nor free—is made real. Our eucharistic solidarity in the prison is in that sense a fulfillment of the liberating presence of Christ, even as it is also only a foretaste of a more holistic solidarity in which all things that separate us, including prison walls and sentences of death, will disappear. Although in a holistic sense, just a glimpse—a limited experience of the reign of God—our table fellowship creates lasting political consequence, since foretastes of the kingdom are the birthplace of hope and courage, themselves political realities that

10. Murphy Davis, "It's About Time," 10.
11. Murphy Davis, "Dorothy Day: The Only Solution Is Love," *Hospitality* 17, no. 1 (January 1998): 8.

foster political acts. The foretaste grants Kelly courage to face death while continuing to live life in love and communion with others inside and outside prison walls, and grants me courage to leave that space and work for concrete political gains.

Ed articulates the relationship between eucharistic solidarity and struggles for justice through his quip, "Justice is important but supper is essential." It is a line most often referenced in relation to the soup kitchen where the Community offers hospitality and food to their homeless friends on an almost daily basis. Yet as Ed and I reflect on our experiences of the vending machine Eucharist, he offers this timely example of its meaning in relation to prison work, specifically in relation to Warren Hill, a mentally disabled man scheduled to be executed a few days later. Ed says, "On Monday, Murphy and I will share food with Warren Hill while the rest of the Community is in the streets holding a press conference and marching for justice for the poor. The Community's work in the streets and at Woodruff Park is important. But on the day of his deathwatch, what is *essential* is to be with Warren. Justice is important but supper is essential."[12]

While the structural changes necessary for justice are not immediately achievable, shared meals and table companionship are always within the present power of the discipleship community. Indeed, for disciples, supper is the foundation for justice, something we learn from Jesus, who was often gathering people to eat, and from King, who sought to realize beloved community both through laws and relationship, with the understanding that societies may legislate justice but they cannot legislate love. Supper is the source of love, and as King teaches, authentic love then works to implement the demands of justice.

Murphy describes this relationship between love and justice through the power of the shared meal and shows how eucharistic solidarity grounds the justice struggle. "When we find the holy in what is ordinary, when we share what is ordinary in love, we become companions," she says. "Companions are those who share bread: from

12. Conversation with Ed Loring, July 13, 2013.

114

the Latin roots *com*—with, and *panis*—bread. . . . If solidarity brings . . . us to the table with the poor, then the grace is that at the table we can learn to love the poor."[13] For Christians who otherwise would remain distant from the people who suffer the most under systematic oppression and grave injustice, table fellowship is where our struggle for justice will likely be born. Without love and relationship, the work of justice too readily dissolves into ideology and moralism, into "a program that we *do* to other people." The shared meal helps guard against this as it creates communities where confession, repentance, and forgiveness may be practiced, where disciples may "confront our own" racism, misogyny, or class hatred. When we do so, we not only "learn how to take on these battles within ourselves," we also are empowered to dismantle external structures as we recognize the ways in which we are complicit in these unjust systems.[14] Privileged disciples may then give our lives to the justice struggle as an act of continual repentance, as an act of personal and social healing that builds beloved community.

When the sacraments find expression beyond the enclosure of a traditional worship service, they proclaim and establish beloved community—that broad reaching, inclusive sociality that King interpreted as the concretization of God's promised reign. At the Open Door, eucharistic solidarity spills out into the streets and prisons, ushering people into beloved community who may not otherwise have found entrance in such concrete ways. Each Sunday as the Community gathers in their dining room for worship, they remind themselves that the Eucharist table around which they are circled extends to the six fold-up tables around which their homeless friends will eat, and that the consecrated bread and juice extend to the soup and sandwiches served that week. The hospitality of the Open Door broadens eucharistic community to include the participation of their homeless friends regardless of whether they were, or ever will be, present at that service. The extension of the sacrament thus affirms God's salvific

---

13. Murphy Davis, "Dorothy Day," 8.
14. Ibid., 9.

care for all human beings—salvation that is unashamedly a gift as it is mediated through the community's works of mercy and struggles for justice. Works of mercy and justice are therefore evangelistic at their core and nonnegotiable for the gospel proclamation. They draw disciples and other human beings into the good news and joyful practice of beloved community, re-creating us together not only as recipients but also as practitioners of God's reign. Visitation on death row is case in point. Whether consciously practiced or understood later as eucharistic celebration, God's presence at prison visitation ushers Kelly and me—ushers the men on Jackson's death row and Open Door Community members—into the concrete performance of beloved community and thus into the promise of the everlasting reign of God.

Beloved community may be established and announced through a variety of sacramental forms. At the Open Door, these practices have arisen from the shared meal, as they have responded over the years to specific needs articulated by their homeless friends. The Community, for example, participates in the sacrament of foot washing during worship at Dayspring farm, where Jesus says to the disciples, "Do you know what I have done to you? . . . If I, your Lord and Teacher, have washed your feet, you also ought to wash one another's feet" (John 13:1–20). Residents and volunteers then continue this sacrament at the weekly foot clinic, when they attend to the blistered and tired feet of homeless people who spend their days walking the streets in search for food or day labor. Likewise, weekly showers baptize homeless friends into the beloved community being worked out at the Open Door, showers that do not merely symbolize but literally become a means of grace for recipients and Community members alike. Nelia shares how one man, after taking a shower, said to her "in a kind of confession, 'This morning I felt so ashamed. . . . I have to ride the bus an hour and a half to get here to get a shower. . . . I felt so bad for the people who had to sit next to me on the bus because I knew they had to smell my stink. It feels so good to get a shower. It feels so good to have that smell washed off me.'" Or, in the words of another man, "I feel like a human being again!"[15]

When the sacrament of baptism finds expression beyond the boundaries of the traditional church, along with the Eucharist, it brazenly announces God's liberating love as gratuitous gift, independent of the disposition of the recipient—generous all the way down. Just as baptism in Anglican and Catholic traditions "mark" the baptized "as Christ's own" regardless of future faith commitments the recipient (often a baby) will or will not make, so too does baptism by shower place the responsibility of faith on the community, not on the individual human being. The recipient is initiated into the gift of God's reign, "marked as Christ's own," no strings attached, while the community is charged with the task of awakening faith in God's reign in others, a task it fulfills as it performs redemption through ordinary acts infused with sacramental power.

By recognizing the showers as baptism, the Open Door carries on the legacy of prophets charged with announcing the reign of God in word and deed. The connection between water and the justice struggle has long been established: the prophet Amos announced, "Let justice roll down like waters and righteousness like a mighty stream" (Amos 5:24); John came out of the wilderness baptizing and proclaiming the nearness of God's reign; and King saw with sacramental vision even the fire hoses intended for harm as waters of baptism establishing communities of justice. In a movement that many identified as the black church on the streets, King attributes the victory of the Birmingham campaign (and thus the Civil Rights Act) to the power of baptism. "[Police Commissioner] Bull Connor didn't know history," he says. "He knew a kind of physics that somehow didn't relate to the transphysics that we knew about. . . . We had known water. If we were Baptist or some other denomination, we had been immersed. If we were Methodist, and some others, we had been sprinkled, but we knew water."[16]

This is the power of baptism spilling out onto the streets, the power of the sacraments more generally to flow over demarcated ecclesial

15. Nelia Kimborough, "The Call of John the Baptist," *Hospitality* 24, no. 4 (April 2005): 10.
16. King, *Testament of Hope*, 281.

boundaries and create new public spaces that reveal God's reign, new communities of human flourishing and belonging: "Come through the water and feel human," says Nelia. "Come through the water and feel renewed and full of God's grace. . . . Come to the water and don't be ashamed anymore."[17] Be free.

## Ordinary Prison Time

During ordinary time, disciples recognize that common acts may be infused with sacramental power, be it washing the soiled clothes of friends from the streets, providing toilets and advocating for public restrooms, offering showers, or sharing a vending machine meal at prison visitation. Visitation itself is an ordinary act of liberation, according to the women in the theology program: "When I get a visit, I am free," says Neka. Through visits, incarcerated people get a taste of the outside world, while visitors are able to hear about the daily realities of prison life they are made to endure, details that help disciples "on the outside" better advocate for structural change that would, in a more holistic sense, "set the oppressed free." The prison theology program serves this purpose, as it is a particular form of visitation and accompaniment.

In an elective course, "Seeing the Sacred: Introduction to Liturgical Art," the women in the prison theology program learn how the liturgical calendar helps Christians mark time as they reflect on ordinary time in prison. On large sheets of brown kraft paper, they draw their life maps, simple lines spiking up the page or down depending on the nature of the memorable event. As they work labeling and dating these hills and valleys, a few of the women I am sitting between share with me sketches of their life stories as they reflect on how time is marked in prison. Tahjae's map is one straight line, like the flatlining cardiac monitor of a patient near death, and only includes her years in prison, 1989 to 2011. Under the line she writes, "Life is just moving along, waiting for an end to this madness."

---

17. Kimborough, "The Call of John the Baptist," 10.

Tahjae explains to me that her map does not include her years before prison because she barely remembers them. She has been inside prison longer than out, having entered the system as a teenager. Although a person of faith, enduring ordinary prison time—for her, a life sentence—is a kind of *Waiting for Godot*, an endless, anti-Advent, and vain attempt to experience time's dynamic movement, a nonexpectant waiting wrapped in absurdity, without purpose. "Prison is just another day after another day rolling on," she says. "We lose sense of time."

Ashley shares that "the day you get locked up is the start of each new year." "There is a shift of universe when arrested," Carla explains. "We try desperately to make connections with each other because our other world is fading away. We do not live in American society anymore but in inmate society." "We make a point of remembering birthdays of people in prison with us," says Sierra. "We try to mark time by birthdays of family and friends [on the outside]," adds Ashley, but it is hard, Tahjae says, since "that world and this world doesn't connect. See, everything stops when you come to prison."

Everything stops. Lives are permanently stilted in totalizing and artificial conditions characterized by intentional, excessive deprivation. "When you come to prison you are stuck in the age when you came," says Carla. "There's no real growth. The system itself produces no real growth. A woman who comes to prison at age fourteen acts like she is fourteen decades later. Janet came at age seventeen and still acts like she is seventeen even though she is thirty-one"—Janet gives a knowing and affirmative nod. At the Open Door, Murphy shares how the same is true for people suffering from addiction. Alcoholics Anonymous teaches that addiction traps people in the ages they were when they started abusing alcohol or drugs. Whether it is addiction to substances or our society's addiction to prisons, the character of oppressive forces remains the same: everything stops, with scant possibility for organic growth and human flourishing. In this way, ordinary prison time seems to betray Murphy's opening admonition that time is a gift.

Yet as they sketch their lives, many of the women place the theology program prominently on their maps. "It saved my life," Carla says. "It stimulates our minds and our faith and tells us we matter, that we have a voice that needs to be heard. It just goes to show the importance of inserting love into someone's life, because most people are acting out of woundedness. It really is true that all we need is to be loved."[18] For Carla, ordinary time is not a gift until the love embodied through the theology program liberates time for a moment, opening up the possibility that she and others can, in Murphy's words, "use the days they have to do good work"—even as incarcerated disciples who, against all odds, may perform redemption now.

18. Conversation with women at the prison, July 29, 2011.

# 5

---

# Lent and Holy Week

Peter went out and wept bitterly.
—Luke 22:62 (Good News Bible)

## Lent as Lament

On Maundy Thursday, four of us from the Open Door stretch out in Woodruff Park, attempting to warm up under the rising sun. At the edge of Georgia State University, nestled among downtown skyscrapers, the hum of activity fills this space with people passing through or pausing for morning coffee, relaxing on the lawn or playing chess. Unofficially renamed Troy Davis Park by local anti-death-penalty activists, the park marks contested space that business professionals, college students, and homeless people daily navigate.[1] Recent beautification projects sponsored by Atlanta Central Progress are noticeable, like the fountain framing one end of the lawn, but there are subtle renovations as well, architectural details intended to make the park inhospitable to people who are homeless: benches

---

1. Woodruff Park was informally renamed in memory of the man executed by Georgia despite international uproar over his probable innocence. See Jen Marlowe and Martina Correia-Davis, *I Am Troy Davis* (Chicago: Haymarket, 2013).

with center divides obstructing attempts to lie down and flower pots lining the marble wall where homeless people once sat. These details are particularly apparent this day to those of us who spent the night on the streets just hours before, celebrating the Open Door's Holy Week sacrament of following the vagrant Christ, a practice that allows us to glimpse the hell of homelessness. We gather in this contested space now to rest and to reflect on our night in light of the lectionary reading—Peter's confession of faith, denial of Jesus, and bitter lament.

In a 1933 sermon on this text, entitled "Peter and the Church Struggle," Bonhoeffer speaks of the one whom Jesus addressed: "You are Peter and on this rock I will build my church."[2] Who is this Peter? Bonhoeffer asks. Peter is the one who confessed his faith. "You are the Christ, the Son of the living God," he says in response to Jesus's pointed question, "But who do you say that I am?" And Peter is the one who "denied his Lord," indeed on "the same night Judas betrayed him."[3] But Peter is also the one who "went out and wept bitterly." Thus, Bonhoeffer concludes, "Peter's church is not only the church which confesses its faith, nor only the church which denies its Lord; it is the church which still can weep."[4]

Lent and Holy Week comprise a season of formation, preparing Christians for Good Friday and Easter, initiating us into the way of the cross and ultimately into the power of the resurrection. If Peter is our guide, indeed our rock and foundation, the only community prepared to face the cross and receive redemptive power is a people that lament. The church of Peter is not merely a body of believers then, a body that acknowledges its sin as a general truth, but is a people shaped by a profound understanding and honest accounting of how it has denied Jesus, the one whom we encounter, Matthew 25 tells us, in the guise of the oppressed. The church of Peter is the church that laments the specific ways it denies and ostracizes those who, like Jesus in his final days, are most despised. The social and political significance of Lent

2. Dietrich Bonhoeffer, *A Testament to Freedom: The Essential Writings of Dietrich Bonhoeffer*, ed. Geffrey B. Kelly and F. Burton Nelson (New York: HarperCollins, 1995), 214. Matt 16:18.
3. Bonhoeffer, *Testament to Freedom*, 215.
4. Ibid.

and Holy Week is precisely this lament—the ability to open oneself up to the pains and needs of the world. This may only happen when we listen to the depth of suffering experienced by people victimized by structural sin and grieve the ways in which we have overlooked or ignored that pain. Embodied lament then takes the shape of political activism and protest—practices that help the discipleship community grow in empathy and solidarity with those who suffer harm. In turn, lament functions as a wellspring of hope. It becomes the force that stimulates active participation in the repair of the world.

## Becoming Peter's Church

In order to become the church of Peter that practices this kind of lament, the humble church that weeps for its sin, we must first examine the ways in which the church's preoccupation with morality has suppressed our ability to lament. Our churches' interpretations of morality, at least in public life, are notoriously individualistic, often focusing not on the sins members of our community struggle with but on those we think we see in others. These interpretations of "right and wrong" deceive us into believing the church is specially positioned as judge over society, which not only ignores the clear command of Jesus in the Sermon on the Mount, "Do not judge" (Matt 7:1), but also makes us blind and deaf to the real needs of the world. As twentieth-century Protestant theologian Karl Barth put it, "We tear ourselves loose from the general unrighteousness and build ourselves a pleasant home in the suburbs apart—seemingly apart! But what has really happened? . . . Is it not our very morality which prevents our discerning that at a hundred other points we are blind and impertinent toward the deep real needs of existence?" For Barth and for Bonhoeffer after him, adherence to morality, especially bourgeois personal morality, separates privileged Christians from the real needs of the world and serves as self-imparted exoneration from present complicity in injustice. Devotion to our own moral image bars Christians from hearing and receiving God's judging word addressed to us that exposes our complicity in the social sin that saturates our world. This religious righteousness—or what is commonly deemed "Christian morality" by some Christians in the public square—deceives us into believing we are exemplars of morality, not beneficiaries and perpetrators of injustice. "There seems to be no surer means of rescuing us from the alarm cry of conscience," Barth provocatively claims, "than religion and Christianity."[5]

"Morality," as Barth and Bonhoeffer define it, not only impairs our hearing the alarm cries of conscience, it leaves us, in Barth's words, "impertinent," dismissive and functionally unsympathetic to the needs of the strangers in our midst. Whereas lament is attuned to the audible and silent cries of the oppressed and despised, and drives us toward solidarity with them, a focus on "morality" creates distance and division. Whereas lament opens the church up to new love, new concern, and new creation, moralism closes Christians off to God and others. Moralism and lament are not only opposite dispositions, though; morality, as Barth defines it, actually cuts off lament. It ossifies faith into ideology—into rigid religious, social, and political beliefs that resist the redemptive movement of the living God. There is no community farther from the church of Peter, from that tenderhearted church that weeps on account of its treatment of others, than the triumphal church that is self-assured of its own moral accomplishment.

This claim—that we do not practice Peter's lament—may be hard for privileged Christians to accept because it is so far removed from the image we often have of ourselves. Perhaps we have denied Jesus in the guise of the poor and oppressed, we may say, but we do practice lament in other ways. We feel deeply for those in our own communities, people who have pain and struggles similar to our own. Furthermore, how could Christians be considered unfeeling when our intent is to live for God, to "be for God" as Bonhoeffer calls it in *Ethics*? There, Bonhoeffer interprets the fall—Adam and Eve's original sin—precisely as the religious desire of wanting to "be for God," which the church does

5. Karl Barth, *The Word of God and Word of Man* (Gloucester, MA: Peter Smith, 1978), 18–19. See also McBride, *Church for the World*, 39–41.

today by defending certain notions of morality or truth. Yet, our defense of God too often comes at the expense of loving real human beings. This religious attempt to "be for God" readily leads to "being against God," Bonhoeffer argues, because it denies the way of the incarnate and crucified Christ whose life is "being there for others."[6] Or as 1 John starkly puts it, "Whoever claims to love God yet hates a brother or sister is a liar, for whoever does not love their brother and sister, whom they have seen, cannot love God, whom they have not seen" (4:20). As many non-Christians readily recognize and have experienced firsthand, the religious desire to "be for God" often leads to being against our fellow human beings because it presumes the church is specially positioned as judge over society. As judge, Christians break our limit as creatures and position ourselves as equal to God and superior to other human beings. When the church presumes it is called to act as judge, morality becomes a power and principality (like those described in chapter 2) used to dominate human beings. Whereas the church of lament accepts God's healing judgment and recognizes that God alone is righteous, the church of religious righteousness sets itself up as judge and as an exemplar of morality. Instead of being the church of morality, the church is called to be a community that laments as it numbers itself with the transgressors.

## Embracing Vulnerability in Order to Lament  *Bruggemann*

"Religion and Christianity" is not the only force, though, that stifles "the alarm cry of conscience" when it comes to how we view and treat others. Our conscience is also shaped by the social location we inhabit. In her essay "Of Soul and White Folks," on growing up white in the racist South, Mab Segrest examines the psychological processes that block lament and silence the conscience. She addresses the questions commonly asked by students when we study historical oppression in the United States from slavery to Jim Crow, or Apartheid in South

---

6. Dietrich Bonhoeffer, *Creation and Fall; Temptation: Two Biblical Studies*, trans. John C. Fletcher (New York: Touchstone, 1997), 74. See also McBride, *Church for the World*, 134–37.

Africa, or the Holocaust in Nazi Germany: How could people do such things? Likewise, how could people remain silent and inactive in the face of such suffering and evil? How could the conscience of self-identified Christians—the majority or dominant citizens in each of these societies—not be stirred? In light of contemporary manifestations of oppression, like mass incarceration and homelessness, the relevant question, I remind my students, is this: How could *we* do such things? How do we find ourselves so utterly unmoved by the pain of, and so easily accepting the reality of, homelessness and mass incarceration? And many of us do this as self-identified Christians, who, like the people we study, occupy various positions of privilege that foster or maintain the status quo.

Drawing on W. E. B. du Bois's 1920 essay "The Souls of White Folk," Segrest speaks of "the psychological wage" of being the dominant or oppressor class and the "personal cost of exploitative systems" even for those who benefit in material ways from an imbalance of power.[7] Namely, she argues that those of us who are privileged lose feelings and practices of love, individually and intergenerationally. In contrast to the excuse we commonly tell ourselves, that in the midst of so much suffering, most of us never act because we feel overwhelmed, pulled in disparate directions given the enormity and number of social issues we face, Segrest presses us to admit that what many of us feel—if we are honest—is nothing. When we are moved, perhaps by a touching story or alarming statistic, addictions and distractions like consumerism, entertainment, or busyness flood the soil where feeling may grow.

Segrest links this void with addiction through the Civil War diaries of Mary Chesnut, the wife of a Confederate general. At times, Chesnut's diary entries betray a growing sense of solidarity between the condition of white women in the patriarchal South and the condition of slaves, which culminates in her description of watching a mother be sold off an auction block. When a flit of emotion surfaces, however, Chesnut takes an opium pill. This allows her, in her own words, to

---

7. Mab Segrest, *Born to Belonging: Writings on Spirit and Justice* (New Brunswick, NJ: Rutgers University Press, 2009), 159.

"quiet" her "nerves" so she can "calmly reason and take the rational view of things otherwise maddening."[8] By anesthetizing herself with opium, Chesnut buries uncomfortable and inconvenient feelings, making room for rational explanations about the world as it is.

Somewhere in the overlapping spheres of our religious, political, and social lives, we too, individually and intergenerationally, have lost our ability to feel compassion toward those who struggle and suffer on account of the policies and social structures we create. We have developed the profound insensitivity that Segrest calls "anesthesia."[9] Local anesthesia impedes sensation, not only feeling but also the ability to perceive correctly, but without inhibiting consciousness. What is left is reason—in our case, Christian answers that we claim are biblically or doctrinally sound but that leave the world as it is. Without lament, Christianity is reduced to reason, or more accurately to ideology, an abstract system of beliefs and morals that explain why the world is the way it is, all the while letting us off the hook to live our lives "apart—seemingly apart!" from places of deep struggle and distress.[10] The problem, though, for us and for those we have denied, is that authentic lament is quite literally our only hope. Lament is the wellspring of hope, the force that pushes us to live into the promises of God—the energy that stimulates active, constructive participation in God's kingdom come. Lament is necessary because, as Segrest says, we cannot know what we cannot feel.[11] We cannot correctly interpret our lives and the life of the world without lament. We simply cannot hope for what we do not mourn.

While morality and ideology impede our capacity to lament for people we deem different from ourselves, we do care for those who share similar struggles. Thus, to become a people that lament, the privileged church must find ways to relate to strangers visible and invisible among us and to reduce the distance between their pain and ours. As one privileged in social and material ways, the gift of lament

8. Ibid., 166.
9. Ibid., 162–72.
10. Barth, *Word of God and Word of Man*, 18.
11. Ibid., 162.

first fostered in me through struggles with depression for much of my adult life. The fruit of the healing process, of learning to cope with this challenge, is that I have been made well aware of human vulnerability to dark forces larger than myself. For privileged people who have a relatively strong sense of control over our lives, this truth is otherwise hard to recognize. At their best, personal experiences like this may serve to foster the sensitivity Segrest names above—compassion or feelings of concrete connection and similarity to all people who suffer under oppressive forces, even of a different nature. Regardless of how it is cultivated, recognition of vulnerability is the vehicle that drives us toward solidarity and moves us into a place where lament is possible.

In a prison theology course on religion and law, students examine two divergent types of vulnerability. On the one hand, vulnerability refers to an imbalance of power, be it acute injustice through which people are made vulnerable by being stripped of the resources necessary to meet basic needs, or be it a state of existence, increased vulnerability to harm because of one's place in society. Children and the elderly are vulnerable in this way, so we attend to them with extra care; likewise, prisoners are inherently vulnerable to harm, in their case, on account of their position within an impersonal system that exerts power over their bodies and lives. This is central to the vulnerability of the cross, examined in the next chapter, where Jesus is in solidarity with all who bear the brunt of impersonal and destructive powers.

On the other hand, vulnerability also may refer to a humble disposition, a way of opening oneself up to another, revealing one's finitude, limits, weaknesses, and pain. As a disposition, it includes the recognition above of human vulnerability to larger forces. Vulnerability in this regard is courageous truth telling about oneself, which invites similar honesty in others, making space for communion, relationship, intimacy, and interdependence. As such, this kind of vulnerability is paradoxically a strength. By fostering community, it makes way for solidarity. Recognizing lament as a force that draws people together and morality as a force that pits us against one another, Sierra writes in a prison theology paper, "If we embrace vulnerability, we embrace humanity." With poignant and courageous words spoken in a place where most officers and inmates (not to mention society as a whole) interpret vulnerability as weakness, she concludes, "If vulnerability were not seen as a bad thing, people would strive to be vulnerable instead of perfect."

Christians often view Lent as a time to perfect oneself, to catalog sins and "get right with God," rather than a time to foster vulnerability. Yet, as the beginning of Lent, Ash Wednesday directs us toward our common vulnerability, finitude, and weakness and announces the truth of human solidarity: "You are but dust and to dust you will return." At the Open Door, we rise early on Ash Wednesday to hear this truth spoken through the imposition of ashes, which come from paper on which we have confessed our sins and burned in a pot used to make soup for our homeless friends. The use of the pot—its sacramental value—is that it helps us recognize at once our sins against fellow human beings and the burden of others we are called to carry. In other words, it helps us acknowledge that we "bear one another's burdens" (Gal 6:2). In this case, those who are homeless bear our sin against them, the sin of the housed that have denied Jesus and lament, while we who are housed at the Open Door bear their need through repentant action. Ash Wednesday thus inaugurates us into what Bonhoeffer calls the "service of bearing," in which "those who bear with others know that they themselves are being borne."[12] This is the "community of the cross," says Bonhoeffer, the community of vulnerability where the sins and needs of all people are made known to one another.[13] The social character of sin bearing is further demonstrated at the Ash Wednesday service when *Atlanta Journal-Constitution* newspapers are added for extra kindling, a particular reminder that we bear responsibility for the sins of the city, for the

---

12. Dietrich Bonhoeffer, *Life Together and Prayerbook of the Bible*, ed. Geffrey B. Kelly, trans. Daniel W. Bloesch and James H. Burtness, vol. 5, *Dietrich Bonhoeffer Works* (Minneapolis: Fortress Press, 1996), 100–103.
13. Ibid., 101.

injustices of our society recorded in those pages. Throughout Lent, these ashes, which make our common vulnerability visible, hang on the cloth of the Open Door's Eucharist table, that place where we acknowledge every week our human solidarity in sin and redemption.

## Lamenting *Han*

Another problem with viewing Lent as a season of self-improvement is that it makes repentance a private end in itself—between the individual and God—rather than an other-centered practice that opens Christians up to the pain and needs of the world. By being preoccupied with individual sin and need, as Bonhoeffer calls it, the church misses the opportunity to participate in God's concrete redemption of this world.[14]

In the theology foundations course at the prison, the women read Andrew Sung Park's *The Wounded Heart of God: The Asian Concept of Han and the Christian Doctrine of Sin*, in which Park argues that the traditional doctrine of sin is one-sided. It emphasizes *my* salvation, that is, the sinner's salvation, and defines sin too narrowly in terms of moral agency and will. This definition overlooks not only the more subtle social and structural manifestations of sin but also the pain of those victimized by that sin. Park seeks to develop instead a doctrine that addresses the profound pain the majority of people experience in our world today: the pain of sexual and emotional abuse; the structural violence of racism, homelessness, and mass incarceration; and labor exploitation, drug abuse, human rights violations, and ecological harm. He also seeks a doctrine that makes sense of the various responses people have to these oppressive situations. Park turns to the Asian concept of *han* to supplement the Western doctrine of sin in order to grasp a more comprehensive picture of the nature of sin and its cyclical effect. He defines *han* as the "woundedness" that comes from being sinned against, the depth of suffering that occurs as a result of the oppressive forces listed above. *Han* is "the wounded heart,"

14. See Bonhoeffer, *Letters and Papers* (Fortress Press), 480.

wounded by repeated external violence, abuse, and injustice that may be expressed actively or passively.[15] Active *han* takes the form of aggressive emotion like hatred, bitterness, and vengefulness while passive *han* is expressed through feelings of depression, helplessness, and self-hatred. The reality of *han* may further be described as "frustrated hope," "condensed feeling of pain," "letting go of all feeling [and] resignation to destructive forces," or "resentful bitterness" that in turn leads to further harm of self or others.[16]

Using the categories above, we may say that when the church of morality thinks of incarcerated or homeless people, it holds a one-dimensional view of sin; it focuses on the sinner's moral agency and will, while the church of lament recognizes the complex, entangled realities of sin and *han*. The church of lament attends to *han* and is moved to take responsibility for it, recognizing that, in the words of Victor Hugo, "If a soul is left in darkness, sins will be committed. The guilty one is not he who commits the sin, but he who causes the darkness."[17] This truth, which King proclaimed, highlights the psychological damage of oppression for the oppressed, something that is common knowledge to people who are oppressed but rarely noticed or noted by privileged whites. Not only is oppression psychologically destructive, it compromises one's capacity to act as a moral agent, a truth absent from the traditional doctrine of sin. As Christian ethicist Marie Fortune writes, "It is often assumed that each of us comes to an ethical decision with equal awareness and resources with which to exercise moral agency. . . . [But] moral agency requires that we possess power and resources. . . . We cannot exercise choice if we do not have options."[18] We may think of *han*, then, as that dehumanizing state in which agency is restricted. Within this context of *han*, the people ultimately responsible for harm are not those who commit certain

---

15. Andrew Sung Park, *The Wounded Heart of God: The Asian Concept of Han and the Christian Doctrine of Sin* (Nashville: Abingdon, 1993), 20.
16. Ibid., 15–20.
17. King, *Testament of Hope*, 192.
18. Marie M. Fortune, *Love Does No Harm: Sexual Ethics for the Rest of Us* (New York: Continuum, 2006), 26–28.

deeds, but the society that refuses to name and address—to shed light on—the darkness.

I assign Park's text to the women in prison in order to provide a more truthful account of sin, namely that they are not only people who have sinned (a reality they are quite aware of) but also are people who have been sinned against, and to invite them to tell a more complete story of their lives than the criminal justice system allows. The women repeatedly share that our study of *han* was a turning point for them because it encouraged them to find their voice, especially in a context in which naming one's victimization (and thus celebrating one's ability to survive) is seen as not taking responsibility for their actions. Natalie writes, "Han relates to the ramifications of being sinned against. I probably knew the concept but reading about it and giving it a name has helped me so much. Because of the readings I have traveled back in my past—opened up some dark and lonely areas—and have begun to deal with the pain." Many of the women say that the concept of *han* not only gives them permission to tell their stories but, like Natalie, helps them come to terms with those stories, since so much of their thinking and action arises from being wounded. Keisha writes,

> In my state of experiencing han, I was affected emotionally to where I committed a serious crime in 2002. Emotional abuse is far worse than physical abuse. . . . My mother used to tell me that I would never amount to anything and my self-esteem was low. Years of emotional abuse that I can't put into essay format tortured me even after I committed my crime. I was so ashamed of my life, my past, and things I'd done that I was in denial my first four years of incarceration. . . . Until I realized and accepted how things affected me, I couldn't see or understand how they affected anyone else.

Accompanying her paper on *han* was a series of poems entitled, "The Animal in Me," in which she tries to make some sense of her crime. "I'm ready to strike / I need a prey," begins part 1.

> If I feel like I'm being closed in
> I attack
> entrapped
> only one thing I c

it's u or me
. . .
It's a survival instinct
2 the animal in me

. . .
backed in a corner what do I do??
fight it out
I open my mouth
2 let out a roar

. . .
face forward
don't turn back
I do this alone
without my pack

. . .
I reached my peak
grounding my feet
I survive
using the animal in me.

In "Animal in Me part 3," Keisha concludes, "the animal in me / is still caged / wanting to be free / I lost the key / so the war's *inside of me.*" Echoing Keisha's experience of being left to her own devices in prison to deal with *han*, Denise says, "We have all suffered at the hands of another, but most often we live with our suffering and never have the opportunity to release the pain of injustice."

The *han* the women share in their papers corresponds with statistics about the alarming number of women in prison who have been sexually, physically, or emotionally abused before their incarceration. "Twenty-five years ago I was embroiled in an extremely brutal spousal relationship," writes one woman. "I did finally escape the situation, at least physically, but the han followed." "I was a victim of child molestation and the han now reverberates in my soul," writes another. "For six months I lived in a prison the monster created. . . . Everyday was a fight for my life. Thirty-two years later I find myself fighting for my life again, just in a different way. Or is it so different? I'm here fighting another monster." For these women, the *han* of prison deepens the wounds they already bear. Patricia writes, "Once you walk into the gates of prison there is a new world. In this world you will feel degraded by the staff that are yelling in your face. Being put down in front of others only brings back the memories of my ex-boyfriend yelling at me and hitting me. I see his face on all the officers' faces. . . . I feel his controlling habits. I start to wonder how I could go from one hell to another." Or as Neka simply states, "Han is what I feel about prison. Now I have a name for my feelings."

The *han* of prison comes in many forms. "Depression knocks at the door of our lives on a daily basis," writes Denise. Sierra writes, "Quite often I feel [what Park calls] 'a sense of helplessness because of the overwhelming odds against oneself, a feeling of total abandonment.'" In an informal conversation with me, Carla observes how the "diagnostic" prisoners who have just arrived stand taller than the rest of the inmates. With some humor, she demonstrates through her posture the weight she carries on a daily basis, like she's "hauling a sack of potatoes," she says, just before her face turns and she wonders aloud if she "will ever be free of it, even if she leaves prison." Describing some of that weight and the negative vulnerability mentioned above, the vulnerability of being stripped of resources necessary to meet basic needs, Gail writes,

> Many, many inmates have severe psychological disorders and medical illnesses upon arrival here and have no choice but to seek help from the prison staff. The majority of the staff is uncaring, lackadaisical and even hateful to the inmates. From my point of view, this mistreatment spins a web of han throughout the prison, showing itself in anger, resentment, and loss of self-conduct. Violent fights, breakdowns, suicide threats and attempts are very common here. . . . Doctors and nurses who once took an oath of caring have become prejudice to our well being due to our circumstances. Imagine being ill, *needing* medicine, *needing* immediate psychological care, *needing* if only a bit of reassurance that they will not let you simply die here, only to be met with hatred. . . . When did our suffering health become part of our sentences?

The weight of suffering the women carry individually is magnified in an environment filled with so much unmet need. "In this small world of prison, han is bound to rear its ugly head in an aggressive way," writes Gail. "Prison has a way of working on us to where we don't see others hurting because of our own pain. We lose compassion," writes Kristi. "But the readings have helped me find compassion again for my fellow women. As Christians we can never get to a place where we forget to love others." A number of the women who struggle, as Kristi does, with compassion for others in this place recall Bonhoeffer's line from prison, "We must learn to regard people less in light of what they do or omit to do, and more in light of what they suffer."[19] Natalie follows this quote with an honest confession: "It is extremely easy to find myself despising humanity here, especially with such close living quarters, so many personalities, bodies, ways. But God does not despise humanity. God knows our pain and suffering."

My intention in assigning *The Wounded Heart of God* was to offer the women a framework beyond the label "offender" that could assist the telling of their stories. What I was not expecting was the way in which a number of them would appropriate Park's criticism to themselves, particularly his argument that Western Christians emphasize the individual's sin against God at the expense of the neighbor. "Since sin was always against God for me, the idea of han is especially intriguing," writes Sarah, a lifelong Christian. "It was a switch for me to see sin not as something done against God only but as an evil done against humans with effects that continue long after the sinful act," says Terri, who grew up in the church as well. "Many of us are quick to seek forgiveness from God for that which we deem sinful," echoes Erika, "yet rarely do we pause to see the human results, the victims of our sin." Tahjae, who was converted in prison, likewise confesses, "I haven't thought of the victim as much as myself and *my* salvation. Yet I do now see and understand that sin is relational."

It may be surprising that these women who have committed crimes, some of which were directly against another human being, have rarely thought about their victims. Yet this blind spot is simply another manifestation of Park's critique of the Western doctrine of sin, as evidenced, in part, by the fact that these women were either already churchgoers before prison or came to faith in prison through the

19. Bonhoeffer, *Letters and Papers* (Touchstone), 10.

evangelism of outside congregations. Like the women, most of us "on the outside" never think of our victims—the effect of the unjust structures from which we benefit—precisely because we are immersed in the same individualistic understanding of sin. Ironically, focus on our own sin is itself a sin, a kind of egoism—or as Luther says, *cor curvatus in se*, the heart turned in upon itself.

Our individualistic understanding of sin—our inability to recognize that the cycle of sin and its effects are social or "relational," as Tahjae says above—in turn influences our Western justice system, which operates within a retributive paradigm rather than a restorative one. Retributive justice, as scholar Howard Zehr maps out, defines crime as a violation of the law and the state as victim, thus neglecting the actual human victim. The process of attaining retributive justice does not encourage the offenders to face the concrete ways they have harmed other people, since they are placed in an "adversarial game" that requires they look out for themselves.[20] As the paradigm most depicted in the Bible, restorative justice, in contrast, focuses on the neighbor relationship, emphasizing that all crime is "a violation or harm to people and relationships" and that the aim of justice "is to identify obligations, to meet needs, and to promote healing" among victims, offenders, and the wider community.[21] The concept of *han* may contribute to the efforts of restorative justice since it offers a conceptual frame for inmates to face the harm they have done and for the church on the outside to stand with the guilty and protest systems like the prison that increase the inmates' *han*. The season of Lent requires that the discipleship community lament this *han* in tangible and constructive ways.

### Lament as Protest

Lament "announces" hope's presence, writes theologian Paul Lutter; for, authentic lament is the force that pushes the church to live into the promises of God, those promises of personal and communal

---

20. Zehr, "Restoring Justice," 26.
21. Ibid., 30.

wholeness and healing—that promise the Bible calls *Shalom*.[22] Because lament is tied to hope, it is, according to Ed, a form of political action. Lament is protest to God in prayer—crying out for God to make God's healing justice concrete—and protest through our embodied lives, through creative acts of justice that increase solidarity with others and participate in God's kingdom come.

In "Of Soul and White Folks," Segrest speaks of protest as a kind of therapy, political activism as a way of healing the psychological wage of oppression for those of us who have maintained the status quo.[23] She is not speaking here of what some people cynically label "white guilt"; rather, she recognizes the truth that there are real spiritual, emotional, and psychological costs to injustice for all people, even for those of us who are privileged and otherwise benefit from unjust systems. Recognizing those costs—like a false understanding of others and oneself—is part of the work of vulnerability and lament.

At the Open Door, lament expresses itself through creative acts of justice in a number of ways. Sometimes the justice work comes in the form of an affordable housing campaign like the Open Door's takeover of the abandoned Imperial Hotel in 1990. This historic downtown building had provided low-cost housing as a single-room-occupancy hotel for years until a developer bought it, closed it, and let it sit neglected and empty for ten years. The Open Door's occupancy, which was enhanced by the activism and leadership of homeless people, was successful on multiple levels, leading to new construction of single-occupancy units and to the reopening of the hotel as a low-income residential living community.[24] Sometimes the creative acts of justice are simpler than an activist campaign; sometimes they involve acts like creating an impromptu shelter for people who are homeless on a particularly cold night. At a Community dinner during an uncommonly cold winter, Ed shares the news that our homeless friend Randy Cook died the night before, frozen to death on the streets. In anguish he says, "Randy's death and the Community's inability to do anything about it

22. Paul Lutter, "Lament: Where Two Realities Collide," *The Lutheran* 23, no. 3 (March 2010): 31.
23. Segrest, *Born to Belonging*, 160–61.
24. See Gathje, *Sharing the Bread*, 201–6.

is mitigated by the fact that we hosted some men last night who were able to get out of the cold and *not* freeze to death." With tears in his eyes and anger in his voice, he says, "We are saved by grace. We do not know by ourselves how to house all the homeless, how to end the death penalty, but we do what we can. We plant mustard seeds." Ed's interpretation of grace parallels Bonhoeffer's in *Discipleship* when he says, "Only those who in following Christ leave everything they have can stand and say that they are justified solely by grace."[25] Only those, we may echo, who lament through prayer and action may know that we are saved by grace.

Lament as political protest takes a specific shape during Holy Week. Every year, members of the Open Door spend the week on the streets in twenty-four-hour blocks to gain a more immediate understanding of the pain of homelessness. "We go out on the streets during Holy Week to remember the Passion of Jesus Christ as we walk the via dolorosa of the homeless poor," says Murphy, who began the practice in 1985 when Palm Sunday fell on the last day of March, the night most shelters in the city of Atlanta would close for the season.[26] Walking this via dolorosa—this way of sorrow—helps those of us who are housed observe firsthand that "homelessness is like a slow execution, [since] the monotony of the day, the exhaustion, the punishment your body takes from the weather, the lack of healthy food, the slavery of labor pools—all lead to death." It also helps us accept responsibility for the fact that "we sentence so many of the citizens of Atlanta to this punishment."[27] Although the gritty and graphic details of street life cannot be experienced or observed in just twenty-four hours or even a week—"for some people every week is Holy Week," one homeless man said to me—and although there are depths of *han* on the streets that we do not wish or try to experience, the practice draws the housed into a more embodied understanding of homelessness, in turn increasing our capacity for lament and for constructive acts of hope.

Holy Week on the streets begins on Palm Sunday when Jesus turns

25. Bonhoeffer, *Discipleship*, 51.
26. Gathje, *Sharing the Bread*, 126.
27. Ibid., 127.

toward Jerusalem and we turn toward downtown Atlanta. Late afternoon, each day of this week, we gather for worship at downtown sites that are significant for those who are poor, either because they are places of power where policies are set or because they are spaces in which poor people abide: the city jail, Woodruff Park, city hall, the state capitol, Pine Street Shelter, and the public hospital, Grady. From these spots, a small group is sent out to learn through our bodies the basic realities of homelessness: the constant walking and displacement, the effects of concrete and sleep deprivation on a worn body and mind, and the bitterness of night temperatures we might otherwise find manageable.

Constant displacement is the dominant theme during my first night on the streets, which begins with a dinner at Safe House, a "feeding" program based on certain conditions—individuals must sit through extended worship before receiving a plate as they are ushered out the door. After dinner in the parking lot, we find a spot to sleep a mile away behind a downtown church, Trinity United Methodist. There until 3:30 a.m. when a thunderstorm displaces us, we walk half a mile to the front courtyard of the shopping district, Underground Atlanta, where we sleep for another hour and a half until we are awakened by a security guard banging from the inside of the window we are up against. By now we have almost made it through the night; at least it is late enough to go to Summit Cafeteria for an eighty-nine-cent coffee that we buy with change panhandled the day before.

My second night on the streets, a few years later, is also filled with intense walking from place to place but this time from small errand to small errand. Once again our first stop is Safe House, but on this particular night it is closed unexpectedly, most likely because a host group did not show, an example of what Ed calls "the institutionalization of homelessness." In place of affordable housing efforts that would work to end homelessness, homelessness has become an institution run mostly by nonprofits and volunteers that provide services now necessary but insufficient nonetheless. With the arbitrary closure of Safe House this night, we are suddenly tasked with finding food, water, and a toilet. About a mile into our journey, we happen upon 7 Bridges to Recovery, a ministry handing out bags of food under an interstate overpass, and then continue on to the water fountain in front of Trinity United Methodist to fill our bottles for the night. The plan is to stop on the way at a city toilet, one of three public restrooms now in downtown Atlanta, but it is closed (as it was during our Holy Week vigil a few years before), even though we are well within its hours of operation. Rerouting our path, we head to the Gateway Center for a bathroom break before searching for cardboard and an unoccupied "cat hole" in which to sleep.

More than learning the basic realities of homelessness, the purpose of spending time on the streets is to follow Jesus, the Jesus of the breadlines whom Catholic Worker artist Fritz Eichenberg so poignantly depicted. The point is not so much to be Jesus to others but to be received by Jesus in this space. It is an act of solidarity, however limited, and a practice that demands community—both the community of the Open Door members who vigil together and the community of homeless friends who watch over and host us in numerous unplanned ways.

When I began worshipping at the Open Door during Lent of 2009, I had not yet built relationships with people from the streets through the work of hospitality. So, although I was immediately drawn to this sacramental act, I did not feel ready to participate. Knowing a number of the men on the streets as friends is central to the practice. Indeed, what makes the practice possible and gives our actions some authenticity are the friendships inaugurated by the Open Door when they welcome homeless people into their space at 910 Ponce de Leon Avenue. As Open Door partner Dick Rustay says, "When we go on the streets, of course we really aren't homeless, but the message to our friends is that we are trying to better understand." Like all nonviolent action for social change, this practice demands preparation—in this case, formation and training precisely through our relationships with those who are homeless. The space of homelessness is not one that privileged people are entitled to, into which we can presumptuously invite ourselves. The practice must be an expression of mutual friendship and come out of a community that has leaders who have navigated the streets before, whether previously homeless or housed.

The morning before my first overnight vigil, James Walker, a formerly homeless man who volunteers daily at the Open Door, strikes up a conversation with me as I am folding laundry in the basement. "It's no joke," he says as if he is testing me, making sure I will not sentimentalize the homeless men I am about to sleep among or overly spiritualize the experience. I am well aware this is not a simulation, evidenced in part by the nightmares I have been having, nightmares that take seriously the reality that "when people are left in darkness, sins will be committed." It is one thing to welcome strangers into a place like the Open Door and make them friends, I think. It is quite another to enter the world of homeless strangers, some of whom I fear as enemies who could do me harm. So that afternoon in Elijah's Cave, the basement closet where we store backpacks and an overflow of donations, I take my time to carefully search—as I have seen many men do before—for the darkest-colored pack that will bring the least attention to me, and I make sure it is big enough and sturdy enough to hold the belongings needed for the street. Here in Elijah's Cave I am already gaining an understanding of the streets through this shared desire for a dark pack and, perhaps more importantly, am gaining patience and sympathy for the men and women who come to the Open Door and are particular about their needs.

In line with the testimonies of prior Holy Week pilgrims, my interactions on the streets with homeless people are, for the most part, not fear inducing. Under the canopy of darkness, any lingering fear is now on account of those who have the power to displace or arrest us for trespassing in a park after hours or urinating in the woods. Not only do our friends meet us with welcome and care as expected, eager to show us their world and give back to us, there also is opportunity for mutuality even among strangers. During my second overnight vigil, our friend Douglass dives into a dumpster to get cardboard for us to sleep on. The next morning, our friend Stanley helpfully identifies himself as our host to the security guard at Pine Street Shelter in order to show us around. At the CNN center the night before, where we passed time along with a smattering of homeless folks, I offered food from the 7 Bridges to Recovery bag to a stranger, Ron. The next day at Our Lady of Lourdes lunch, Ron walks by as a server and asks if I was the woman at CNN last night. "Thanks again for the food!" he exclaims; "Thank you for this food!" I say back as I think of Ed's words at worship the night before, "It is hard to do the right thing in the wrong place." Thanks to the community of the Open Door, I am in the right place to do the work of the gospel—the work of mutuality and peace—at least to some small degree. This work demands, as Ed says, a change of position, a new situation, an expansion of familiar space.

The homeless and the housed have divergent relationships to space, a realization that becomes clear my first time on the streets. A group of us are sleeping behind Trinity United Methodist Church for a few hours until we are all awakened at 3:00 a.m. by a great gush of wind that seconds later brings with it lightning, thunder, and a torrential downpour. We knew there was a possibility of a thunderstorm, and before going to sleep we took notice of the lit parking garage across the way. As the wind howls and the rain begins, resident volunteer Quiana Hawkins and I quickly gather our things, and with skullcaps on our heads and cardboard tucked under our arms, we take off toward the well-lit garage as two homeless men sleeping yards away from us bolt into the darkness in the other direction. We arrive as a security guard behind glass jumps out of his seat, and assuming we are homeless, frantically waves his arms and says, "No! No! No! You can't be here!" To which Quiana responds instinctively and with a tone that conveys the obviousness of the situation, "But there's lightning and it's pouring down rain." "Please, may we stand here?" I plead in a tone that, like Quiana's, demands basic human decency. "Just until the storm passes?" With a deeply confused look on his face, as if he is now noticing that we are not homeless and yet knew that we had been sleeping by the church across the way, the attendant sits back down without explicitly giving us permission but nevertheless allowing us to stay.

As the rest of our group makes their way to the garage, Quiana and I stand there processing what has just happened. To the attendant, we undoubtedly looked homeless as we slept by the church and then raced across the concrete with our dark clothes and cardboard in hand, but perhaps upon arrival in our encounter with him, we did not have the presence of those who are homeless. For instead of hiding from police and security lest we wind up in jail, we had a basic sense of claim to the parking garage. It was raining and we needed shelter, simple as that. What I take immediately from that experience is the different relationship that those who are housed and those who are homeless have to space. For the housed, there is some basic sense of belonging, a basic sense of a right to be somewhere. For the homeless, there is experience after experience of exclusion with the clear message that they do not have that same right simply to exist somewhere.

In Atlanta, this is made explicit through numerous signs—"No Trespassing," "No Loitering"—and, more recently, through blue-light security cameras on almost every downtown street corner. The cameras have successfully done their intended work of controlling the movement of homeless people, pushing them deeper into hiding, while also communicating to people like me to beware of "people like them." This message of exclusion is communicated in a unique and extreme way to the Morning Prayer gathering of the Church of the Common Ground, an Episcopal worshipping community that seeks to be "a sacramental presence on the streets." Maundy Thursday of our Holy Week vigil, we attend what happens to be the last service in their storefront space in a part of downtown where the reality of homelessness is impossible to miss. There we hear the everyday prayers of chronic and episodic homeless people, many of which include concerns about jail and prison. "Lord, give us our daily bread," one woman prays. "We thank you that we are hungry but not starving, homeless but not locked up." The next week, the congregation has to move its gathering to the corner of an adjacent parking lot, where they say their prayers under a tree that provides enough shade for all—until the owners of the lot cut the tree down.

Holy Week is a time when the community responds to the call of Romans 12 to "present our bodies as a living sacrifice" in an intentional and concentrated manner, that admonition that Ed calls "the disciple's primary method of social analysis." This methodology helps Christians "be not conformed to the pattern of this world" (in this case, to the pattern of exclusion) "but be transformed by the renewing of minds" in order "to discern . . . the will of God." In regard to the right to belong somewhere, or more specifically, the human right to housing and shelter, it only took one night on the streets for my mind to be renewed.

I am in a profession where knowledge is gained mostly in the classroom through books, by reading and debating multiple and opposing arguments, many of which can sound quite convincing, all at the same time. The social analysis that comes from embodied engagement often proves to be the clarifying factor. In a theology or ethics course, for example, one may read a school of thought that argues "rights" language is detrimental to Christian ethics because the language of rights is too individualistic or bolsters democratic liberalism, which some argue leaves no room for particular Christian commitments in the public realm.[28] When I first heard these arguments in graduate school, they gave me pause. Maybe as a Christian I should not speak of a "human right" to such things as housing, I thought. There are other lines of thinking that appeal to realism and argue that while the notion of human rights may well serve as a common moral language across cultures and faith traditions, not everything, like housing, can or should count as a human right. We have to be realistic, so the argument goes, about if and how a society could pay for something like housing if it were deemed a right. "Good point," I have thought in the classroom.

But what I learned through my body the night of Holy Wednesday on the streets of downtown Atlanta amid a threatening storm is that I believe that shelter is a right. I believe it is a right for me. When faced with someone who was trying to deny me this, I thought, "Are

28. For example, see Stanley Hauerwas, *The Work of Theology* (Grand Rapids: Eerdmans, 2015), 191–207.

144

you kidding? You're not going to let us get shelter in an empty parking garage?" "There's lightning and it's pouring down rain," voiced Quiana. If I hold this deeply embedded belief in the right to shelter for myself, I must hold it for others. I must work for it for others. Because of this embodied knowledge, I now have no problem claiming unequivocally that it is the will of God that all be housed because housing is a human right. By placing my body in a new situation, in unfamiliar space, my mind has been renewed.

## The Shared Space of Belonging

When the Open Door invites homeless people into their home, perceived enemies become friends. Those friendships in turn expand and transform space, not only during Holy Week as they give us entrance to the streets where we would not otherwise go, but also in our everyday lives as we see homeless friends around the neighborhood and in adjacent localities—in all the various places where their presence is scorned at worst and tolerated at best. Different in kind from the profound intimacy and connection I have with the women in prison, my friendship with the homeless men is rooted simply in a shared space of belonging, specifically the shared space of the Open Door that then envelops other places where our lives as housed and homeless overlap—in parks or on the sidewalks of neighborhood cafés. The most common place of overlap for me is my daily running path down Freedom Parkway, where I have the opportunity to stop and chat with a number of the men I know from the Open Door or simply pause and offer a sweaty hug. Because of these friendships, I am more likely to speak to other homeless men I do not yet know, further expanding the possibility of friendship and a mutual sense of belonging.

This is not to claim that the streets are first and foremost the streets of the housed that we then share with the homeless. Open Door leader Mary Catherine Johnson and I discussed how different the streets felt after we spent the night on them. They became more intimate, more meaningful, than simply a way to get from point A to point B. As housed professionals, we presume ownership over these downtown streets, an entitlement that affects our perception of others. Even as we deny them affordable housing, we see the homeless as invading our space and inhibiting our ability to get from here to there with comfort and ease. After a consistent twenty-four hours on them, though, the streets possessed a certain familiarity to us as "homeless" people; they became the space in which our lives occurred: there is the space we found shelter from the wind, there is the space we stood in line for food, there is the space we held conversation with others, we said evening prayer, we laid our heads. In this very tangible way, the streets belong to the homeless even as they remain spaces of marginality, survival, and exclusion. To say that the streets belong to homeless people, though, is not to perpetuate the myth that they want to be there, all things being equal. "Help me get housing" was a phrase that rang multiple times in our ears: "Help me get housing," we overheard one homeless man say to our homeless friend Jermaine. "Help us get housing!" an elderly woman shouted from the steps of Immaculate Conception as we walked by. The streets are intimate but not safe or desirable; they are familiar but not spaces of belonging—not a home. Nor are they the shared space of belonging—the space of social flourishing and transformed relations—that defines beloved community.

We find that shared space of belonging back at the Open Door during the Saturday night Easter vigil. After a cookout, homeless friends are invited to spend the night in the front yard with members of the Community and wake up to an extravagant Easter brunch. Although I have little experience falling asleep to the constant noise of traffic and the bars across the street, when I see the watchful eye of Calvin Kimborough, who is tasked to stay awake and protect that space, I feel safe and am better able to rest. While lying on the streets, I was quite aware of the position of my body, the least vulnerable position being on my back, but in the front yard I am able to relax and get more comfortable. I glimpse why homeless people who come to worship can barely stay awake, often dosing in and out of sleep. Because homelessness requires constant vigilance—sleeping with one eye open, so to speak—exhaustion often takes over in safe and welcoming space.

The journey toward beloved community begins with this transformation of space that resists alienation and exclusion. It begins with the creation of shared spaces of belonging, which may come in various forms from services of Morning Prayer to houses of hospitality. For the housed, it includes a journey toward the streets, a journey of embodied lament that then makes the fight for decent and affordable housing—the repair of the world—urgent and concrete.

# 6

---

# Good Friday

For the message of the cross
is foolishness to those who are perishing,
but to us who are being saved
it is the power of God. . . .
We proclaim Christ crucified. . . .
For God's foolishness is wiser than human wisdom,
and God's weakness is stronger than human strength.
—1 Corinthians 1:18–25

When they came to the place that is called The Skull,
they crucified Jesus there with the criminals,
one on his right and one on his left.
—Luke 23:33

## The Message of the Cross

On October 20, 2009, the Open Door Community stands with Georgians for Alternatives to the Death Penalty, Central Presbyterian Church, and others on the steps of the state capitol, holding candles in vigil for Mark McClain. He had shot Domino's Pizza manager Kevin Brown in the chest during a robbery that amounted to $130, killing him, and is being executed by the State this very hour. It is approximately the one-hundredth time the Open Door Community has hosted a vigil on these steps for a condemned criminal, given the number of temporary stays and executions in Georgia over the last thirty years, but it is my first time to stand in outward solidarity with them as I wear their black T-shirt bearing a bloody handprint and the words, "The death penalty makes killers of us all." The next day the *Atlanta Journal-Constitution* runs a story about the vigil, and the online version includes a picture of twelve of us among the crowd, some, including me, wearing the provocative and graphic T-shirt. I read the story thinking about the bumper-to-bumper traffic edging by on Washington Street the day before, the drivers staring blankly at us or occasionally shouting harsh words of disapproval. As I peer into this online picture of solemn and mournful faces, most looking up toward the sound of the church bell tolling at the moment of execution, me looking down into the flame of my candle, I think, "We must look crazy to care about the life of a man who committed such a senseless act of violence." I feel sick to my stomach, acutely aware of our bizarre witness.

The answers to most controversial issues, the ones that get closest to the heart of the matter, are often discovered in a third way forward beyond mutually opposing and polarizing positions. Yet the impracticality and immorality of the death penalty, it seems to me, is fairly straightforward. There is an enormous amount of data that supports the side of death-penalty abolitionists, both from an ethical and a purely practical perspective: the high cost of executions on taxpayers, the 156 people nationwide whose innocence has been established by DNA evidence after serving time on death row, the arbitrariness of the penalty's application, the racial and class disparities, its lack of deterrence, not to mention that the United States is the only developed country in the Western world that puts its own citizens to death, a fact expressed in the words of Senator Kwame Raoul after Illinois abolished its death penalty in 2011. "I'm happy to say today we've joined the rest of the civilized world," he exclaimed.[1]

1. "Illinois Coverage of Repeal," *The StandDown Texas Project*, March 10, 2011, http://tinyurl.com/j9wumw3.

What remains true, however, in what seems so obvious to the Open Door and other abolitionists on moral and practical grounds—summed up in slogans like "an eye for an eye makes the whole world blind" or "the death penalty makes killers of us all" and even in Jesus's own words, "You have heard it said 'an eye for an eye' *but I say* . . . love your enemies,"—is how outrageous, how audacious, our witness is. What is outrageous is not the fact that we are against the death penalty as such, but that there on the steps of the capitol building we are mourning and standing with the guilty criminal, with a particular man—in the case of October 2009, with Mark McClain, who was convicted of a senseless act of violence—and that we have the gall in the face of the death of Mark's victim, Kevin Brown, whom we also mourn, to use the same term for Mark, a *victim* of state violence. The concreteness of our stand *is* offensive. It is a stumbling block for many Christians and non-Christians alike, a stumbling block at times even for those of us who firmly oppose the death penalty. For, although we can point to the immorality and impracticality of the death penalty as such, our stand with the convicted criminal disrupts our moral bearings, our commonsense understanding of right and wrong, of good and evil. It is important for all of us—whether abolitionists, defenders, or the undecided—to glimpse how outrageous it is, how offensive and foolish it is to stand with the guilty criminal, because if we do not understand this, we cannot understand the full power—the meaning and message—of the cross. When Paul says to the Corinthian church that "the message of the cross is foolishness to those who are perishing but to us who are being saved it is the power of God," he invites Christians to consider anew what exactly the meaning of the cross is, why the cross as a central symbol of our faith is a stumbling block, and how it is that we are being saved through this foolish proclamation.

This chapter addresses these questions through focused attention on the social and political meaning of the cross. The social and political significance of Good Friday is found in the cross, where Jesus becomes a victim of state violence and is in solidarity with society's victims. A central claim of the chapter is that the crucified Christ commands that we turn to his cross for salvation and see in him all of society's victims; for when we turn toward our victims in repentance and reconciliation, we transcend the victim-oppressor cycle and are liberated into beloved community. The chapter initiates this turn by helping us see the incarcerated Christ through the testimonies and insights of women in prison.

## Beyond Substitutionary Atonement

Paul's letter to the Corinthians invites reflection on the message of the cross and presses us to ask anew what Christians are announcing when we "proclaim Christ crucified." Because these questions are central to our faith as Christians, we may be quick to think the answer is well known and that we know. In reality, like all truths of Christian faith, the meaning and message of the cross is one we have to live into continually, learn and learn anew. For if the cross is a central point of encounter and intimacy between God and fallen humanity, then it must be bursting with a multiplicity of meaning.

Those of us who have grown up in the church have likely heard the meaning of the cross expressed through what theologians call the "theory of satisfaction" or "the substitutionary atonement theory." The satisfaction theory was first articulated by the medieval theologian Anselm in the eleventh century, later developed into a theory based on penal substitution by Reformation thinkers like John Calvin in the sixteenth century, and is now the dominant and popular understanding of the meaning of the cross among North American Protestants. Most Christians are familiar with this way of thinking about the cross, even if we only know it in its popular formulations like "Jesus died for my sins." This theory so dominates our theological imaginations that most North American Christians today cannot think of the cross outside of this paradigm, cannot fathom that there are other ways to understand the cross's theological meaning, some of which directly challenge aspects of this atonement theory, at least in its classical articulations. Anselm's atonement theory arose out of his medieval context of feudal lords and their serfs and the medieval culture's understanding of law and order, in which a serf's disobedience dishonors the feudal lord. What Anselm understood as honor, later theologians came to understand as wrath. Because a serf's disobedience dishonors the feudal lord, satisfaction must be paid or there will be punishment. In the same way, the theory goes, human disobedience dishonors God and so satisfaction must be paid or punishment will follow. Because sinful humanity cannot make satisfaction, God becomes a human being and pays the price on our behalf. God satisfies the debt owed to God.

As do all theories of atonement articulated and developed over the course of Christian history, the satisfaction theory has roots in scripture, in certain biblical passages like the suffering servant in Isaiah 53 and in Paul's letter to the Galatians where he writes that Christ redeemed us from the curse of the law by becoming a curse for us (3:13). These passages suggest that human beings are redeemed through vicarious suffering—someone suffering on behalf of another—which includes the idea of substitution, what Luther called the "happy exchange," God's righteousness substituted for our unrighteousness. "God made him who had no sin to be sin for us, so that in him we may become the righteousness of God," Paul writes in his second letter to the Corinthians (5:21).

Yet the cross is bursting with a multiplicity of meaning and the various metaphors scripture uses to make sense of it are evidence of this. No doubt, the theory of substitutionary atonement developed by earlier generations of Christians expresses important truths about who God is and who we are, about God's love being shown in the fact that the sinless one became sin for us, took our sin, and through the Holy Spirit imparts upon us God's righteousness. Without a doubt, a central message of the cross is that Jesus died for, or better, on account of, our sin. But there are also some serious flaws and limits to these theories about the cross, as feminist and womanist theologies articulate most consistently, especially if the substitutionary or satisfaction theory is the only lens through which we come to understand the cross.[2]

2. See, for example, Rosemary Radford Ruether, *Sexism and God Talk: Toward a Feminist Theology*

To name one flaw, the satisfaction theory tends to glorify suffering as it reduces Jesus's mission to his death, rather than emphasizing that Jesus's cross was a result of a life he chose to live in solidarity with outcasts and in resistance to the prevailing social order. To name another, substitutionary atonement tends to make God's wrath rather than God's love central. The cross is necessary to appease God's wrath, because like the feudal system of lords and serfs, if God's wrath is not appeased, there will be punishment. Wrath and punishment thus become the driving factors of God's movement in the world instead of God's strength to love and God's capacity to straightforwardly forgive erring human beings.

Perhaps most importantly, though, for members of the Open Door who visit men and women on death row, who come to know someone like Mark McClain not simply as a man who committed a senseless act of violence but as a man of repentance and faith, this dominant and popular theory of atonement described above fails to address what we are acutely aware of—the cross as an instrument of state execution and violence. If we are to know the meaning God has given this instrument of state violence, the meaning God has given the cross through Jesus—in other words, if we are to understand the cross theologically (from the standpoint of God), we first need to understand its meaning and function in this world, its anthropological meaning, the meaning that fallen and sinful human society first gave it. This is a meaning that classical atonement theories rarely address.

### The Cross as the Place of Collective Violence and Victim Making

The most helpful way to explore the cross from the standpoint of human society is through the groundbreaking study of Christian anthropologist René Girard. Girard studies ancient myths and has

(Boston: Beacon Press, 1983); Julie M. Hopkins, *Toward a Feminist Christology: Jesus of Nazareth, European Women, and the Christological Crisis* (Grand Rapids: Eerdmans, 1995); Katie Geneva Cannon, *Black Womanist Ethics* (Atlanta: Scholars Press, 1988); Delores S. Williams, *Sisters in the Wilderness: The Challenge of Womanist God-Talk* (Maryknoll, NY: Orbis Books, 1993); and Karen Baker-Fletcher, *Dancing with God: The Trinity from a Womanist Perspective* (St. Louis: Chalice Press, 2006). Also see J. Denny Weaver's discussion of this in *The Nonviolent Atonement* (Grand Rapids: Eerdmans, 2011), 151–217.

found in them a reoccurring pattern that he calls "the cycle of mimetic violence" or "the single victim mechanism."[3] The ancient myths begin with society in a state of extreme disorder, in the midst of a crisis or a conglomeration of smaller crises that come to a head, that bubble up and reach a breaking point and threaten the order of society. The society then overcomes its fragmentation and conflicts by finding unity through a collective violence that eliminates someone among it—an innocent victim, a scapegoat—who is blamed as the source of social trouble, deemed guilty, and held responsible for societal conflict and disorder. Finally, there is catharsis, a sense of relief, and a new social cohesion fostered by the unanimous condemnation and expulsion of an innocent victim. The chosen victims in the myths are those whom "no one will mourn," for the drive behind the victim mechanism is to pacify conflict not to stir it up. Thus, the victims are, as Girard says, "social nobodies: the homeless, those without family, the disabled and ill, abandoned old people," and we must, of course, add "the hated," those on death row who are all too easily demonized.[4]

Girard then shows that this single victim mechanism is also at work in the Gospel accounts of the crucifixion. There is social crisis that leads to collective violence against an innocent victim. Girard argues that the Bible reveals—exposes—the victim mechanism that lies behind the ancient myths and that also is at work in human cultures in all times and all places. The similarities between the ancient myths and the Gospels serve to highlight the differences between them. Whereas the myths justify collective violence, always taking the side of the violent crowd and condemning the innocent victim, the Gospels are unique in that they expose this pattern and take the side of the victim, Jesus. As societies perpetrate mimetic violence, they are unconscious of the process they are caught up in. The myths themselves are unaware of the process they describe, Girard argues, and the fact that the social group has deceived itself is what gives the single victim

3. René Girard, *I See Satan Fall Like Lightning* (Maryknoll, NY: Orbis Books, 2009), 19–31.
4. Ibid., 76.

mechanism its power. With words that sound as if he is specifically describing the death penalty in the United States, Girard writes,

> In us and about us scandals proliferate; sooner or later they carry us along toward . . . the single victim mechanism. It makes us unknowingly the accomplices of unanimous murders, all the more deceived by the devil because we are not aware of our complicity, which is not conscious of itself. We continue to imagine ourselves alien to all violence. . . .

> . . . The single victim mechanism only functions by means of the ignorance of those who keep it working. They believe they are supporting the truth when they are really living a lie. . . . Persecutors [of the single victim mechanism] think they are doing good, the right thing; they believe they are working for justice and truth; they believe they are saving their community. . . .

> . . . In revealing the self-deception of those who engage in violence, the New Testament dispels the lie at the heart of their violence . . . our belief in our own innocence. The Gospels are well aware of what they are doing.[5]

There is an amazing similarity between the ancient myths and the Gospels. Jesus's death is one example among many others of the single victim mechanism, writes Girard. What makes the Gospel accounts different, though, is that as God incarnate, Jesus offers an end to the pattern of collective violence and victim making, which is what the cross represents as an instrument of state violence. As a human instrument, the cross *is* the place of collective violence and victim making. Jesus offers an end to this pattern of violence by transcending the victim-oppressor relationship. Jesus becomes the victim. He then returns as the Resurrected One to his judges in Jerusalem—to the very people who condemned and excluded him—and instead of continuing the process, of then making them victims of condemnation and retaliatory violence, he offers them forgiveness, reconciliation, the opportunity to repent and become cobuilders of the kingdom of God.[6]

So the meaning of the cross from an anthropological view is this: the cross is the place where an unjust and self-deceived society makes

---

5. Ibid., 41, 126–27.
6. Rowan Williams, *Resurrection: Interpreting the Easter Gospel* (Cleveland: Pilgrim Press, 2004), 1–5.

its victims. The cross is not first or initially an instrument of God for salvation. How preposterous! What an insult to the character of God, who is love, to claim that God would need an instrument of state violence to forgive human beings and bring about salvation. No, the cross is first an evil instrument of human societies bent on condemnation, exclusion, and destruction, bent on blaming others for its conflicts and crises in order to substantiate its own innocence. It is then reclaimed by God as an instrument that exposes this very evil and that offers an end to the cycle of oppression and victim-making. In the crucified Jesus, we find all victims of collective condemnation, exclusion, degradation, rejection, and blame. When we proclaim Christ crucified, we proclaim that, as an Open Door T-shirt reads, "Jesus was a victim of the death penalty." We proclaim that God identifies with, and takes the side of, society's victims.

Girard argues that because of Christianity's great influence on Western civilization we now live in a culture that values concern for the innocent victim. This may be seen, for example, in the response of many citizens who poured into New Orleans in 2005 to attend to the victims of Hurricane Katrina. But what about our concern for victims who are also guilty? If society's victims were innocent like Jesus, there would be little offense in taking their side today. Yet the victims of state violence that the Open Door stands with and for on the capitol steps are often not innocent of the crime with which they are charged. They are at once victim and oppressor.

In courageous truth telling that pushes Christian belief in the forgiveness and reconciliation of Jesus to the extreme, Open Door leader Emma Stitt highlights the horrific nature of the crime in a particularly difficult vigil in June 2014. Marcus Wellons was a friend of the Open Door Community before committing his crime (he had even spent a Christmas season decorating Open Door cards sent to men on death row) and was visited on a regular basis by a number of Community members after his crime. At his vigil, Emma says,

What we're doing here tonight isn't simple. In fact, standing here together in affirmation of the life and humanity of Marcus Wellons is an act of fierce and dangerous hope.

It isn't easy hope, though we have that, too. Easy hope is hoping for a last minute stay or a Supreme Court intervention. Even if it would take a miracle for these things to happen, hoping for them isn't difficult for death penalty abolitionists like us.

What is difficult is standing here affirming the life of a man who is guilty of the crime for which he was sentenced to death. Marcus Wellons raped and murdered a fifteen-year-old girl. He ended her life and in doing so tore apart the world for everyone who knew her and loved her. He broke trust with everyone who knew and cared about him. His sin was the worst of the worst.

Martin Luther King said that "capital punishment is society's final assertion that it will not forgive."[7] Our standing here tonight is a proclamation that we believe that even in the wake of the worst thing that could possibly happen, there is hope for reconciliation.

Marcus Wellons has lived out this hope, working everyday in numerous and creative ways for reconciliation. I know that he reached out to his victim's family, and as far as I know they haven't responded, which of course we understand—reconciliation is a difficult path to choose. So Marcus has found other ways to work toward wholeness. He leads Bible studies on the row and has even been a minister for some of the guards. He buys stamps for prisoners who don't have any resources. He helps find pen pals and visitors for men who don't have any connections outside the walls of that prison.

He has built up his own community outside of the prison with pen pals and visitors from all over the world including Switzerland and Australia and the Open Door. He has repaired and maintained his relationship with his own family. His mother and daughter, son-in-law, and grandchild visit him regularly.

This is Marcus Wellons. He is a son and a father and a grandfather, a friend, and a pen pal. He has lived on death row for over twenty years with a fierce hope for reconciliation. We stand here tonight with that same difficult hope.

This "fierce and dangerous" hope is based on God's promise and on

---

7. King, *Strength to Love*, 42.

God's previous acts. It brings into focus scriptural texts like God's protection of the murderer Cain or God's determination to make murderers like Moses and Paul central to the divine drama of salvation. It is a hope not only for transformed individuals but also for transformed social relations—for the creation of beloved community—which means it is a hope that envelops us all.

Like Marcus Wellons, the guilty victims of state violence are simultaneously victim and oppressor—victim of collective violence and perpetrator of unthinkable harm. But isn't what is true of the guilty criminal also true of us, if only in varying degrees? "Where is the pure victim to be found?" asks former Archbishop of Canterbury, Rowan Williams. Echoing our discussion in the last chapter on *han* and building off of Girard's study of the single victim mechanism, Williams argues that the line between victim and oppressor runs down the center of each of us. He writes, "The human world is not one of clearly distinguishable bodies of oppressors and victims, those who inflict damage and those who bear it. . . . The problem is that in ordinary human relationships, boundaries are very fluid indeed."[8] Williams suggests that Christians are comfortable speaking about "concern for the poor" if it is done in an abstract, sentimentalized manner that fits neatly into our moral and religious categories. However, sentimentalizing "the poor" as purely innocent is unrealistic since they, like us and like the guilty victims of state violence, are both victim and oppressor in a complex web of human relationships. Indeed, the power of sin is its constant, cyclical effect: I am abused or injured and so I injure. The one whom I have sinned against sins against another out of that wounded state that I have caused, that we as a society have caused or contributed to or failed to address. It appears to be a cycle that has no end.

The cross of Christ does offer an end to this cycle, but the end is found not simply in the notion of the forgiveness of my sins, as substitutionary atonement implies. That my sins are forgiven does not account for the fact that I am a part of a society that continues

8. Ibid., 6–7.

to make victims every time we exclude, condemn, isolate, reject, and dehumanize. The cross of Christ offers more than the forgiveness of my sins. It offers an end to the victim-oppressor cycle of which I am a part, because as we turn to Jesus's cross for our salvation, Jesus the victim commands that we see in him all of society's victims.

## Transcending the Victim-Oppressor Relationship

Our salvation, that is, our entrance and participation in the kingdom of God, the beloved community, requires that we see ourselves as guilty of making victims and that we turn toward our victims in concrete ways. Jesus, the convicted criminal, the excluded and rejected one, calls us to face our victims because when we turn toward them in repentance and reconciliation, we transcend the victim-oppressor relationship. Rowan Williams says it this way: "I am not saved by forgetting or canceling my memory of concrete guilt, the oppressive relations in which I am in fact inextricably involved. And so I must look to my *partner*: to the victim who alone can be the source of renewal and transformation."[9]

It is this dynamic—the dynamic of turning toward our victims and in them finding partners—that is powerfully at work at 910 Ponce de Leon Avenue as the Open Door turns toward those who are homeless. Instead of condemning, excluding, dehumanizing, and rejecting, instead of continuing to make victims, the Community makes friends through hospitality in its home, through warm showers, hot meals, clean clothes, through shared conversation in the living room or over coffee in the yard.

It is this dynamic that is powerfully at work as I and other teachers in the theology certificate program venture to the women's prison to hold courses on theology and biblical studies. We bring texts and tools to foster critical thinking and the women bring their experiences and voices. They add their insights to thousands of years of biblical and theological reflection, and in this process we teachers and student-inmates alike are all, as Paul says, "being saved"—being liberated into

9. Ibid., 6. Italics mine.

beloved community through our partnership. The depth of li'
that is being experienced by both teachers and students c;
explained through a simple paradigm of "prison ministry," that is, of
"us" ministering to "them." It can only be explained by the cross of
Christ, which has the power to stop the victim-oppressor cycle and
replace it with the politically potent notion of friendship, summed up
so beautifully by that sign that hangs in the Open Door hallway: "If
you have come to help me you are wasting your time. But if you have
come because your liberation is bound up with mine, then let us work
together."

This dynamic of turning toward our victim in a concrete way is also
at work every time members and friends of the Open Door stand on the
steps of the capitol building in vigil for an individual being executed
by the state. We stand on those steps in our pitch-black T-shirts with
bloody handprints, we turn toward the sound of the church bell tolling,
and we face our victim. In doing so we proclaim Christ crucified. We
stand with the criminal found guilty of a heinous crime, with the guilty
criminal who is also the victim of state violence, and we proclaim that
in this moment God is on the side of this victim and all victims. It is an
offensive proclamation. It "is foolishness to those who are perishing"
under and see no alternative to the victim-oppressor cycle. "But to us
who are being saved" through our participation in the kingdom of God,
the beloved community, to those of us who have tasted the liberation
that comes from transformed human relations—to us "it is the power
of God."

When we turn toward our victims in repentance and reconciliation,
we hear unsettling truths, sometimes words of indignation, like Erika's,
boldly spoken in the first Theology Foundations course at the prison.
"God doesn't live here!" Erika proclaims in exasperation to a room
full of women holding tight to their faith. "God does *not* live here."
Formerly a "PK," a pastor's kid, Erika recoils at any hint of "jailhouse
religion" that could serve to bolster the dominant structure of the
prison system by making it appear to be an institution of rehabilitation,
a place where "bad" or "immoral" people could find God. The other

women in the class vehemently disagree and offer testimony of God's presence with them at key times during their incarceration. No doubt the women are right to hold tight to palpable moments and their everyday faith, which is anything but a show. "If my strength wasn't in the Lord," says Kristi, "I would easily crumble." But Erika's resolve conveys an important truth as well: prisons are godforsaken in that they oppose the reign of God, as Jesus's gospel proclamation of liberty for prisoners makes clear. To me, Erika's fiery words also express what Bonhoeffer calls "ultimate honesty," the perplexing and paradoxical fact that God's presence is often hidden in spaces like the godforsaken cross.[10] Thus Erika's words convey, perhaps unwittingly, a central truth in Martin Luther's theology of the cross, the truth the rest of the women affirm through their testimonies and experience as a comfort. God is "hidden," meaning God is present in the most unexpected places, the places that seem the farthest from God and from which most human beings turn away. God hides in humiliation and suffering, be it on the cross or behind prison walls, a point Bonhoeffer stresses when he says that Jesus drank the cup of suffering "to the dregs" on the godforsaken cross.[11] This notion of a hidden God combines Erika's crucial insight of the godforsaken nature of the prison with what the other women certainly know but are not articulating in such a stark manner: God is present there not because the prison serves or pleases God but because God seeks out and enters godforsaken places (and then calls disciples to do the same). God does this in order to be in solidarity with human suffering, expose destructive powers that cause the suffering, and redeem.

The experiences of Erika and the other women press us to examine further the message and meaning of the cross, especially the way that the cross addresses social sin like mass incarceration and leads to the dynamic of liberation and reconciliation described above. The women's experiences in prison compel us to examine the way in which the message of the cross—solidarity with society's victims—is, according

10. Bonhoeffer, *Letters and Papers* (Fortress Press), 478–79.
11. Bonhoeffer, *Discipleship*, 90.

to Paul, "the power of God" that interrupts the victim-oppressor cycle and transforms human relations.

## Bonhoeffer's Jesus

Bonhoeffer is a good guide for those of us who are schooled in substitutionary atonement but want to reexamine the meaning of the cross. He is a model of a theologian who works deeply with classical Western categories, with which the majority of North American Christians are most familiar, but also allows his understanding of the cross to be expanded as he learns from oppressed African Americans in Harlem and then applies that knowledge to Jewish oppression in Germany. He articulates the cross's meaning in a way that both retains the classical concepts rooted in Paul's letters and also incorporates into his understanding liberation accounts that attend to the Gospel narratives and identify Jesus's cross as a work of solidarity. Liberation theologies see in Jesus's cross the crosses of all of society's victims, as depicted, for example, by the black Christ that hangs on a crucifix in the Open Door's dining room/worship space or by the vagrant Christ that hangs on the Community's Holy Week cross. Specifically, Bonhoeffer's theology centers on Christ as the vicarious representative of humanity rather than on Christ as the vicarious substitute. In doing so, his Christology avoids some of the problematic aspects of substitutionary atonement, like God's alleged need for punishment to calm God's wrath, and provides a more seamless link between classical theories and liberation theologies.

For Bonhoeffer, Jesus is representative in that he is, as 1 Corinthians says, the second or final Adam. Whereas Paul sees the first Adam as a representative of humanity whose disobedience had ontological repercussions for us all, Jesus is the representative of humanity whose obedience to God and love for the world has the same expansive and inclusive reach.[12] Specifically, Jesus is the representative of humanity in his incarnation, crucifixion, and resurrection. Through the

12. Bonhoeffer, *Ethics*, 231–32, 253.

incarnation, all of humanity has been accepted; through the crucifixion, all of humanity has been judged; and through the resurrection, all of humanity has been reconciled to God. Bonhoeffer writes, "In becoming human we recognize God's love for the world toward God's creation, in the crucifixion God's judgment on all flesh, and in the resurrection, God's purpose for a new world."[13] First, Jesus became the "real" human being who "experienced in his own body the essence of the real" and thus is in solidarity with all human beings who navigate the complexity and messiness of this-worldly existence.[14] Then, because real human beings are also fallen human beings—humans that oppress and injure others, humans that endure wounds and act out of *han*—Jesus accepts guilt and takes responsibility for sin on the cross. In doing so, he exposes the sin that needs to be judged.[15] God's judgment is a divine "No!" to anything that distorts human flourishing and so is in the service of God's "Yes" to human reconciliation and concrete redemption. God's judgment is not in the service of divine punishment, as the satisfaction theory claims, but of divine promise, specifically the promise of reconciled and redeemed community. Because of the work of the incarnate, crucified, and risen God, Bonhoeffer concludes, "It is no longer possible to conceive and understand humanity other than in Jesus Christ. In Christ we see humanity as a humanity that is accepted, borne, loved, and reconciled with God."[16] Disciples are then called to conform to Christ—to participate in his already accomplished work—by being in solidarity with their fellow human beings (conforming to the incarnation), taking responsibility for sin (conforming to the crucifixion), and manifesting God's reconciliation and redemption in concrete ways (conforming to the resurrection).

By focusing on Jesus as the representative of humanity, Bonhoeffer makes human participation in Christ's completed work central to the way salvation unfolds in this life. Whereas substitutionary atonement

13. Ibid., 157.
14. Ibid., 263.
15. Ibid., 91. See McBride, *Church for the World*, 104–8.
16. Bonhoeffer, *Ethics*, 253.

tends to make human beings passive recipients of salvation, Bonhoeffer's focus on vicarious representative action includes within it the human capacity to participate in Jesus's already accomplished work, and Bonhoeffer does so without giving up the Reformation truth that salvation is God's initiative and deed. Whereas substitutionary theorists tend to diminish human responsibility in the work of salvation, representation provides a better frame for human participation in God's liberating transformation of this world. Human participation is folded into God's prior participation in human experience, what Bonhoeffer calls "the suffering of God in the world."[17] Suffering, as we have seen, is not a punishment God demands but is a way of life God chooses in a fallen world. God chooses suffering both to be in solidarity with those who bear the brunt of destructive powers and to stop destructive forces like the victim-oppressor cycle. It is God's suffering love for others and our participation in that love that overcomes these powers.

This theological truth that Jesus is the representative of humanity makes Jesus's solidarity with real human beings central to his person and work, from the incarnation to the resurrection. As theologian Reggie Williams argues, Bonhoeffer's interpretation of Jesus as the human representative in solidarity with real human beings and his focus on God's hiddenness in suffering prepared him to readily embrace a fresh understanding of Jesus that arose from his engagement with oppressed people. Specifically, Bonhoeffer engaged the concept of the "Black Christ," which deems Jesus a representative of black suffering at the hands of white domination. Bonhoeffer encountered this depiction of Jesus in Harlem while studying at Union Theological Seminary and attending Abyssinian Baptist Church in 1930–31, toward the end of the Harlem Renaissance. At the time, Harlem was the home of tens of thousands of southern black migrants who had journeyed North after World War I, a migration that, as Reggie Williams writes, "signaled the dawn of the poor inner city black neighborhood, in the context of what Langston Hughes described as 'a

17. Bonhoeffer, *Letters and Papers* (Touchstone), 369–70.

dream deferred.'"[18] There, the German Bonhoeffer built relationships with black middle-class Abyssinian members as well as their impoverished neighbors, and he engaged Harlem's literary movement. In doing so, he models for us a way of being open and attentive to the Christological insights of others, which his own social location prohibited him from otherwise gaining. He models a self-critical posture that enabled him to revise and deepen his previous thinking about the meaning and message of the cross.

While in New York City, Bonhoeffer listened to slave spirituals and studied popular African American literature from the Harlem Renaissance. Some of the most popular works—W. E. B. du Bois's 1920 *Darkwater,* Claude McKay's 1922 poem "The Lynching," and Countee Cullen's 1929 poem "The Black Christ"—connect Jesus's suffering to black oppression, the latter two works specifically linking Jesus's death on the cross to black men lynched in the South.[19] Likewise, the haunting intimacy of the spiritual "Were You There When They Crucified My Lord?" sung by slaves and their descendants, exemplifies the degree to which crucifixion is an accurate image for the continued experience of unjust suffering: "Sometimes it causes me to tremble, tremble, tremble," sings a people crucified at present by injustice, "were you there when they crucified my Lord?" Through his embodied engagement in Harlem, Bonhoeffer gained a new understanding of the gospel in light of African American oppression, and its impact was immediate and lifelong. A year after his return from the United States, it sounds as if Harlem was on Bonhoeffer's mind as much as Germany suffering under worldwide depression. In his sermon "Lazarus and the Rich Man," he says,

> Blessed are you outcasts and outlaws, you victims of society, you men and women without work, you broken down and ruined, you lonely and abandoned, rape victims and those who suffer injustice, you who suffer in body and soul . . . for you have a God. Woe to you who live happily in

18. Reggie L. Williams, *Bonhoeffer's Black Jesus: Harlem Renaissance Theology and an Ethic of Resistance* (Waco, TX: Baylor University Press, 2014), 85–86.

19. Ibid., 53–75. We do not know precisely what Bonhoeffer read, but we do know he immersed himself in the most popular literature of the Harlem movement and wrote an essay on it that is now lost. As a thorough German scholar, he likely read all of the most important pieces.

luxury and are respected yesterday and today. That is the most concretely good news of God for the poor.[20]

Without negating previous and subsequent claims that Jesus is the representative of all of humanity, Bonhoeffer emphasizes in this sermon that God's kingdom come demands a concrete gospel, good news for the poor in their particular circumstances.

> We have spiritualized the gospel—that is, we have lightened it up, changed it. Take our gospel of the rich man and poor Lazarus. . . . The frightening thing about this story [is that] there is no moralizing here at all, but simply talk of poor and rich and of the promise and the threat given to one and the other. Here the external conditions . . . are taken unbelievably seriously. Why did Christ heal the sick and suffering if he didn't consider such external conditions important? . . . And where do we get the incredible presumption to spiritualize these things that Christ saw and did very concretely? We must end this audacious, sanctimonious spiritualization of the gospel. Take it as it is, or hate it honestly!

Voicing this honesty, Bonhoeffer continues,

> We disdain the masses of Lazaruses. We disdain the gospel of the poor. . . . But if just one of these would really meet you face to face—the unemployed Lazarus, Lazarus the accident victim, Lazarus whose ruin you caused, your own begging child as Lazarus, the helpless and desperate mother, Lazarus who has become a criminal . . . can you go up to him or her and say: I disdain you, Lazarus. I scoff at the good news that makes you glad?[21]

He then turns his attention to his privileged audience and asks, "Who is the rich man" and what is his good news? Bonhoeffer continues, "Certainly *we* are not rich. *We* are not full and satisfied. *We* do not live happily in luxury. . . . Do you mean that seriously? Even when you meet Lazarus? . . . We should see—see poor Lazarus in his full frightening misery and behind him Christ, who invited him to his table and calls him blessed."[22]

The good news for "the rich man" is just as concrete as it is for

20. Dietrich Bonhoeffer, *The Collected Sermons of Dietrich Bonhoeffer*, ed. Isabel Best (Minneapolis: Fortress Press, 2012), 36. Sermon based on Luke 16:19–31.
21. Bonhoeffer, *Collected Sermons*, 35, 37–38.
22. Ibid., 40. Italics mine.

poor Lazarus. It is the promise of abundant life and transformed human relations. In the words of Luke 4, the good news is that the blind will see. We will see Jesus—find, listen, relate to Jesus—hidden in oppressed people on godforsaken crosses. We who are privileged in various ways cannot recognize the good news as good, though, if, as Bonhoeffer says above, we disdain the gospel of the poor—that good news that Jesus is in solidarity with those who are oppressed, working to end their suffering by overcoming injustice. Perhaps this is why Jesus says, "It is easier for a camel to go through the eye of a needle than for a rich person to enter the kingdom of God" (Matt 19:24). We cannot receive the good news and participate in beloved community if we reject the black Christ, the vagrant Christ, the incarcerated, drug-addicted Christ.

## Seeing the Incarcerated Christ

The image of the incarcerated Christ became a part of Carla's consciousness when she was strapped down to a hospital bed, each wrist in handcuffs, causing her body to lie flat in the shape of a crucifix. She was waking up from cervical cancer surgery, was in pain, alone, and humiliated by the hospital's presentation of her. Internalizing this experience while trying to make some sense of her entire incarceration, she painted the incarcerated, drug-addicted Christ: a woman wearing a black-and-white striped, state-issued uniform, held up on a cross by drug needles piercing her wrists and a stake being driven into her feet by a gavel that reads "justice for all." A courthouse lies in the background, and under her feet in the grass are the words, "life with the possibility [of parole]," "mandatory minimum," and "no eligibility." "I drew this picture," Carla says, "thinking about the relationship between drug addiction and injustice in the judicial system. The picture is an attempt to convey this injustice and connect it to the meaning of the cross. . . . I am deeply affected by these issues, which is why it was important for me to create this picture, which can often convey more than words alone." She continues with her own story of drug addiction and incarceration, a story worth hearing in full.

I try as hard as I possibly can to take responsibility for my life. I also try to put an equal amount of energy into accepting the reality of the circumstances that I am in. As time goes on, it becomes more and more difficult to do both. My burden is heavy and now seems absurd that it should rest on my shoulders alone. It makes less and less sense as I examine myself (my past, present, and future) and as I am forced to take an honest look around me. My situation becomes less unique as I take in the hundreds here (and I hate to think of the tens of thousands nationwide) that are similar to myself. I by no means can excuse my choices or the participation I took in my own experiences, yet there is clearly a larger problem, multiple problems, beyond my own accountability.

My story starts at home. I was cared for as a child by my paternal grandparents who were wonderful people. Driven by the desire to know my wayward mother, I moved into her home at age eleven. My mother, father, stepfather and older stepbrother were all drug addicts who had each served time in a correctional facility at some point. Starting at the age of twelve, these four people introduced me to basically every drug on earth and I used them regularly, mainly marijuana, Xanax, Lortab, LSD, and cocaine. This drug abuse was inseparable from other forms of abuse—sexual, emotional, verbal, and physical. I knew that my environment was bad for me and was fortunate enough to have alternatives. (I could have moved back into the safety and sobriety of my grandparents' loving home.) Yet I stayed to continue to use the drugs that had become a gripping part of my daily life.

When I was 14, I ran away from home after only three years of regular drug use. I hid at a friend's house where I was found and brought home. The police had been called and an officer was there to talk to me upon my return. I told him *everything* that went on in my house, expecting help for myself and for my family. He told me that I couldn't just get mad and leave. Before he left, my stepfather gave the officer a large amount of cash to ignore me. After that incident, the only thing that changed at home was that my access to the drug supply was increased and I was pacified beyond my grievances.

When I was 17 years old, after years of rape and neglect, I moved away. I stayed with friends in an attempt to graduate from high school the following year. Despite the heavy drug use, I did well academically and was musically inclined. I developed dreams to attend Juilliard and pursue a career as a professional flutist. But without the constant supply of drugs from my family I had to find them, find money to buy them, and then figure out how I was going to get more. My energy for school along with all my other goals quickly faded away. I became a stripper with a severe cocaine problem and drank alcohol constantly. This spiraled out of control. I contacted my family, who let me into their trafficking endeavors, to increase my ability to remain high.

By the time I was 22 my life was beyond description, beyond comprehension. Being raised with substance abuse as a normal part of my home life, I emerged as a young adult with serious addiction problems, a lack of coping skills, and a natural indifference to the law. By 22 years old, I was a high school dropout, a stripper, and a raging alcoholic with a $1000 a day crack cocaine habit.

Knowing that I was beyond any place of destruction I had ever been, I sought help. First, I went to a local detox center to admit myself, but they could not accept me. The state would not allow them to treat individuals with cocaine addictions due to the medical fact that stopping cocaine use will not kill you; there is no physical withdrawal process that is dangerous. So they turned me away. Later, I took myself to the emergency room of a nearby hospital and explained that I could not stop and was afraid for my life. A man from the mental health department came and talked to me and made me an appointment at an Advantage Behavioral Health Clinic six weeks into the future. With my appointment card, they sent me back into the streets I had come from. I lost the card, forgot the appointment, and couldn't have cared less. Later, my grandmother took me with her on a vacation to Florida. Thinking it would help to be in a different place, I went with a hopeful attitude. I was clean for almost 24 hours when I went into the streets of Panama City looking for crack that was easy to find. Driven by my lack of control over myself, I called 911 there in Florida asking for immediate intervention. An ambulance and police officer responded to my call. They wrapped me in a blanket and convinced me to travel home with my grandmother and seek help after arriving there. I traveled home and another appointment was made for the distant future.

There are small windows of clarity where the need for help is obvious and desperate within the addicted person. In that window, everything is open and honest and ready. It passes quickly, and if it is ignored, it is lost to the more powerful grip of addiction.

In the end of September 2004, nine months after smoking crack for the first time, I found myself in a situation that changed many lives forever. A crack dealer and two of his acquaintances proposed that I go and dance for a man to earn money to buy more crack. I rode with the three boys, but the man wasn't interested in a stripper. Instead he wanted to have sex with me for twenty dollars, which I refused. The crack dealer convinced me to allow the man to pay for sex in advance, assuring me that we would leave with the money he gave me without me having to perform. The man gave me the twenty dollars. I was excused from the house by the dealer who brought me.

I went to the car, started it, and waited to leave. Because I would not make money to buy crack, the boys I had ridden with decided to rob the man and beat him to death while I was in the car unaware and insulted by the lack of respect for my body. When they came out of the house, one of the boys was covered in blood. They put a gun to my head and told me they would put me in a ditch if I said anything now or later.

Three years later we went to trial. The young man pled guilty for actually killing the man and received sixteen felonies. At my trial, he admitted that he said he would kill me if I told and that he meant it at the time. I was charged with being a party to the crime of his sixteen convictions and was convicted of all of them by a conflicted and confused jury. The jury was all white, mostly women between the ages of 30 and 50, and were certainly not my peers. They held occupations like gardener, kindergarten teacher, correctional officer, and librarian. I was presented as a crack addicted, lesbian stripper who lurked in innocent neighborhoods with thugs in the night. After my own attorney put me on the stand, the jury's perception of me changed. It became clear that I was actually a messed up girl that had at one time shown, and still possessed, a great deal of potential. It became clear that I needed help more than anything, so the District Attorney changed his strategy to one that offered me help if I got convicted. The jury was told that I would get back on the right track and get the drug treatment I deserved if they convicted me, so they did. The first two accounts were mandatory life sentences. When the sentence was read in the courtroom, the jury members were shocked and some wept, unaware of what implications went with their sentencing. I received ongoing support from the staff of the jail and the court as the injustice was apparent and irrevocable. It was my first felony. In the past decade of incarceration, I have not been offered or allowed any drug rehabilitation or counseling. Any program related to drug recovery is extremely limited within the system and offered to very few.

So, this is the point: who is guilty specifically when it comes to the outcome of my life thus far? I have to take A LOT of responsibility for my choices and their consequences, but beyond that, it is clear that it is impossible to accept that the events of my life happened in isolation from many, many other influences. I am the only one serving a life sentence in the penal system based on party to the crime convictions of conspiracy charges. Yet, what about my family (who all still use/abuse drugs to this day) and whom I have no contact with? The clinics and hospitals that neglected to help me on several occasions after desperate cries for assistance? The powers that govern the policies for clinics and hospitals that turn people away? The officer who accepted the bribe? Whoever may be responsible for the manufacturing and distribution of drugs to begin with? The larger international forces at work in the drug trade?

In our society there is a desperate need for healing, help, and support. Instead, there is a vicious judicial system that funnels brokenness into punitive consequence, engulfing a body of people who are convicted and forgotten. I, a member of that great body, have been incarcerated since 2004 and will become eligible for parole for the first time in 2024. We here are the harvest of the "war on drugs," the "zero tolerance." We are the voices who are never heard, the ones that never had a chance and possibly never will. I am one of the two million Americans buried alive, taking the guilt of myself and everyone else, as a nameless, faceless number in the growing masses who are incarcerated.

Like Girard's scapegoat who is the victim of collective condemnation and blame, Carla's drug-addicted and incarcerated Christ is society's victim, made to bear the guilt of the collective whole. The incarcerated Christ begs us first to see Jesus in the guise of the prisoner, and then in Jesus all victims of the War on Drugs and mass incarceration. Simply by offering her painting for view, Carla assists us in the process of transformation that Rowan Williams describes above. In order to transcend the victim-oppressor cycle, in order to experience "the power of God" of which Paul speaks, we must turn to Jesus's cross for our salvation, which means we must turn toward our victim and see ourselves responsible. Describing her painting, Carla says, "Christologically, the prisoner stands in the place of all who are guilty and calls the world to repentance."

The incarcerated Christ calls the world to recognize the blurred character of innocence and guilt, as Jesus demonstrates in his own person and work. Even as the sinless one—or, precisely because he is the sinless one—Jesus lives for others and shows his love in a fallen world by taking responsibility for the sin that harms fellow human beings. As a convicted criminal, Jesus is in solidarity with sinners to the point of becoming sin on the cross (2 Cor 5:21). Following Luther, Bonhoeffer says that Jesus exists as a "sinner among sinners," even as "the worst sinner," and yet as "sinless among sinners."[23] Jesus demonstrates his "genuine guiltlessness," Bonhoeffer says, "precisely by entering into community with the guilt of other human beings for their sake."[24] Bonhoeffer writes, "Because he loves them, he does not acquit himself of the guilt in which human beings live. A love that abandons human beings to their guilt would not be love for real human beings . . . it is God's love that lets Jesus become guilty."[25] The discipleship community is called to participate in Christ's accomplished work and unfolding salvation by taking responsibility for sin like Jesus does, but with one defining difference. The discipleship community not only accepts responsibility for the sin of others but also confesses its own complicity in social sin and the maintenance of unjust structures. Bonhoeffer writes,

> Confession of guilt happens without a sidelong glance at others who are also guilty. . . . When one calculates and weighs things, an unfruitful self-righteous morality takes the place of confessing guilt face-to-face with the figure of Christ. Christ conquers us never more strongly than by completely and unconditionally taking on our guilt and declaring it Christ's own, letting us go free. Looking on this grace of Christ frees us completely from looking on the guilt of others and brings Christians to fall on their knees before Christ with the confession: *mea culpa, mea culpa, mea maxima culpa.*[26]

Carla's picture thus illustrates an understanding of Jesus and his cross—an atonement theory—that combines classical Pauline concepts with liberation frameworks, in turn helping us address social sin like mass incarceration. Because Jesus has accepted guilt and taken responsibility for sin on the cross, the discipleship community is able to carry on the work of Jesus by also taking responsibility for sin and acknowledging our complicity in an unjust society. When we, like Jesus, take responsibility for sin, we can no longer look to another person's guilt to establish our own innocence. The power of God for salvation is unleashed instead when we see the incarcerated Christ,

23. Bonhoeffer, *Christ the Center*, 107–8. See McBride, *Church for the World*, 73–76.
24. Bonhoeffer, *Ethics*, 234.
25. Ibid., 233.
26. Ibid., 136.

turn toward our victims in repentance, and find in them partners in God's redemptive work.

## Jesus Was a Convicted Criminal

To speak of "the incarcerated Christ" is not simply to speak in metaphor, since Jesus was in actuality a convict. After the Theology Foundations course disperses one Friday afternoon, an officer making his rounds wanders into the classroom and reads in a dubious tone the chalkboard announcing this historical fact, "Jesus was a convicted criminal?" "Yeah!" interjects Janet. "It's right there in the Bible!" she exclaims, referring, of course, to Jesus's arrest in the garden, trial before the Sanhedrin, and sentencing before Pilate and the angry crowd—central events in the Gospel accounts that rarely get narrated as Jesus being "a convicted criminal." We had been studying *God of the Oppressed* by James Cone, the father of black theology, who, like the Harlem Renaissance authors, argues that Jesus is in a certain sense "black," a title meant to be both metaphorical and literal. It is literal in that Jesus literally becomes one with "the least of these," and in the United States, Cone argues in 1975, the least of these are black. It is metaphorical since Jesus's solidarity with the oppressed and his presence in their struggle for liberation are not limited to African Americans. Cone recognizes "that 'blackness' as a christological title may not be appropriate in the distant future or even in every human context in our present." Still, it is accurate to say today, half a century after the civil rights movement that "the least in America are literally and symbolically present in black people."[27] This is evident, for example, in Michelle Alexander's argument (discussed in chapter 1) that mass incarceration is paradoxically a racial caste system that includes all people of color, black and brown, as well as poor whites.

Although it would be just as accurate today to claim that Jesus is black, metaphorically and literally, in the Theology Foundations course we discussed Cone's argument in an altered form: "Jesus is a convicted

27. James H. Cone, *God of the Oppressed* (Maryknoll, NY: Orbis Books, 1997), 125.

criminal." Cone derives the title "Jesus is Black" from an analysis of "Jesus' past identity, his present activity, and his future coming."[28] He maps out the dialectical relationship between his past, present, and future in the following way: "Jesus is who he was"; "Jesus is who he is"; and "Jesus is who he will be."[29] Thus, in Cone's terms: Jesus was a Jew; Jesus is black; and Jesus is the coming liberator; and in our alternate application: Jesus was a convicted criminal; Jesus is a convicted criminal; and Jesus is the coming liberator—a message that excited Janet because it located her specific identity, experience, and hope concretely within the person and work of Christ.

By "Jesus is who he was" Cone means that "there is no knowledge of Jesus Christ today that contradicts who he was yesterday," that contradicts, in other words, "his historical appearance in the first-century Palestine."[30] Cone writes,

> The biblical emphasis on Jesus' humanity in history [is] the starting point of christological analysis. For without the historical Jesus, theology is left with a docetic Christ who is said to be human but is actually nothing but an idea-principle in a theological system. We cannot have a human Jesus unless we have a historical Jesus, that is, unless we *know* his history. That is why the writers of the four Gospels tell the good news in the form of the story of Jesus' life.[31]

Central to that history is Jesus's identity as a Jew, a member of a particular people who knew God as liberator of the oppressed from bondage. Jesus's Jewishness, Cone argues, "connects God's salvation drama in Jesus with the Exodus-Sinai event. . . . [Jesus] was a particular Jew who came to fulfill God's will to liberate the oppressed."[32] Salvation through Jesus is liberation—a liberation that comes through his life, death, and resurrection.

"Jesus is not merely a historical person," Cone continues, "who once identified with poor people" in his life under imperial rule and in a death reserved for rebels and the poor. Because he is risen, he is

28. Ibid., 122.
29. Ibid., 106–22.
30. Ibid., 106.
31. Ibid., 109.
32. Ibid., 109.

also present today with those who struggle for liberation.[33] Through the resurrection, God affirms that Jesus stands in solidarity with the outcasts and oppressed in order to make a way for transformed human relations that will liberate human beings from sin and death into a restored and just community.

The quip "Jesus is who he is" also refers to personal testimonies that Jesus is present with those who suffer injustice, be it past slaves or the incarcerated today. In a passage where "black slaves" could easily be replaced with "incarcerated people," Cone says,

> For many black slaves [read: incarcerated people today], Jesus [becomes] the decisive Other in their lives who provide[s] them a knowledge of themselves, not derived from the value system of [the prison]. How could [incarcerated people] know they [are] human beings when they [are] treated like cattle? How [can] they know they [are] somebody when everything in their environment [says] they [are] nobody? . . . Only because they [know] Jesus [is] present with them and that his presence include[s] the divine promise . . . to liberate the oppressed.[34]

Whether slaves or inmates, the identity that the oppressed have in Jesus sharply contradicts their present status. In turn, "this new knowledge about themselves and the world, as disclosed in and through the resurrection, requires that the poor practice political activity" and resist oppression. "Not to fight is to deny the freedom of the resurrection," Cone says.[35] He concludes that Jesus is known "through his present activity with the oppressed" in their struggle for freedom in various concrete ways.[36] Finally, Cone argues, "Jesus Christ is who he will be. He is not only the crucified and risen One but also the Lord of the future who is coming again to fully consummate the liberation already happening in our present."[37] As prison theology student Sierra says, "When the world imprisons, God sets free." The oppressed and their allies struggle for liberation now "because it is a

33. Ibid., 110.
34. Ibid., 119–20.
35. Ibid., 115.
36. Ibid., 120.
37. Ibid., 116, 121.

sign of Jesus' presence with us and of his coming" redemption of "all humanity."[38]

While the cross is political in that it is the place where society makes its victims, Cone shows that the resurrection is also political. It is a politics of liberation that counters and resists the politics of oppression. Significantly, Jesus announces the politics of the resurrection precisely from the cross: "Today," he says to his fellow convict, "you will be with me in paradise."

## The Liberation Proclaimed from the Cross

One afternoon, when the theology courses are unexpectedly canceled so that the inmates can attend a newly instated Good Friday service, I hear those words above powerfully spoken inside the prison. Natalie and Sierra are hesitant to go to the service, unsure what the message of the cross will be this day, but they decide it would be good to go together and invite me along. I know not to expect a proclamation of the gospel that has direct social and political consequence—the kind of discourse that happens on a regular basis in the theology courses—and so I prepare myself to receive this simply as a special liturgical time to share with friends. As we make our way to the front of the chapel, I am pleasantly surprised by the liturgical sensitivity and the ambiance created by the seminary interns leading the service—dimmed lights, tea candles lit on the altar railing, and Taizé music playing the repetitive tune, "Jesus, Remember Me When You Come into Your Kingdom." The leaders read a reflection on the power of the resurrection and lead us through an exercise where we write down what attitude, thought, or behavior we need to lay before the cross. Neither Sierra nor I have paper on which to confess our sin, so she turns to me and whispers, "I've recently become consumed with jealousy for what other people have." I whisper back, "I need to finally give up anxiety about my future." She then finds a scrap of paper, writes "anxiety about the future," and hands it to me to place in the

---

38. Ibid., 122.

bowl coming around. Even though the gospel proclamation focused only on the inner life and individual behavior with no mention of the sociopolitical dimensions of the cross, I think, "This is powerful," as I receive Sierra's act of burden bearing and glance around the packed chapel. In place of a sermon, the interns then read three passages from the passion narrative, with the Taizé music still playing off and on in the background. By the time one of the interns gets to the third reading, you could hear a pin drop. She reads,

> One of the criminals who were hanged there kept deriding him and saying, "Are you not the Messiah? Save yourself and us!" But the other rebuked him saying, "Do you not fear God since you are under the same sentence of condemnation? We indeed have been condemned justly, for we are getting what we deserve for our deeds, but this man has done nothing wrong." Then he said, "Jesus remember me when you come into your kingdom." Jesus replied, "Truly I tell you, today you will be with me in Paradise" (Luke 23:39–43).

Before she can complete the sentence, "today you will be with me . . ." a collective sigh and audible release—"yes . . ."—reverberates throughout the sanctuary and hovers there for a moment. Whether intended or not, the gospel is political, I think, it is concrete, and these women know it. Precisely on the cross, in that godforsaken space, Jesus proclaims liberation to convicted criminals.

Cone describes the liberation Jesus brings to the oppressed in four overlapping levels. First, there is liberation through relationship with God, what some call "inner liberation." Fellowship with God through prayer and worship is "the beginning and end" of the Christian practice of liberation, Cone argues, because without the knowledge that comes through a relationship with God, the slave, the prisoner, the homeless person, would not know that "what the world says about them is a lie."[39] Second, there is liberation through the transformed human relations I name above, the reality that liberation for the oppressor and oppressed are tied together. This is true on a social scale, as we speak of entire demographics: "the privileged," people

39. Ibid., 130, 132.

who are systematically advantaged, and "the oppressed," people who are systematically disadvantaged in various interlocking ways. This is also true on an interpersonal scale, as we speak of a victim and an oppressor in a particular situation. Jesus's work of liberation envelops all of humanity, liberating both victims and oppressors from the powers of sin and death, since oppressors must be liberated from known and unknown participation in these powers as much as the oppressed need to be released from their harm. Being saved from destructive forces, from structures of sin and death, enables human beings and human relations to flourish—to be what they were created to be.

That second level of liberation is related to the third, what Cone calls "the struggle for freedom in history."[40] According to Hebrew scripture, salvation is "a historical event of rescue," says Cone, "and is identical with God's righteousness" or justice—God's will and ability to make right that which is not. This "historical character of liberation" is also "an essential ingredient" in the way Jesus enacts salvation as he heals the sick and feeds the hungry. "Jesus struggled against the things that kept people in bondage in this life and made people vulnerable" to destructive powers, Cone says. For Jesus, salvation was not "an abstract, spiritual idea or a feeling in the heart." It was granting "physical wholeness" to those who are suffering.[41] The liberating gospel, therefore, demands struggle for this-worldly transformation. The work of historical liberation includes, for example, inmates literally being set free from prison and those of us on the outside working to overturn structures and policies that bolster the prison system and usher specific demographics into it. Thus Cone concludes, "Any view of liberation that fails to take seriously a people's freedom in history is not biblical."[42]

Each of these levels is rooted in the fourth: eschatological liberation, God's future fulfillment of total liberation, which envelops relationship with God, relationship with all of creation, and the just ordering of

40. Ibid., 139.
41. Ibid., 140.
42. Ibid., 141.

society. Indeed, the promise of God's future coming is the energy behind historical liberation. Liberation is not limited to what happens in history nor to what humans can accomplish. It is eschatological, the fulfillment of the Lord's prayer and promise, "Thy kingdom come on earth as it is in heaven." This promise frees disciples from despairing over what has yet to be accomplished and drives our present struggle as we anticipate Jesus's final coming to make things right once and for all. Disciples live into that promise knowing that God's eschatological liberation breaks into our world even now in concrete ways. Thus, as we studied Cone, the relevant and incredibly complex question for the women was—and continues to be—how to live into the promise of liberation inside the prison.

### Free on the Inside

"I hate it when my mama says, 'You can be free on the inside' and have inner liberation even in prison," Sierra says during the first class session on Cone. A week later, as we review the previous readings, she says in an upbeat voice, "Like my mama always says, you can be free on the inside." When I remind her of what she said the week before, we laugh and then acknowledge Cone's dialectic playing out right there in her seemingly contradictory thoughts.

Sierra is correct to both critique and accept the notion of inner liberation. If she were to focus only on the inner life, she would deny her bodily existence and the real pain of being incarcerated (and thus deny God's affirmation of embodiment through the incarnation, which does not allow a split between the spiritual and the material). At the same time, if she denies her experiences of inner liberation and the possibility of some measure of freedom on the inside, she gives too much power to destructive external forces and neglects the semblance of agency she has, even in that place, to resist them—at least in some way. The driving question thus becomes how to navigate this tension inside the prison. Sierra's struggle to do so not only shows how necessary it is to understand liberation in the holistic way Cone describes, but also adds a layer of textured complexity to his framework.[43] Over the course of the next few years, Sierra and I discuss this complexity, a conversation that culminates in an essay she writes for me that redefines what it means to be "free on the inside." "I hope it inspires you to tell our story," she says. "I hope it liberates the minds of others."

What I saw as "free on the inside" two or even five years ago is different from what I see today. . . . When I first started my time, my mama used to tell me all the time, "you can be free on the inside. There are people out here that are more locked up than the people in prison." I went for this encouragement for a long time. I sought many ways to be liberated from within. . . . In the county jail I had time to focus on God and build my relationship with the Lord. The Word brought comfort. I studied the Bible fervently page by page. I read many spiritual books. Literally, I thirsted for God "as a deer longs for streams of water" (Psalm 42:1). This thirst was quenched and this living water brought freedom.

That worked for a while. I sold that dream to many. . . . I used myself as an example. No one in my jail had it as bad as I did. No one was facing life or life plus 10 at that time. No one smiled or sang more than I did. In a lot of ways I am still this way. I exhibit my faith in how I act. I encourage all that I can. . . . If I am not singing or making noise, I must be sick or severely depressed. That has stuck with me all these years and gotten me through. I can't just focus on my own misery. I am not the only one miserable.

But I got weary. I had been in this jail for 19 months and my anger was growing. . . . All the complaining really grated on my last nerve. I was just happy to be alive and these people who had it much better than me constantly complained—to me! I just wanted to be around people like me. . . . My happiness to be alive faded and I wished I had died instead.

Then I came to prison. Everything I studied and learned helped me to be mentally sharp, but this whole new world away from the world was its own thing. In diagnostics I needed God's strength to survive literally. . . . They yelled at us, called us stupid for answering a question wrong. They yelled even more if we were inaccurate about our clothing size. (Hey, most of us put on a little weight in county and these bra and underwear sizes were not the same sizes at the regular store. But try telling them that.) It felt like being attacked every which way. I was scared as hell and I tried not to show it. . . .

---

43. Delores S. Williams makes a similar critique of Cone through her analysis of "survival" and "quality-of-life" in *Sisters in the Wilderness*, 153–61.

When I first got to prison I stayed true to reading and studying the Word, but *I wanted more. I wanted to live again.* I already felt like life for me was over. Would I ever love again? Get married? Have children? . . .

After trying everything you can in prison—popping others' prescription drugs, having sex, being engaged in the drama and gossip on a day to day basis, lockdown, and then facing your mother in shame trying to hide your secret life in this other world, I decided to seek out something good. Prison was making me sick. I had to find a way to be true to myself and accept my place in this prison world. By this time I attended church regularly. I signed up for Bible study groups to be around positive people. I joined the choir. I asked God to bless me with good friends. And I was good for two years. Then I got tired. I got tired.

I got tired of hearing the same thing at church, of singing the same songs, of walking the same paths to the same buildings with the same people in the same clothes. I definitely got tired of the same message: "you can be free on the inside." I heard this too many times to count and it began to infuriate me. This is just something people who have never done time say to people in prison trying to comfort them. But this statement brings pain. It is a painful reminder of how planted we are in this place. How forced we are to live inside of death.

The same routine all the time made me even more bound than my addiction to running the streets. . . . I yearn for responsibility. . . . All I have control over is my behavior, my bed, and my locker. I have no bills, no property worth much, no job to earn income to take care of myself, no real relationships in here. I'm at the mercy of others to provide my basic needs. If my family chooses to remain in my life and aid me through this painful process then that adds to the ease and pain of this sentence. . . . Just wondering if your family will stick by your side adds to your inner turmoil. . . .

"No you can't just be free on the inside!" my heart screams. I'd rather be free and depressed, free and addicted, than locked up. I'd rather be free on the outside with issues, with struggle, with pain, abuse, whatever, than be in here with these things or in here without them. . . . You are forever lost in this bottomless pit trying to either adhere and become prison or fight against it and remain human with some dignity and self-respect. How do you live free on the inside if your hope of freedom on the outside is slim to none for at least 20 years?

I finally found the answer. You have to seek a freedom that free world people know nothing about. I began to see this prison world for what it is and I started to live into it. . . . I made my own free: that is, creating a home away from home, a life, a purpose that resembles a life you once had or wish you had.

People in prison try to live out their lives as if they were free. You see boyfriend/girlfriend, husband/wife, brother/sister, auntie/niece/ nephew, mother/daughter, big sister/little sister type of relationships acted out everyday. This is the only freedom you have to try to live into this environment. . . . You may see a husband/wife couple cooking a meal on a flat iron made for hair and doing things a typical husband/wife may do in the free world including arguing, watching TV, being intimate, and just being there for each other and existing as one. You have women who take pride in their appearance and make it a habit to do their makeup and hair. You find people trying to make their uniform stylish and different from others. We take nothing and make something. . . . We create products and sell them. . . .

But the parties, these are the best. When parties take place for whatever reason—a birthday, holiday, just for the fun of it—imaginations flow. People make outfits and decorations out of anything. For a fly outfit we use sheets, T-shirts, coats, uniforms, anything that can be cut and sewed into some replica of something seen on TV or in a magazine. To change the color it gets interesting. I had a bunkie pay a girl who was a certified artist to make a "Hello Kitty" shirt with a "Louis Vuitton" background made out of coffee, creamer, Kool-aid and markers. It was beautiful! Imaginations flow. . . . The food gets pretty artistic too. I've seen big teddy bear cakes made out of 92 honey buns plus other stuff. . . . Name it, it can be done! On these party days people come together to celebrate, to have fun, to create that feeling of freedom, if only for a moment before the police (correctional officers) come and break it up. People have been transferred or locked down because of these parties. But it was worth it!

I have found that when you live in this place as a person who is alive, not dead, then you are free. If you can live life like you're still in motion and not stand still, you are free. If you can love and find love in a loveless environment, do so at all costs. It's often erotic but it doesn't have to be, it can be nurturing, like my relationship with my two "children." My children are two girls younger than me that I took under my wing and love them just because. I give them gifts, I talk to them about life, I teach them, I encourage and uplift them. I yell at them when they do wrong and I play spank them to let them know they need to do better. I hug them and hold them when they need me to. Their families on the outside do not support them and I have taken it upon myself to be their family . . . because people thrive on relationships.

I got locked up at age 20 and I cannot see living 20 years without intimacy and real human contact. I buck the system and love, share, hug—even when it is forbidden. I am not going to give up and surrender my humanity, dignity, sexuality, or intimacy. I need them to survive. . . .

I have let a lot of passion in my life die and I sometimes struggle in my relationships because I am scarred from my past like most women in prison. I am afraid to love and be loved inside these walls. Yet I still take the chance with caution because some people prey on the ones who love them for selfish gain. You have to take that chance or else you are not living. People take a chance on me and vice versa because they have those same fears. It's important to remain as human as possible and never stop living, like Kelly Gissendaner.

Now I am free on the inside. I am free because I live into the world in which I exist. There are still things that have me bound, but that doesn't matter. What matters is that I am struggling to be alive and I possess some joy. . . . I am as free as I can be inside these walls because I focus on living life, not my prison time. . . . I think about today. I prepare myself each day for what lies ahead. I find fulfillment in the most unfulfilling circumstances because I look for God in places most think he cannot be found. . . . Living life continuously is being free on the inside of prison.

I find Sierra's essay brilliant and beautiful as she demonstrates the way in which authentic inner liberation presses toward external freedom, driving one to struggle against outward circumstances that demean one's worth. As Cone argues above, the liberation that comes through prayer and worship is not meant to make us passive and accept the unacceptable, for that is nothing more than Marx's opiate of the people. Rather, inner liberation is the energy behind the struggle against oppression, dehumanization, and death.

Sierra's essay is also upsetting and uncomfortable. As we have seen before, the meaning of the cross does not fit neatly into our predisposed categories of morality. Proclaiming liberation in the midst of oppression sometimes means "bucking the system"—breaking rules in prison, being accused of having behavioral problems by the staff, and paying the consequences of lockdown and disciplinary reports, all for the sake of affirming some level of human normalcy, of maintaining relationship and a sense of play. Keisha tells the story of chatting outside with a friend one afternoon when three women burst out of the gym clutching scores of chocolate bars—a hilarious scene reminiscent of those comedic movies and shows that depict the absurdity of prison, like *Orange Is the New Black*. The women had just broken into the visitor vending machine, and they offered Keisha some chocolate as they ran past. "Of course I took one," she says, as we giggle and acknowledge the overwhelming power chocolate has over many of us. "Was it worth it?" I ask in a joking tone, all the while knowing that it led to many days in lockdown. "Absolutely," she says with emphasis, and we laugh some more. Our laughter is simply a shared recognition that playing into the absurdity of the situation—of the entire prison—is sometimes the only way to expose this ridiculous system of control and affirm one's agency despite it. "When you come to prison, everyone including yourself assumes you are as good as dead," says Sierra. "You've got to find a way to live again."

Sometimes in order to live with integrity, to keep their values, the women have to break prison rules—give a T-shirt to someone in need or a hug to someone in pain. Other times, to "stay alive" they "have to adapt." They have to adjust "how they would have lived their lives if prison had not happened," especially in relation to their "personhood and bodily existence." Sierra says, "If I had a determined day that I was getting out, and not one decades into the future but a reasonable date, I could be stronger and not compromise. Those of us who would not be intimate with other women on the outside and are uncomfortable doing so still do because we need to feel loved holistically. The person you're intimate with is often the only person you can trust." "We are just getting through this the best way we know how," Keisha adds. "It's a survival tactic that is discarded once most women leave prison but it's necessary while we're here because loneliness eats you up."

What is most upsetting about the reality Sierra depicts is that she and others must seek freedom in a context of utter scarcity, artificiality, and survival. It's a level of freedom that carries with it the compromises of "a soul left in darkness" by a society that abandons people to such impossible situations. As we talk about some of the compromises Sierra has made consciously before God—under Jesus's cross of solidarity—I ask if they are expressions of lament, protest, or liberation. We concur that they are a combination of all three that is hard to name and untangle. What is clear is that the choice Sierra and the other women have—the choice we as a society have given them—is this: deny embodiment and be buried alive or live into the absurdity the best they can. Sierra chooses, and encourages others, to resist being buried alive by being free on the inside.

# 7

---

# Easter

When they came back from the tomb, they told all these things to the
Eleven and to all the others. It was Mary Magdalene, Joanna, Mary the
mother of James, and others with them who told this to the apostles.
But they did not believe the women, because their words seemed to them
like nonsense.
—Luke 24:9–11

And Saul approved [of their persecution]. . . .
Now as he was going along and approaching Damascus,
suddenly a light from heaven flashed around him.
He fell to the ground and heard a voice saying to him,
"Saul, Saul, why do you persecute me?"
He asked, "Who are you, Lord?"
The reply came, "I am Jesus, whom you are persecuting.
But get up and enter the city and you will be told what you are to do." . . .
Saul got up from the ground, and though his eyes were open,
he could see nothing. . . . Now there was a disciple in Damascus named
Ananias. . . . He laid hands on Saul and said,
"Brother Saul, the Lord Jesus, who appeared to you on your way here,
has sent me so that you may regain your sight
and be filled with the Holy Spirit."
And immediately something like scales fell from his eyes,
and his sight was restored.
—Acts 8:1–9:18

## Believing the Women

In a letter describing the details of a particularly challenging situation in prison, Natalie writes to me, "It does no good to complain, no one cares, and I don't want to go to lockdown for making a complaint. I could be at my wits' end but I'm praying to be strong." Conscious of not wanting to burden her family with the realities of prison life, she concludes with words reminiscent of the Gospel text, "Thank you for letting me dump. I can't tell anyone else. WHO WOULD BELIEVE ME?"

"Do you believe the women?" Ed shouts in the Open Door's front yard as a steady stream of traffic attempts to drown out his Easter-morning message. "Do you believe the women?" he asks again and again as he pivots to address each corner of the circle containing Community members and a small smattering of homeless friends. For Ed, the women in Luke's text represent the people we are most likely to dismiss—like the women and men in prison or on the street—whose testimonies about their lives "seem like nonsense," an idle tale, when interpreted through our middle-class perspectives. The women in the biblical text were living into the struggles of their present existence the best they could by going "to the tomb, taking the spices that they had prepared." Although they shared their stories of how they were "perplexed" and "terrified" upon arrival with the very people who should have had the capacity to understand—who should have been able to empathize with their experience of the empty tomb and angelic presence—the men rendered them mute by denying them authoritative voice.[1]

This Easter text in Luke presses us to give an honest account of whether or not we believe the testimonies of the women and men in these pages, who are often rendered mute by their homelessness and imprisonment. A testimony like Sierra's in the preceding chapter is so unfamiliar and parts so disruptive to our middle-class values that our gut response is often to silence the complex truths we need to hear by blanketing them with heavy-handed moral principles. Sierra's

1. See Luke 24:1–11.

testimony and struggle is a perfect example of what feminist ethicist Lisa Cahill calls "adverse virtue" and womanist theologian Katie Cannon refers to as alternative virtues. Cahill describes an adverse virtue as an attempt "to act with integrity in the midst of unavoidable conflict and adversity," and Cannon describes an alternative virtue, like a subversive act, "not as an ideal to be fulfilled but as a balance of complexities so that suffering will not overwhelm and endurance is possible."[2] According to womanist theology, subversion is itself a virtue in unjust conditions because it resists destructive and dehumanizing forces and reveals the injustice of the situation. In order for privileged people to participate fully in the power of the resurrection, we must seek to understand these unjust contexts and honor the struggles of women and men in them. We must "believe the women," discarding postures of skepticism and distrust, and seek to understand their lives. Only then may we comprehend the full power of Easter and unleash it in our lives.

Alongside the women met with suspicion in the biblical text are people blind to the new things God is doing in the world. They are blind to the meaning and power of the resurrection. Those who are blind are not "unbelievers," people who claim no relationship to God, as religious folks may be tempted to assume. They are the male disciples on the road to Emmaus, wary of the women's story, and pious elites like Saul, driven by a sense of religious loyalty to God. Luke and Acts juxtapose the women with these men not through the metaphor of hearing as we may expect (they did not believe what they heard). Rather, the Gospel writer uses the metaphor of seeing—the theme of perception, of new insight and understanding. This theme harkens back to Jesus's first public speech in Luke 4 where he announces that his person and work usher in the kingdom of God, the beloved community, which is intended for all—indeed requires all—whether formerly oppressed or privileged. In that inaugural speech, Jesus proclaims that he brings good news for the poor, liberty to the

2. Katie Geneva Cannon, *Katie's Cannon: Womanism and the Soul of the Black Community* (New York: Continuum, 2003), 92; Lisa Sowle Cahill, *Theological Bioethics: Participation, Justice, and Change* (Washington, DC: Georgetown University Press, 2005), 119.

captives, and freedom for the oppressed, as well as "sight for the blind." His speech suggests that liberation for some and clear-sightedness for others are intimately intertwined.

In Luke, the blind include those two disciples walking along the road to Emmaus who do not recognize the resurrected Jesus in their midst. "Their eyes were opened," though, when Jesus breaks bread at the table with them, a familiar scene in scripture that exemplifies the fellowship of beloved community. This fellowship cannot happen without including at the welcome table those whom we have dismissed or cast out.

"The blind" also includes Saul, the religious enthusiast in Acts, who both "approved" of the persecution of the marginalized group (8:1) and actively participated in their oppression (8:3). In order to show Saul his lack of perception, he is literally made blind by a divine light accompanied by the voice of Jesus, "*whom you are persecuting.*" Jesus's identification here with Roman society's outcasts echoes the words of his ministry where he identifies with "the least of these"—the stranger, the sick, the hungry, and the imprisoned—and bases the judgment of the nations on their treatment of these most marginalized people. Jesus's identification with the outcasts also echoes the crucifixion discussed in the previous chapter, where he is in solidarity with all of society's victims. The representative character of Jesus is now apparent in a new way during the conversion of Saul to Paul, when Paul comes to know Jesus precisely by encountering him in the risen form of the persecuted. Whether in his life, death, or resurrection, Jesus is not only a specific human being but also the representative of humanity. He is the real human being, as Bonhoeffer says, who at all times and in all states of existence—in the flesh, on the cross, and even in risen form—is in solidarity with those who suffer most. In *Resurrection*, Rowan Williams says it this way,

> Saul is stopped on his journey by a vision of power and judgment: blinding light, an accusing voice. . . . The Lord names himself not only as Jesus, but as Jesus embodied in the particular present victims of Paul's violence: he *is* those whom Paul has oppressed, hurt, or killed. And yet . . . the Lord who judges is the Lord who saves; the Lord who vindicates his oppressed

witnesses also comes, in their words and hands, to save their oppressors—who are his as well.[3]

Before Paul can live by the power of the resurrection and preach the resurrection to the ends of the earth, he must face his own religious blindness and moral misconceptions—and repent. So it is with us. Before we privileged Christians can live by the power of the resurrection we must hear the Lord name himself as Jesus embodied in Sierra, Carla, Marcus—the particular present victims whom we as a society have oppressed, hurt, or killed. Jesus "comes in their words" to save us, who are his as well.

This chapter argues that the social and political significance of Easter is rooted in the power of the resurrection unleashed in this life. This power convinced Saul of his blindness and ignited in him a living hope grounded in Easter's central proclamation. Through Easter, God reveals the triumph of life, love, and liberation over the powers and principalities of death. Disciples participate in resurrection power through embodied hope—the revolutionary vision and energy through which they live into the possibilities and promises of God and resist all that contradicts these promises. In other words, Christians participate in God's movement in the world through concrete acts of discipleship that anticipate Easter liberation and embody the good news of the promises of God. The chapter turns to the prison theology program as an example of Easter liberation, particularly as it demonstrates the power of listening to and affirming the voices of marginalized people. It then concludes with an account of embodied hope, demonstrated through advocacy efforts for Kelly Gissendaner. As it narrates the fight to overturn Kelly's sentence from death to life, the chapter addresses the relationship between God's action and human effort, between God's movement in the world and human participation in that movement.

3. Rowan Williams, *Resurrection*, 4–5.

## Confronting Our Blindness

Before we may live by the power of the resurrection in concrete ways that have this-worldly consequence, privileged Christians must confront our own blindness. In *A Strength to Love*, a collection of sermons preached in black churches but edited for white audiences, King discusses the theme of blindness in multiple ways. In the sermon "Love in Action," he examines Jesus's words on the cross, "Father, forgive them for they know not what they do" (Luke 23:34). King argues that Jesus's prayer acknowledges the "intellectual and spiritual blindness" of human beings. He says, "We must recognize that Jesus was nailed to the cross not simply by sin but also by blindness. The men who cried, 'Crucify him,' were not bad men but rather blind men. The jeering mob that lined the roadside that led to Calvary was composed not of evil people but of blind people. They knew not what they did. What a tragedy!"[4]

This tragic blindness reverberates throughout history, King says, and expresses itself "in many ominous ways in our own day."[5] King distinguishes between evil people and blind people, but he never denies that the effects of our blindness are severe. They lead to crucifixions, advancing the powers of evil and death. In order to participate in the power of the resurrection, we who are privileged must confront the ideologies and myths that keep us blind. In *Disrupting Homelessness*, for example, Laura Stivers directly addresses "the social myths that pervade our collective consciousness" about homelessness. "The dominant ideology is that people are homeless because they have a personal fault," most commonly that they are lazy, incompetent, or unreliable. We assume that those who are homeless do not have or want jobs and presume they would rather "leach off the welfare system" than work, an image advanced in part by racism. In turn we base our social policies on stereotypes and half-truths.[6] As shown in chapter 1, "our ideologies lead us to individualistic solutions

4. King, *Strength to Love*, 42–43.
5. Ibid., 43.
6. Stivers, *Disrupting Homelessness*, 48–49.

that focus on transforming the poor, rather than structural solutions that challenge the social domination and inequality in our nation."[7] This individualistic ideology is driven by certain common myths, including meritocracy or "the pursuit of the American dream," the myth that individuals may achieve socioeconomic success through hard work regardless of social location. Meritocracy denies the vast role of unearned privileges on the one hand and entrenched structural barriers on the other when trying to explain the success or lack thereof of particular groups of people. When social barriers are identified, another myth is activated: the idea that any talk of unjust structures creates a victim mentality that discourages individuals from taking responsibility for their lives. The truth is that oppressed people may be at the same time victims and agents, people who endure real victimization while navigating the injustices the best they can. Like the women at the tomb, we affirm human agency when we listen to people share the truths about their lives, including the real barriers they face, and believe them. Unfortunately, as Stivers shows, privileged Christians tend toward disbelief. Most well-known Christian responses, while born of good intentions, buy into ideologies that further stigmatize homeless people and exacerbate the problems they are trying to address, even when the stories of those they seek to serve discredit dominant interpretive frames.

Because sincerity and good intentions "are not enough," King argues that the church must never "tire of reminding [its people] that they have a moral responsibility to be intelligent." He says, "If we are to call ourselves Christians, we had better avoid intellectual and moral blindness. . . . We are commanded to love God, not only with our hearts and souls, but also with our minds."[8] King defines the intelligence that wards off blindness as "open-mindedness, sound judgment, and the love for truth." He says, "One does not need to be a profound scholar to be open-minded, nor a keen academician to engage in an assiduous pursuit of truth."[9] Loving God with our minds does require effort,

7. Ibid., 4.
8. King, *Strength to Love*, 46–47.
9. Ibid., 47–48.

though, "to rise above the stagnation of close mindedness."[10] A closed mind often takes the form of conformity, as King argues in his sermon, "Transformed Nonconformist," which examines Romans 12:2. "Do not be conformed to this world but be transformed by the renewing of your mind." King writes, "Nowhere is the tragic tendency to conform more evident than in the church, an institution . . . [that has] sanction[ed] slavery, racial segregation, war, and economic exploitation."[11] The Apostle Paul gives Christians the mandate to be nonconformist in an unjust society and to instead conform to "God and his kingdom of love."[12]

For King, it is not so much intellectual inability as intellectual laziness that drives conformity and keeps us blind. In his sermon "A Tough Mind and a Tender Heart," which examines Jesus's paradoxical command to be "wise as serpents and innocent as doves," King says, "Rarely do we find [people] who willingly engage in hard, solid thinking. There is almost a universal quest for easy answers and half-baked solutions. Nothing pains some people more than having to think."[13] Instead of cultivating a tough mind, we are soft-minded, deeming anything that bolsters our preconceived notions "final truth" even when it is driven by false facts and irrational fears.[14] Soft-mindedness is "one of the basic causes of race prejudice," King says. It is perpetuated when people critique the effects and not the causes of injustice, which happens when we confuse the source of an unjust event with the victim's response to that injustice.[15] Because the origin of a particular unjust force reaches generations back, the root of the matter at hand is hard to immediately recognize, while a victim's response to the injustice is more readily on display. The systemic nature and complex inner workings of racism and other unjust powers defy "easy answers and half-baked solutions."[16] Indeed, a power like

10. Ibid., 47.
11. Ibid., 25.
12. Ibid., 22.
13. Ibid., 14.
14. Ibid.
15. Ibid., 16; see King, *Testament of Hope*, 290.
16. King, *Strength to Love*, 14.

racism often perpetuates itself by denying its own existence. Thus, sight for the blind demands focused and willful study—investigations of the historical roots, structural evolution, and present manifestations of evil forces.

Some of our blindness is better defined as intellectual and doctrinal arrogance rather than mental laziness, although the two may be related. In our highly partisan political context, we may pride ourselves on tough-mindedness, on "incisive thinking, realistic appraisal, and decisive judgment," but lacking humility, we refuse to alter long-held political or religious positions.[17] We reject "new truth" with "dogmatic passion," King says, which is why tough-mindedness demands a tender, malleable heart.[18] Refusing to unlearn certain positions and be formed anew is itself a kind of hard-heartedness, which is why Jesus commands his disciples to combine the serpent's acumen with the dove's humility. The tough-minded yet hard-hearted Christian is detached from the concrete hopes and struggles of real human beings who consistently endure suffering, like homeless and imprisoned people, and lacks the empathy necessary for recognizing truth. This lack of empathy is painfully on display today, for example, as white audiences watch black children be killed and harassed with alarming regularity by people charged to serve and protect. Lacking basic empathy to see these unarmed children as our own, ordinary whites across the country and pundits on cable news silence the complex truths about race that white Christians must heed in order to participate in concrete restoration and be saved into beloved community. When Christians lack empathy to mourn these and other people, when we deny those who suffer authoritative voice, when we critique a person's response to injustice as if it were the root problem, when we deny the role of the powers themselves, with Saul we "approve" of their persecution. Our hope lies in the power of the resurrection, that power that convinced Saul of his blindness in the voice of the oppressed.

17. Ibid., 14.
18. Ibid., 15.

## Easter Vision

As the narratives of the male disciples and Saul show, Easter begins in darkness, in blindness, but it does not stay there. The "scales fell from [their] eyes." For the men on the road to Emmaus, it was through table fellowship and broken bread; for Saul, it was his encounter with the disciple Ananias. Easter begins in darkness and despair, in failure and divine judgment, but it transitions to a living hope when our sight is restored.

Through renewed Easter vision, disciples live into the promises of God and resist all that contradicts these promises. "It is not for nothing," Moltmann writes, that 1 Peter uses the phrase "born again to a living hope."[19] As Moltmann argues, biblical hope does not give up on this life for something better beyond the grave. The God of the Bible is no "extra-worldly God" but the God who is making all things new "here and now, today" (Rom 15:13; Rev 21:5).[20] Hope, therefore, "revolutionizes and transforms the present," as it arouses "passion for the possible."[21] Its adherents live into the kingdom of God now—into God's intended social order "on earth as it is in heaven" (Matt 6:10). This is the hope of the psalmist who "looks for the goodness of God" in this life (Ps 27:13), the hope that Kelly Gissendaner proclaims through her favorite verse, "I shall not die but live, and declare the works of the Lord" (Ps 118:17). A living, embodied hope in God's promises "throws open the future" as it recognizes that things are not as they have to be, and envisions an "alternative future" based on the promises of God.[22] This vision brings disciples "into contradiction with the existing present" even as it draws them into a deeper love for this life.[23] Living into the "possibilities and promises of God" demands anticipatory, concrete action that has this-worldly consequences since God's promises include the kingdom come (Matt 6:10), the reconciliation of all things (Col 1:20), the total restoration of this world (Eph 1:10),

---

19. Jürgen Moltmann, *A Broad Place* (Minneapolis: Fortress Press, 2008), 105.
20. Moltmann, *Theology of Hope*, 16; Moltmann, *A Broad Place*, 105.
21. Moltmann, *Theology of Hope*, 35.
22. Moltmann, *A Broad Place*, 101, 103.
23. Ibid., 103.

and that nothing is lost (John 6:39). All our energies are gathered like patchwork into the tapestry of God's restored community. Or, as Bonhoeffer says, through our "fragmentary" work—through the building blocks and shattered pieces of lives lived in genuine "this-worldliness"—God is designing the "mosaic" of a new world.[24]

Thus, the significance of Easter is so much more than mere belief in the resurrection. Plenty of believers readily affirm that Jesus rose from the dead even as they maintain the status quo and deny the possibility of substantial this-worldly change. The significance of Easter is embodied hope—the revolutionary vision and energy by which the risen Jesus intends his disciples live. "God promises a new creation of all things," but human beings act "as if everything were as before and remained as before," writes Moltmann.[25] New creation unfolds in the present moment even as it has already been accomplished, "for no matter how many promises God has made, they are Yes in Christ" (2 Cor 1:20). Easter vision recognizes the power of the resurrection in this life, which is unleashed not through mere belief but through discipleship. Anything less than abiding by the reconciliation and redemption accomplished by Christ is a fanatic belief in death, Bonhoeffer says starkly, and a functional denial of the resurrection.[26] He writes, "Christ gives up nothing that has been won but holds . . . in his hands" even the world fallen "under the control of Satan" (1 John 5:19). "There is no part of the world, no matter how lost" that has not been accepted by God and reconciled to God through Jesus Christ. "The power of death has been broken. . . . The miracle of the resurrection and new life shines right into the world of death."[27] Because of the resurrection, the world's fallen nature no longer determines what is possible. This resurrection power drives the social and political engagement of disciples; its raison d'être is the life of the world.

While believers profess the truth of the resurrection, disciples participate in its power. The power of the resurrection is made

24. Bonhoeffer, *Letters and Papers* (Fortress Press), 301, 303, 541.
25. Moltmann, *Theology of Hope*, 23.
26. Bonhoeffer, *Ethics*, 92.
27. Ibid., 65–67, 92.

manifest now in the concrete triumph of life over death, the large and small triumphs, that is, of the kingdom of God, the beloved community. The power of the resurrection is at work anytime the forces of life that constitute beloved community overcome the forces of death—anytime love overcomes hate, liberation overcomes bondage, flourishing overcomes diminution, abundance overcomes scarcity, repentance or forgiveness overcomes sin, belonging overcomes estrangement, and relationships of trust overcome suspicion. Indeed, this dynamic power is unleashed every time human beings move toward these realities while placing their bodies in the spaces that contradict them most.

## Unleashing Resurrection Power through the Voices of Incarcerated Women

"If Jesus were to come back today he would appear first to the women in prison, and no one would believe them," Murphy said in affirmation of the tension I was feeling. I had been teaching in the prison for almost a year and was processing the contradiction between my growing relationships with these women through our academic program and the prison staff's explicit directive not to trust them. The institutional posture of distrust served not only to muffle their voices but also to cast doubt on my own integrity and maturity, on my ability as a volunteer to relate to incarcerated people in strength and truth. I began to wonder if my confidants on the outside shared the prison system's presumption of my naivety. Although other instructors felt similarly, it seemed as if I was holding the weight of these raw and rich interactions in prison on my own.

What I came to realize is that trust begets trust. Foundations of trust are laid through postures of trust sustained over time, and the theology program created the rare and unique space necessary for that to happen. Grounded in academic commitments to critical thinking and conducted loosely through a liberation theology frame, the program affirms the liberating power of finding one's voice—of having one's insights encouraged and affirmed. As all the different streams of liberation theology avow, the social location of nondominant people provides them unique perspectives, ways of interpreting scripture and tradition that often challenge misperceptions embedded in the tradition, and thus they offer a vital and fresh perspective on the gospel truth. As Moltmann writes, "Reading the Bible with the eyes of the poor is a different thing from reading it with . . . a full belly. If it is read in the light of the experiences and hopes of the oppressed, the Bible's revolutionary themes—promise, exodus, resurrection and Spirit—come alive."[28]

In the prison program, the Bible is read "in light of the experiences and hopes" of incarcerated women, who come to see that their biblical and theological reflections can be a gift to the wider church on the outside as well as in prison. By studying historical and contemporary Christian thinkers, they enter the conversations that make the Christian tradition dynamic. They ask honest questions about their relationship to God, others, and the world. They read scripture and grapple with centuries-old theological questions. They learn that this courageous questioning is not antithetical to faith in Jesus but central to it, as captured in Anselm's famous phrase, "faith seeking understanding."[29] In a course on Bonhoeffer, for example, the women write theological letters from prison sharing what they have learned in the yearlong program with family or friends on the outside. In an Old Testament course, they write their own lament Psalms and risk honest words boldly directed at God. In a womanist theology course, they attend to unnamed women in scripture and explore the texts from their perspectives, granting the biblical women voice even as they grant themselves the same. In a restorative justice course, they learn how to lead mediations and circle processes to heal conflict. In a homiletics course, they write sermons, some of which are later preached in the prison chapel in the presence of officers and fellow inmates. The women not only discover their authentic theological

28. Moltmann, *The Church in the Power of the Spirit: A Contribution to Messianic Ecclesiology* (Minneapolis: Fortress Press, 1993), 17.
29. See Daniel L. Migliore, *Faith Seeking Understanding: An Introduction to Christian Theology* (Grand Rapids: Eerdmans, 2004), 2–7. This was the main text for the Theology Foundations course in the prison theology program.

voices but also exercise agency in the midst of this work. As Sarah poignantly writes, "You encouraged me to read works with a deeper meaning, to think beyond the obvious, to question if I feel the need. You pushed me to write from the depths of my soul, to share thoughts rather than to hide them."

At the 2011 theology graduation at the prison, Professor Moltmann affirms the core truths undergirding the certificate in theological studies in his keynote address. This internationally influential theologian knew these truths not because he had taught in the prison program but because, like the women, he began his theological vocation there. Moltmann says, "When I first heard of your study of theology in prison, pictures of my youth and the beginning of my own theological studies emerged from the depth of my memory." Connecting their paths from guilt toward healing to his own, he shares how he came to terms with his participation in the German war effort as a Hitler Youth. "Yes, I remember," he says.

> My theological studies started in a poor prisoner-of-war camp after World War II. . . . In a camp of forced labor in Kilmarnock, Scotland, I read for the first time in my life the Bible and encountered Jesus. I had not decided for Christ, but I am certain Christ found me there when I was lost in sadness and desperation. He found me, as Christ has come to seek what is lost.
>
> I tried to understand what had happened to me. We had "a theology school behind barbed wire." . . . Excluded from time and the world, imprisoned professors taught imprisoned students. . . . We studied the Bible, church history and theology, but we also tried to come to terms with our death experiences near the end of the war. Theology was for us at that time an existential experience of healing our wounded souls.
>
> This was the beginning of my theological studies and my first experiences of the church of Christ: the church in prison camps. Later I became a pastor and professor of theology, but deep in my heart, there is still a frightened and sad young prisoner of war.[30]

Moltmann's improbable connection to incarcerated women in Georgia is rooted in the shared context of prison. His solidarity is also rooted

---

30. Jürgen Moltmann, "The Church in the World and the Church in Prison," *Hospitality* 31, no. 1 (January 2012): 1, 6.

in a shared understanding that theology's transformative power arises from gut-wrenching existential questions that resist easy answers, but when honestly explored, "heal our wounded souls." The latter is the ground upon which my solidarity with the women has grown, as is true, I dare say, for most of us who have taught in this context. For as Moltmann says, whether inside or outside prison walls, "Theology has only one problem: God. God is our pain, God is our joy, God is our longing. We are theologians for God's sake." Affirming their theological contributions to the "worldwide fellowship of all theologians, . . . the age old community" that includes "Augustine and Thomas Aquinas, Martin Luther and Dietrich Bonhoeffer," Moltmann continues,

> Every Christian who believes and understands is a theologian, not only the professionals at Candler or Tübingen. Every Christian! . . . You are really theologians and in fact excellent theologians. I have read a paper that Jenny McBride sent me, and I was impressed. My students at Tübingen could not have made it better. . . .
>
> . . . I would like to encourage you. . . . You must not only learn from other theologians, but develop your own thoughts. We need your spiritual insights and theological reflections. . . . We need you: the theology in the world needs the theology in prison. . . . You are the church! We are sisters and brothers in Christ Jesus.[31]

The significance of this for beloved community is clear. Together as we wrestle with God, our selves, and one another, together as we arouse passion for the possible in light of the promises of God, we are freed into a fellowship that is itself a concrete manifestation of Easter liberation.

## Prison Theology as Easter Liberation

Moltmann not only connects the women's studies to the age-old community of theologians from Augustine and Luther to Cone and Cannon, he also connects them to the radical tradition of prison writing. Theology from prison, penned by political prisoners like the

31. Ibid., 6.

Apostle Paul, Bonhoeffer, King, and Dorothy Day, has advanced discipleship movements grounded in a liberating faith. It is not a stretch to include the women in this radical tradition at the heart of Christianity, especially given what Megan Sweeney calls "the political significance" of writing and reading practices in prison.[32] Based on her participatory research leading fifty book discussions in various penal institutions around the country, Sweeney shows that under certain conditions prison education may "enhance critical thinking and social consciousness."[33] As she explores "the specific ways in which reading enables some women prisoners to gain self-knowledge, contextualize their experiences in relation to larger frameworks, mediate their histories of victimization and violence, and develop an understanding of the limits and possibilities of individual agency," she identifies many dynamics that are present in the theology program as well.[34] The political significance of reading can be seen in the way the class discussions resist the forces of isolation, abandonment, and insularity that are part and parcel to the prison environment, and the way reading connects the women to the outside world, which, as new research shows, is absolutely necessary for restoration and rehabilitation. Reading and discussion serve "as a bridge to the larger community, enabling women to feel like they are a part of a conversation that usually goes on without them."[35] Furthermore, the book discussions, like those in the theology certificate, provide "a rare opportunity to gather for conversation" and to build some semblance of trust and community in a place where it is extremely hard to do so.[36] Thus reading and education in and of themselves may be acts of resistance to incarceration, all the more so given the energy it takes to overcome the unrelenting noise, overcrowded space, and regimented schedule, which offers little to no time for sustained study.

For the majority of women in the theology program who only hold

32. Sweeney, *Reading Is My Window*, 17.
33. Ibid., 6.
34. Ibid.
35. Ibid., 240.
36. Ibid., 236.

GEDs, who rarely have had others recognize their genuine insight (some of whom were prohibited from even speaking in their conservative southern congregations), and who now exist in an environment in which they are strictly forbidden to question authority, this communal experience of academic theological inquiry is profound. In an environment built to constrain agency—to constrain self-expression and human connection—their studies unleash resurrection power. Easter liberation is manifest in the theology program not only as the community of women grow together in intellectual freedom but also as they grow in an interrelated psychological freedom. As King acutely understood, exercising agency requires growth in self-esteem. In order to resist oppression, recipients of abuse must be able to assert their humanity and internalize the truth of their created and personal worth. Sierra, for example, tells the story of being invited as a building representative to a meeting with a deputy warden. When asked about concerns inmates have, she respectfully suggested they serve healthier food. Instead of considering this request, Sierra was transferred on the spot in spiteful irony to the dreaded overnight kitchen-prep detail, the consequence of expressing her opinion even when asked. In her farewell to me, with this work detail in mind, while referencing her coursework, she proclaimed, "I am still determined to have a voice even if it is just a piece of paper on Friday mornings." Years later, Sierra has not given up her vision as she works on a formal proposal for women to grow a garden on prison grounds that would provide dignified work and healthier food for incarcerated women.

While simultaneously attuned to the psychological and pastoral needs of the women, the academic nature of the theology program is central to its power; its emphasis on critical inquiry guards against turning the women into a religious project or a project of Corrections. The academic frame also allows any woman to find entrance into the theology program regardless of a commitment to Christian faith. While the pilot course consisted mostly of self-identified Christians, the program has also attracted "seekers" as well as practitioners committed to other faith traditions. At a time when the popularity of liberal arts education is declining in colleges and universities across the country—deemed impractical and even under political attack—these women in prison are engrossed in its liberating power.

As an educator, the values of the liberal arts have been self-evident to me: foster critical inquiry, enable lifelong learning, and help students recognize the contributions they offer to the local community and society at large. Their repetition in the mission statements of liberal arts institutions had been predictable enough to seem trite, until I began teaching in prison. In this context of forced conformity, deprivation of resources, dehumanization, and isolation from the outside world, the transformative power of critical inquiry is palpable and unceasing. "I feel like I am part of something larger than myself," writes Keisha. "The major realization I've come to over the past few months is that it is normal to question," writes Sarah. "I've come to see that unquestioned embedded thinking is almost like a bondage or prison—no freedom to form new ideas. As I allow myself to open up, I am free," echoes Natalie. "Thank you for freeing my mind while my body remains bound. Thank you for giving me a voice." As the program has "given" them voice, the women simultaneously have helped me discover mine. They are the ones who have charged me to write about our time together, to trust these experiences, and to continue to live within their unfolding truth.

Crucial to genuine critical inquiry—as well as to the creation of beloved community—is the possibility of growth for all participants, of mutual transformation for students and instructors alike. This dynamic of mutual transformation became clear in a meeting evaluating the first few years of the certificate in theological studies as instructors shared how the program has helped them grow in solidarity and develop new sight. Crystal, a law student poised to begin practicing in a firm, says that for the first time she was "confronted with what it really means to be put behind bars," even though she had formerly participated in a Bible study through Prison Fellowship Ministries. Juxtaposing her class discussions on vulnerability with the

Bible study in prison, Crystal says of her church group, "We never really *heard*."[37]

Shively, a doctoral student in biblical studies, shares that before the course she "had some reservations, was nervous, and didn't know what to expect." What she instantly realized, though, was how much the women desired to be in the Biblical Foundations course and "gain another way to see." She says, "They want to be there and know the material. They are okay with the difficulties and ambiguities in the text, and it's so refreshing. I come in and they're like, 'What do you have for me; what do you got?' In the classroom, Shively says, "all the images and presuppositions melted away. I found my voice for advocacy. I know I wouldn't have found it any other way." Cathy, a seminary graduate, similarly shares, "They are so hungry for this chance to engage their minds. I watched their confidence develop and my confidence developed too. On a personal level, it has been a profound experience. It made me confront my ideas of the other, like the murderer, whom I would have been prone to demonize." Likewise, Jessie, a doctoral student, shares how "the complexity of their lives became more and more evident" as the class unfolded. Halfway through her course on comparative religions, "the pain of their own lives really started to come through, as well as what evil looks like for them." She explains, "One of my students went into solitary confinement. She was frustrated with her living situation and her only choice or agency was to go deeper into isolation. This is now on her permanent record. To further silence herself was her relief." David, a biblical studies professor, agrees as he observes that the women in prison "understand biblical themes of exile, power, and authority in a much different way than [his] seminarians do." He says, "I notice the power issue most strikingly when a deputy warden comes in and they spring to attention." Kris, who taught a course on the Book of Revelation, shares one such well-timed moment. "We were talking about the two beasts," he says, "how one represents the Roman military, and . . . the second represents the emperor cult." Right in the

37. Meeting of prison theology program instructors, author's audio recording, January 28, 2011.

middle of their discussion on emperor worship, the captain walks in "and they snap to attention." Making the connection, Amy says right after the captain leaves, "We do have a choice. We don't have to stand up like that, but they have a nice little cell for us if we don't."[38]

Lisa, who has been teaching in the prison for over a decade, reflects on how extended time on the inside has helped her think more clearly about the prison system and be more precise in her critique, which she aims at the system itself rather than at the officers and staff "who inhabit the power structure." In doing so, she models King's crucial insight that nonviolent resisters should direct our attack "against forces of evil" not people also victimized by the evil systems in which they work. As King says, "The tension is, at bottom, between justice and injustice, between the forces of light and the forces of darkness."[39] Lisa explains, "The role of the officer is very complicated to me. I'm always struggling with this. A lot of these officers are only one paycheck or one act away from being in the situation the women are in. They aren't that far apart." Lisa names how difficult it is to hold together the varying and complex ways the totalizing conditions distort the personalities of both officers and inmates. "It takes ongoing negotiation," she says. Michelle speaks to the realities the women must negotiate daily and shares how much it meant to her that they wanted to introduce her to the details of their incarceration. "They cared enough about me as part of their group that they want me to *see*." She says, "Sometimes I'm just driving in my car and an insight will come to me from something a woman said or wrote or preached. In that classroom, I'm sitting with my theological peers; everyone in the class is teaching. By the time they get to the elective courses they are bringing the heat!" She continues, "They are teaching me and my church community." As a result of her relationships with them, "there are now prayers in my church for these women. Never before was that language coming out."[40]

The space of mutual insight and transformation created by the

38. Ibid.
39. King, *Testament of Hope*, 18.
40. Meeting of prison theology program instructors, author's audio recording, January 28, 2011.

theology program does not preclude mutual challenge. Indeed critical analysis requires participants to "push back" on certain claims instead of accepting every presupposition, proposition, or conclusion without question. While always affirming and learning from the truths of their subjective experience, I push back when I suspect that someone's idea expresses some form of internalized oppression, some common myth or stereotype about themselves or others that perpetuates harm. I push them, and they push me. They push my thinking forward and together we come to new understanding, a third way, a synthesis of meaning. In my course on public witness, for example, graduates from the yearlong program read portions of my book *The Church for the World,* aimed at an audience that is decidedly privileged, which I assign as an example of a constructive use of Bonhoeffer's thought. When some of the women relate my argument to their prison context, I worry out loud that they are too harsh on themselves, and I am quick to remind them that incarcerated people are not my audience. Carla, in particular, pushes back and ends up articulating her argument in a critical review of my book that is published in Open Door's *Hospitality* newspaper, which has a readership worldwide of approximately forty thousand people inside and outside prison. Emphasizing our relationship of mutual learning and challenge, Carla writes, "McBride works with communities, organizations and real human beings like me. As an incarcerated person I have had the opportunity to know her, learn from her and teach her over the years." She continues,

> During the summer of 2012, she taught a course on Public Theology with *The Church for the World* as a text. Although she emphasizes that her intended audience is privileged North American Protestants, her message holds a significant weight for us all who believe.

At the heart of her work McBride writes,

> While some theologians involved in conversations about public witness want to ground witness in the church's identity as forgiven sinners, it is unclear . . . how the knowledge of the forgiveness of *my* sin . . . makes intelligible God's love for all of humanity. . . . This is especially a problem given the quietism and apathy that too readily arises from Christians . . . who are so familiar with the message that we are a forgiven and redeemed people that

> this good news no longer awakens us to the ways that we remain complicit in sin. . . . Under these circumstances the church stands before the world not as forgiven sinners, but as a body needing to confess and repent for things done and left undone (pg. 121–122).

This means each Christian must raise a hand in acknowledgment that he or she is a part of a giant problem. McBride argues that certainly people who live in comfort and privilege have more hands to raise and more responsibility to bear, but even as someone in prison and vulnerable under an unjust system, I examine myself. I find too many times I have turned away from issues in this place that "don't concern me," where it is easier to remain silent and uninvolved. This especially occurs in my life when the issues arise from a system or structure much larger than my protest. After considering McBride's argument I must re-think my own responsibility to the world regardless of my position in it, and believe that without my own hand raised and my confessions heard, I remain only a part of the problem, neglecting the world and my membership in the church body, the crucified form of Jesus Christ.[41]

Carla presses me to acknowledge more fully the scope of her agency even as one "vulnerable under an unjust system" and invites other inmates to more deeply consider their own agency. Given the power differentials between instructors on the outside and students on the inside, the truth of these words may only be activated through a voice like Carla's behind prison walls. Indeed, these words are really only true when spoken by her, since truth, as the Word Made Flesh reveals, is not so much propositional as it is relational and contextual.[42] Only through our dialogical space was new insight unleashed—for me, for Carla, and for the thousands of people who read her review.

## When Prison Ministry Fails to Liberate

The transformative experiences above are basic to educational programs rooted in the humble recognition that free individuals cannot possibly know how to speak into the context of mass incarceration without imprisoned people as our guides. Through them and with them we learn and teach. Because of this, the aim of the

41. Carla Simmons, "Existing in the World, Living for Others: Review of *The Church for the World*," *Hospitality* 32, no. 5 (May 2013): 3. Emphasis in the original review.
42. See McBride, *Church for the World*, 25–29.

theology certificate is not to indoctrinate incarcerated people with specific views on religion or morality in hopes that they think or behave in certain predetermined ways. From both a historical and a contemporary perspective, this makes the theology certificate rare in the world of prison programming and prison ministry. In Megan Sweeney's history of reading practices in prison, she demonstrates that questions about "reading and reform," "reading and citizenship," and "reading and subjectivity" have shaped US penal policy since the founding of the penitentiary by Christian reformers in the late 1700s.[43] Sweeney shows how often reading has been used as "a tool of discipline and normalization," while also arguing that education on their own terms enables incarcerated people to intentionally resist "penal control of their minds and spirit."[44] Reading practices, prison education, and prison ministry may either serve to foster prisoner conformity or play a liberating role.

The act of reading, especially the act of reading religious texts, has been used to discipline and control people for the vast majority of penal history. In the late eighteenth century, Christian reformers created the penitentiary to counter the brutality of corporal punishment that they inherited from England, and the original purpose of the prison was to give lawbreakers an opportunity to practice penance. In the United States, prison authorities instantly adopted a model of reading called bibliotherapy, the selective use of reading for therapeutic treatment. While this model rightly recognized the healing potential of reading, it restricted approved texts to biblical passages, prayer books, and religious materials that focused on the prisoners' alleged moral failings, the aim being to induce moral change in accordance with narrow social norms. In doing so, reformers turned incarcerated individuals into religious projects, relegating people made in the image of God "to the status of things," as King says, to objects instead of subjects of their own healing, thus degrading their personhood.[45] The therapeutic model remained in effect until the 1970s

43. Sweeney, *Reading is My Window*, 20–21.
44. Ibid., 53.
45. King, *Testament of Hope*, 293.

when it began to overlap with a disciplinary model, which viewed reading as a privilege—not a right—and endorsed reading only when it advanced the state's goals and objectives. A final shift from rehabilitation to retribution caused both a substantial decline in prison libraries (space as well as holdings) and extensive restrictions on prison education, which were accelerated by Congress's elimination of Pell Grants for prisoners in 1994.[46]

It is no small matter that it was Christians who created the modern institution of the prison. Reformers did so because they presumed that self-reflection in forced confinement over a long period of time would be more humane than the public spectacle of flogging. While at the time it was a mark of progress in some regards, they created what was ultimately a misguided and nonsensical project: a Christian prison. In *Beyond Retribution*, Marshall argues that a Christian prison or "biblically based" prison is a contradiction in terms since "God's purpose is to break open prison cells and set the captives free."[47] The New Testament writers mention prisons "remarkably often," he says, but always with criticism. "The Bible has nothing good to say about prisons, and anyone who listens carefully to what it does say should not be surprised at the 'failure' of the prison system today," writes Marshall.[48] Citing fellow biblical scholar Lee Griffith, he continues, "The Bible identifies the prison with the spirit and power of death. . . . Whenever we cage people, we are in reality fueling and participating in the same spirit we claim to renounce. In the biblical understanding, the spirit of the prison is the spirit of death."[49]

Law professor Melvin Gutterman describes this spirit—or "the basic dysfunction of the prison itself"—in more detail.[50] He says, "Today, as in the beginning, the most serious social consequence of the prison system is the disintegration of the human personality of those

46. See Sweeney, *Reading Is My Window*, 27–53.
47. Marshall, *Beyond Retribution*, 14.
48. Ibid., 13–14.
49. Ibid., 14. Marshall quotes Lee Griffith, *The Fall of the Prison: Biblical Perspectives on Prison Abolition* (Grand Rapids: Eerdmans, 1993), 106.
50. Norval Morris and David Rothman, eds., *The Oxford History of the Prison* (Oxford: Oxford University Press, 1995) xii, quoted in Winnifred Fallers Sullivan, *Prison Religion: Faith-Based Reform and the Constitution* (Princeton: Princeton University Press, 2009), 5.

committed to its confines." Because prison deprives one of autonomy, presents a serious threat to self-image, and reimposes the subservience of youth, "imprisonment may not be much of an improvement over corporal punishment. Even public flogging did not contribute to the degradation and disintegration of the human personality as much as conditions do in our prisons today."[51] Criminologists Morris and Rothman agree:

> Most students of the prison have increasingly come to the conclusion that imprisonment should be used as the sanction of last resort, to be imposed only when other measures of controlling the criminal have failed or in situations in which those other measures are clearly inadequate. . . . Research into the use of imprisonment over time and in different countries has failed to demonstrate any positive correlation between increasing the rate of imprisonment and reducing the rate of crime.[52]

On both religious and secular grounds, imprisonment has little to no redemptive value.

Retrieving the eighteenth-century project of institutionalized penance, conservative Christian organizations like Prison Fellowship Ministries attempt to fill the rehabilitation gap by establishing Bible studies, participating in "faith and character" programs sponsored by the state, and even on occasion contracting with the Department of Corrections to run a faith-based prison wing or facility. ("We were able to take over a large section of a state prison and run it according to biblical principles," boasts Prison Fellowship founder Chuck Colson.)[53] While sincere and conscientious, they are doing so, it seems, with little to no critical attention to the ways in which they advance the specific mistakes of the early Christian reformers. As prison abolitionist Angela Davis warns, while we "should work [to] create more humane, inhabitable environments for people in prison," we should do so "without bolstering the permanence of the prison." Davis charges reformers, whether secular or religious, to "passionately attend to the

---

51. Melvin Gutterman, "Prison Objectives and Human Dignity," *Brigham Young University Law Review*, 1992, p. 906, cited in Sullivan, *Prison Religion*, 5.
52. Morris and Rothman, *Oxford History of the Prison*, xii, quoted in Sullivan, *Prison Religion*, 5.
53. Cited in Sullivan, *Prison Religion*, 32.

needs of prisoners"—by advocating for less violent conditions and an end to sexual assault, for improved physical and mental health care, greater access to addiction programs, better education and work opportunities, more connection with family and communities, and shorter sentencing—while also calling for "alternatives" to imprisonment itself.[54]

Christians have the resources to imagine alternatives and to partner with others through the power of the resurrection, but we are also the demographic most poised to bolster the prison system since it was our idea in the first place. Seemingly unencumbered by church-state concerns, prisons on the whole welcome partnerships with Christian congregations and organizations because they view them as "largely benign" manufacturers of morality and thus promoters of subservient "good behavior."[55] In *Prison Reform: Faith-Based Reform and the Constitution,* Winnifred Sullivan calls this the "'naturalizing' of religion in the U.S." Religious programming is encouraged, deemed natural and benign, "unless it appears to be clearly aimed at undermining prison authority."[56]

Christians bolster the prison when we assume the authority of the prison is the authority of God, when we presume prisons are God's instruments of justice and that God's justice is based in retribution. While there are places in the Bible that speak of justice in retributive terms, divine justice is definitively restorative. Marshall says,

> It is one thing . . . to identify certain retributivist dynamics in biblical law and narrative; it is quite another to read out of the text a wholly retributivist theory of punishment that can be transferred directly into the secular criminal justice system today. . . . The ultimate counter-theme [to retribution] is the Christian gospel, where the whole notion of just deserts and repayment in kind is turned on its head. . . . "The New Testament, far from underscoring retributivism, actually deconstructs it."[57]

54. Davis, *Are Prisons Obsolete?*, 103–4. See also Gilligan, *Violence,* 163–90.
55. Sullivan, *Prison Religion,* 2.
56. Ibid., 2, 15.
57. Marshall, *Beyond Retribution,* 127. Marshall quotes Timothy Gorringe, *Gods' Just Vengeance: Crime, Violence, and the Rhetoric of Salvation* (Cambridge: Cambridge University Press, 1996), 58.

Our misguided belief in retributive justice tends toward an "exaggerated individualism" that locates wrongdoing in individual people without acknowledging our own complicity in the societal injustices that create criminogenic conditions. Christians bolster prisons when we advance the myth that society's problems are primarily rooted in the deviant behavior of individuals, not in unjust structures, and thus presume that prisons are necessary instruments for societal reform.

In order to participate in resurrection power—that revolutionary energy that stands in contradiction to present injustice—Christians must dispense with faulty ideas about prison and punishment that impair genuine solidarity. As previously shown, solidarity is impeded in programs and ministries that treat incarcerated people more as passive recipients than equal participants in the cultivation of beloved community, or that focus their concern on spiritual, but not physical, liberation. To be sure, the women I know consistently express their gratitude for each church group and every visitor that comes into the prison on their behalf. Their disposition is always generous, as they appreciate any opportunity to be "a part of something positive." They know these volunteers do not have to leave the free world and venture into this unfamiliar space, and they are moved by their obedience to Jesus. Still, a lack of genuine solidarity is not without harm, for the women exert unnecessary effort trying to make sense of well-meaning but trite claims about the faith—processes that are worked out in part in theology classrooms, those places where the power of the resurrection has already been unleashed. As we have seen, the revolutionizing energy of the resurrection creates spaces for trust and authentic voice; it is the power that creates unlikely community through shared pain and mutual transformation. It is also, as emphasized below, embodied hope—the energy by which disciples respond to what they have heard and live into the possibilities and promises of God.

## Is the Gospel Stronger? The Relationship between
## Divine and Human Action

Will Campbell, the white Southern Baptist renegade preacher, civil rights activist, and compatriot of King's, tells the story of a man who came by his house for a visit. Campbell, who helped found the Southern Prison Ministry that Murphy directs, asked the man, "Do you believe the Bible literally?," to which the man responded affirmatively, "Yes, my brother, word for word." Delighted, Campbell said, "Well fantastic."

> I didn't know there was anyone else in the world who believed the way I do. The Bible says that the day has come to proclaim the opening of the doors of the prison and letting the captives go free. I've been looking for years to find someone who agrees with the literal interpretation of *that* scripture 'cause there's this prison in west Nashville and I can't tear the thing down by myself, but if there's 15 million folks out there who believe in the literal interpretation of Scripture, we can get them all together and raze that prison to the ground.[58]

With the same intent to tear the prison down, Ed asks the question in a slightly different way: Is the gospel stronger? Like Campbell's, his is an honest and urgent question about the power of the resurrection. Is the gospel stronger than homelessness, mass incarceration, and capital punishment? Is the gospel strong enough to resist these forces of death and diminution, and dismantle their stronghold? In other words, are Christians willing to become disciples who embody the good news and unleash resurrection power? If not, we are left with an otherworldly religion, with Bonhoeffer's cheap grace that has little consequence for this world. The central proclamation of Easter, though, is that the powers of life, love, and liberation are indeed stronger than the powers of death, which Jesus has conquered. Disciples live by that resurrection power when we obey Jesus's commands, when we take literally his mandates to love enemies, welcome strangers, make peace, have mercy, and do justice.

It is no coincidence that the most prominent leader of the civil

---

58. Will D. Campbell, *Writings on Reconciliation and Resistance* (Eugene, OR: Cascade Books, 2010), 74. Italics mine.

rights movement believed in the revolutionary power of God, nor is it a coincidence that this social movement, which made significant concrete political gains, was comprised of thousands of people who took Jesus's gospel commands quite literally. King believed that ordinary human beings could participate in God's transformative power, a power that he referred to most often as love. Love is "the most durable power in the world," he says, "a creative force . . . working to pull down the gigantic mountains of evil."[59] Although appeals to love are sometimes deemed sentimental and naive, King's commitment to God's revolutionary power is driven by realistic thinking about the entrenched nature of evil in this world. In his sermon "The Death of Evil on the Seashore," King says that there is "something about evil that we must never forget, namely that evil is recalcitrant and determined, and never voluntarily relinquishes its hold short of persistent, almost fanatical resistance."[60] From Frederick Douglass, he learned the importance of that resistance: "If there is no struggle, there is no progress. . . . Power concedes nothing without a demand."[61] As a member of the oppressed group, King clearly avoids naive thinking. Even when concrete gains are made on account of persistent struggle, "we must be careful," King says, not to rest in shallow optimism. "All progress is precarious, and the solution to one problem brings us face to face with another," he says. "But just as we must avoid a superficial optimism, we must also avoid a crippling pessimism."[62]

In "The Answer to a Perplexing Question," King locates this pessimism in certain doctrines about human nature that emphasize human corruption at the expense of human response and responsibility. Without a firm sense that we can respond to evil in constructive ways and take responsibility for this world, Christians wait passively on God to cast it out, believing "that in his own good time God alone will redeem" the situation. This was the sentiment expressed by white moderates who told King that, although they

---

59. King, *Strength to Love*, 56, 143; King, *Testament of Hope*, 252.
60. King, *Strength to Love*, 79.
61. Frederick Douglass, *Two Speeches* (Rochester, NY, 1857), 22.
62. King, *Strength to Love*, 83.

theoretically supported integration, they believed it would not come "until God wants it to come."[63] Sharing King's critique of a passive and functionally fatalistic faith, Bonhoeffer writes from prison that being "Christians today" demands two things: "prayer" and "doing justice among human beings."[64] In an essay in which he reflects on a decade of resistance to the Nazi regime, Bonhoeffer writes, "I believe that God is no timeless fate, but that he waits for and answers sincere prayers and responsible action."[65]

Bonhoeffer and King agree that "the real weakness" of passive faith is its "false conception" of both God and human beings.[66] The God of the Bible is not a distant figure who casually takes his time; neither are human beings helpless creatures who "can do nothing but wait on God." This sense of human helplessness leads "to a callous misuse of prayer," King contends, where prayer becomes a "dangerous substitute" for embodied discipleship, and "God becomes little more than a 'cosmic bellhop' summoned for every trivial need."[67] King's "bellhop" conjures up images of Bonhoeffer's god of the gaps, the deus ex machina figure in ancient plays who descends on scenes of human complacency at just the right moment, delivering human beings from consequences of our own sinful making.[68] Instead of presuming that God will clean up the mess we have carelessly made, Bonhoeffer says that the responsible human being, in contrast, tries to make his whole life "nothing but a response to God's question and call."[69] God calls for divine-human "cooperation," King says, through which humans become the "instrument" of God as we pray earnestly and work diligently by offering up concrete acts that anticipate Easter liberation and embody the good news of the promises of God.[70]

This question about the gospel's strength consumes me in the last weeks of winter 2015. I knew the call from her lawyers would come

63. Ibid., 130–31.
64. Bonhoeffer, *Letters and Papers* (Fortress Press), 389.
65. Bonhoeffer, *Letters and Papers* (Touchstone), 11.
66. King, *Strength to Love*, 132. Bonhoeffer, *Letters and Papers* (Fortress Press), 479.
67. King, *Strength to Love*, 131.
68. Bonhoeffer, *Letters and Papers* (Fortress Press), 366.
69. Ibid., 40.
70. King, *Strength to Love*, 135.

sometime in February telling me that Kelly had received her death warrant, including the precise date of the execution, which was set for two weeks later, Wednesday, February 25. Since the US Supreme Court had denied her last appeal in October, Kelly had been living in an intensely liminal space, fearing that each call or visit from her lawyers bore the bad news. A month earlier, she and I had set up fifteen-minute collect calls to add some structure to her week, to provide her a small amount of extra support and me an opportunity to feel less removed from the situation, which, regardless of the geographic distance between us, was now fully occupying my mind. I had known for a while that I would speak at her clemency hearing, scheduled the day before the execution, and at the prompting of her dedicated team of lawyers, who guided her case for seventeen years through the appeal process, I had already written the letter submitted with her fifty-four-page application, uniquely filled with testimonies from officers, inmates, prison volunteers and staff, and a former warden.[71] Now, in haste, I make arrangements for my courses and buy a plane ticket back to Atlanta, assuming my primary role will be to accompany Kelly through visits and to speak at the clemency hearing on her behalf.

When I arrive in Atlanta the weekend before the scheduled execution date, I learn that although I am on her "death watch" list and thus able to visit her the day before and the day of the execution, I am not allowed to be added to her regular visitation list. I spend the weekend instead meeting with her lawyers and practicing my clemency speech alone in my room ad nauseam. As time draws closer, I realize that I am terrified of speaking before the Board of Pardons and Parole, terrified not only of their authority but also of my inability to speak authentically into a situation that is inherently arbitrary and nonsensical. I will be addressing five men who have the incomprehensible power to take or save Kelly's life, who need not show any guidelines or reasons for their opinions, and who work more

---

71. Kelly Gissendaner's declassified clemency application may be found at the Georgia Board of Pardons and Parole website, http://pap.georgia.gov or go directly to http://tinyurl.com/jf6k7np.

on a political timetable (granting clemency on average once every five years) than on the basis of the specific case before them. The whole process has a wave of inevitability about it, interrupted only by moments of hope grounded in the reality of who Kelly has become.

My letter to the board shares this reality: how I first met Kelly one morning in early January 2010 in the classroom where she arrived beaming with excitement for the experience she was about to undertake, how she told the class that she was excited to be a part of a community and grateful for this opportunity to explore the Bible and theology in a rigorous manner that would challenge and nurture her devotional life. I tell them that the image of her on the first day of class is so vivid to me because it captures the core of who she is—who she has become—someone full of contagious joy and gratitude, someone full of openness to others and to new experiences for growth.

In that letter, I tell the board how Kelly serves as a model for courageous reflection. I share how we read theological texts through the bars of her cell, including one by the Archbishop of Canterbury, Rowan Williams, who describes healing and restoration as the act of facing our memories, "the ruins of the past," and building from them here and now. Restoration, Williams writes, "is going back to the memories of the painful, humiliating past and bringing them to redemption in the present . . . to Christ [who] comes to repair the devastation."[72] I tell the men on the so-called "mercy board" how Kelly had done and continues to do this incredibly difficult work, how she has gone back to her painful memories, increasingly taken responsibility for them, and shown profound remorse. I tell them of our most recent visit on Christmas day, how she wanted me to know more fully her involvement in the crime, not just who she is now but who she was then. I had met her long after her process of transformation had begun, which was shortly after she arrived in prison following her conviction for planning the murder of her husband, Douglas Gissendaner. A pastor began visiting her and

72. Rowan Williams, *A Ray of Darkness: Sermons and Reflections* (Cambridge, MA: Cowley Publishing, 1995), 64–67.

initiated a series of difficult yet compassionate conversations that urged Kelly toward courageous self-reflection. Her commitment to Kelly over the past seventeen years, along with that of the prison chaplain and chaplaincy interns, provided steady, ongoing love that fostered change. So by the time I met Kelly in 2010, she had already undergone a significant transformation. Still, for most of that time, Kelly could not speak directly about the crime because the case was pending, and her counsel wisely advised that she not talk about it with anyone except the legal team. But once the appeal process was over, Kelly wanted me to know. The power of these moments, where she looked me in the eye and confessed concrete sins, where in turn I proclaimed to her the depth of God's forgiveness, will stay with me forever.

I tell the board how Kelly and I read books by Jürgen Moltmann, how she was so influenced by his writings that she wrote him and a friendship quickly ensued. Professor Moltmann was so impressed with Kelly that he asked me if I would bring him to meet her when he traveled from his home in Germany to Atlanta, where he would be delivering the Reformation Day lecture at Emory University. This is what led to Moltmann giving the keynote address at the theology graduation in October 2011 and to a two-hour pastoral visit with Kelly and me. I tell the board that the time I shared with the two of them in that small visitation room will remain one of the most significant experiences of my life. On the one hand, it would be hard to find two people more different in this world—a German academic who is one of the most widely read and respected theologians of the twentieth and twenty-first centuries and the only woman on Georgia's death row—yet I was struck by how similar they are and how real the connection is between them on account of their "faith seeking understanding." I tell the board how Kelly has an extraordinary ability to create community, seen by the fact that Professor Moltmann not only sought Kelly out, but also, on account of their friendship, chose to spend one full day of his three-day visit honoring her and her fellow graduates. Her ability to create supportive community is seen in the testimonies of the women she has encouraged while on death row, who have inhabited rooms in lockdown next to her. It is seen in her ability to appreciate that she is on a pilgrimage and to recognize her companions along the way. It is seen in a photograph taken at graduation of her student colleagues looking at her with such admiration and respect as she delivers her speech. In that letter, I tell them I share that admiration and respect, fostered through our journey together, as I consider her a central figure in my own development as a Christian and a human being.

Aware that my words are imperfect and incomplete, I practice my five-minute speech one last time early Tuesday morning. I head downtown and shuffle my way into a small courtroom filled with people advocating on Kelly's behalf, a community of people, most of whom I know: pastors, chaplains, theology instructors, a formerly incarcerated woman, and Kelly's children, also victims of the crime, who beg these five men to spare their mother's life. For over four hours, together, we document the fruits of her redemption: reconciliation with her children, ministry to inmates full of despair whom no one else could reach, counsel to troubled youth who visit the prison, and daily concern for others. As I sit in the back row waiting my turn, I listen to the truth of her life being boldly proclaimed. The air is thick with the presence of God in this truth-filled speech.

The air is also thick with a cloud of suspicion demonstrated, no less, through the theological assertions made by the board. Kelly's lawyers had advised our community of religious advocates that although it was appropriate to tell Kelly's story in the language of her transformation—the particular language of Christian faith—we should do so without making sweeping theological proclamations or engaging in theological debate, a request with which we all heartily agree. We are not there to preach, nor are we advocating that Kelly should be given mercy because she is a Christian but because she is a restored human being who has an enormous amount to give if granted life in prison. In a startling dismissal of church-state separation, though, the board initiates a series of theological questions, interrogations that reveal, as Bonhoeffer says, their fanatic belief in death. "What about the thief on the cross? Jesus could have used his power to get him down, but he didn't," one member says with conviction. "Doesn't the fact that Jesus died on the cross show that good can come from death?" asks another in earnest. Later, in a prayer vigil for Kelly, Reverend Yolanda Thompson responds to these questions with appropriate indignation. She says, "We were asked, why would Jesus not stop his own execution on the cross. Really? In the Bible belt in Georgia, you're asking a room filled with pastoral leaders *that* question? Really? Why did Jesus die on the cross? *Why?* So that Kelly can *live*" and "declare the works of the Lord" (Ps 118:17).[73] After the hearing, holding in tension apprehension and hope, I race to the prison to see Kelly before visitation ends, the first opportunity I have to see her since Christmas day. There, she and a few companions are anxiously awaiting news of the hearing. "Your children were amazing," I say as others arrive, and together with nervous excitement we share the details of every testimony we can recall.

Early Wednesday morning, I make my way back to the prison under a winter advisory warning, unsure what the day will hold. By the time I arrive, the execution scheduled for that night has been postponed five days because of the possibility of snow, but we still await the board's decision. To pass the time, our small group of visitors play "I Spy" with Kelly in a small and completely bare visitation cell, fully aware of the absurdity of the game and our attempt to distract ourselves from the pending news. To stay hopeful, we playfully imagine what it will be like for Kelly once she is living in "general population," sharing visitation space with the rest of the inmates the next room over. We joke about the crowds of visitors swarming the vending machines, her pushing up against the rope like the rest of the inmates, calling out over the commotion, "They're out of burgers? Okay, get me the pizza instead!" Then the call comes that stops us in our tracks.

Kelly is ushered into the next room to take the call from her lawyers.

---

73. See *Vigil of Light, Life and Solidarity for Kelly Gissendaner*, Emory University, March 1, 2015, video recording, 54:41, http://www.kellyonmymind.com/videos/.

The five of us in the visitation room grab each other's hands, stare stoically at the wall, and take deep breaths as we wait to hear if this woman full of life and purpose will be executed by the State in just a few days. Minutes later, Kelly walks past the window of the visitation cell and turns the corner shaking her head. "We lost, we lost," she says underneath a stream of tears. Her daughter slams her fist on the table and falls into a heap on the floor. Hours later, reflecting on the horror, Kelly will say to me, "I had to pick my baby up off the ground." Leaving her alone with her children, we huddle together in the hallway and, holding onto one another, weep.

In the weeks before the clemency hearing, I reflected on how my mind and body might process all of this, wondering if I would be able to wrap my head around the surreality of it enough to feel any emotion at all. As one who has struggled with depression, I have known inner darkness, a dark night of the soul that at its worst feels like an abyss, an interior hold that seems as though it may never be lifted. Until this moment, though, I had never experienced this abyss outside of myself—the finality of what transpired, the knowledge that no amount of trying can budge this external reality, this abysmal place where there is no turning back, where there is no person to whom you may direct your complaint, where no amount of mustered energy counts, where nothing can stop what is now, in all absolute terms, inevitable. This is the power of death. This is what it means to be surrounded by the powers and principalities of death, to be hemmed in on all sides. As others rotate back into the room with Kelly, I sit in the vast, empty visitation hall weeping into this void. Our last hours of visitation are spent mostly in shared silence as we all continue to absorb the news together, a silence broken only by sporadic words addressed to Kelly: "Your life is so valuable. We love you so much."

Then, toward the end of visitation, two members of Kelly's legal team burst in, breaking through the silence. Her investigator marches straight up to her, stops Kelly's attempt at a consoling hug and instead grabs her face, pulls her close and says, "Listen, we are not giving up. Remember Daniel in the lion's den? You are in the lion's den my friend, but this is not over." Her fervor startles me out of despair, and I breathe in new life. I do not know when it exactly happens, perhaps sometime in the hour-and-a-half drive back from the prison, not too long after the void, but a renewed resolve wells up within me, a determination that Kelly's execution will not happen in silence, behind closed doors, without the world watching. I do not necessarily think her life can be saved, except by her lawyers who are working around the clock, but I do think her story can be told. We can raise her voice, demand that her life be witnessed and this execution be condemned. When I get home to my brother's house, without much of a plan, I reach out to a colleague at the New York Times, simply wondering if the theology certificate and the story of Moltmann's friendship might be of interest for his weekly religion column. As I do so, I notice Facebook and cell phone messages from a few close friends. A group of about fifteen, all of whom are connected in various ways to the prison theology program, are already gathering to strategize next steps—faculty, theology instructors, pastors and priests, doctoral students and seminarians, and a former inmate, Nikki Roberts, who credits Kelly with her own transformation. That night, in the living room of a dear friend, the #kellyonmymind campaign is born. Bolstered by the embodied hope of her lawyers and these companions, I write on social media that night: "Our message is the beauty and concrete value of Kelly's life. . . . We still cling to a sliver of hope."

In that living room, we meet every night to strategize under the organic leadership of pastor/scholar/activists, who, although not professional organizers, draw on our previous activism and knowledge of social change. Within a day or two, the New York Times piece is out, getting picked up by other media outlets from CNN and the Washington Post to Fox News and the Christian Broadcasting Network.[74] Kelly's story is impacting Christians across the political divide, pushing the logic of Christian faith to its outermost limits, pressing us to reexamine and reaffirm the truths we proclaim about repentance, forgiveness,

74. Mark Oppenheimer, "A Death Row Inmate Finds Common Ground with Theologians," New York Times, February 25, 2015, http://tinyurl.com/h3dwuh3.

redemption, and hope. In the five short days leading up to the scheduled execution, we launch a major social media campaign reaching over four million people, write for *Huffington Post* and CNN.com, gather letters from religion scholars around the world who advocate for Kelly as their sister theologian, start faith leader and Groundswell petitions, and deliver over eighty thousand signatures to the governor's office. We map out talking points, make targeted phone calls, publish press releases, hold a press conference and an action at the state capitol, produce short documentaries, host a prayer vigil and spark vigils in seminaries across the country, and respond to numerous local and national interview requests. The movement is happening so quickly we can barely keep up. Each strategic decision bears enormous weight, and one risky decision about messaging, timing, or placement leads to another. Casting aside our day jobs as much as we can, we throw ourselves into the work, every concrete act arousing passion for the possible and throwing open the future. This is our participation in the revolutionizing energy of the resurrection, already revealing itself in threats of snow. This is our "fanatic resistance" to evil and death.

We tell Kelly's story everywhere and every way we can, most poignantly in a series of short documentaries, one of which quite literally raises her voice. "Because Kelly is behind bars she cannot speak to you herself," the documentary begins, "so we ask you to listen to the words she has written as we lend our voices to lift her story." Drawing on the art of the spoken word, diverse voices present portions of her clemency confession and graduation speech:

It is impossible to put into words the overwhelming sorrow and remorse I feel for my involvement in the murder of my husband, Douglas Gissendaner.

There is just no way to capture the depth of my sorrow and regret. I would change everything if I could.

I will never understand how I let myself fall into such evil but I have learned first hand that no one, not even me, is beyond redemption through God's grace and mercy.

Hope is still alive, despite a gate or guillotine hovering over my head. I still possess the ability to prove that I am human.

Labels on anyone can be notoriously misleading and unforgiving things,

but no matter the label attached to me,

I have the capacity and unstoppable desire to accomplish something positive and to have a lasting impact.

Even prison cannot erase my hope and conviction that the future is not settled for me, or anyone.

I have placed my hope in the God I now know.

I rely on the steadfast and never-ending love of God.[75]

Driven by resurrection energy, the documentary ends, "As long as Kelly has breath, hope is still alive. So we must act while there is still time. Tell Governor Deal he DOES have the power to halt this execution. Tell Georgia's Board of Pardons and Parole that there is STILL TIME to reverse their decision." Because the Georgia legislature had passed a law removing the governor's power to commute sentences from death to life a few years earlier, there is no obvious place to direct our complaint. Indeed, the Governor's public response to the flood of messages he is receiving is to appeal to his lack of authority and wash his hands. We seek to expose his Pilate-like response and flood his office nonetheless, reminding him that he does have political influence over the board since he appointed its members. At the Sunday-evening vigil, I read Luke 18, particularly relevant since the Governor had released a statement earlier that week telling people to "quit bothering" him about Kelly.

Then Jesus told them a parable about their need to pray always and not lose heart. He said, "In a certain city there was a judge who neither feared God nor had respect for people. In that city there was a widow who kept coming to him and saying, 'Grant me justice against my opponent.' For a while he refused; but later he said to himself, 'Though I have no fear of

75. See *Kelly Gissendaner*, YouTube video, 2:25, posted September 17, 2015, http://www. kellyonmymind.com/videos/.

God and no respect for anyone, yet because this widow keeps bothering me, I will grant her justice, so that she may not wear me out by her continual coming.'" (Luke 18:1–7)

"We have come here tonight to bother Governor Nathan Deal," I say to a packed chapel. "We have come here to wear out the Board of Pardons and Parole with our cry for justice—restorative, merciful justice. We have come here tonight because we are not giving up."

Earlier that morning, I had visited with Kelly one last time, rotating in and out of the visitation room with family and close friends, since she planned to spend Monday's short morning visitation alone with her children. Kelly is living the best she can in the present moment, soaking in the time together—laughter leads seamlessly into tears and back again. I watch as she and her stepmother, her last living parent, say goodbye: grasping hands, wailing, and pleading with one another to remember how much they are loved. "You've given me so much," Kelly sobs, holding their hands clasped across the table. "I know, Kelly, I know." Later I go to make a phone call to ask my ride to pick me up a bit later, since visitation lasted longer than I thought. An officer had given me permission to use a phone at the prison entrance, but I unknowingly cross an invisible line that ends my visitation, and I am not permitted to go back. "I didn't even say goodbye," I say in a state of shock to an unyielding officer. That night, as I drive to the prayer vigil, Kelly calls. I pull off I-75 into a hotel parking lot and speak to her for the fifteen minutes the collect call allows. "Kelly, this doesn't feel real; I don't know how to say goodbye. We are still fighting for you," I say, as I try to share all the beautiful things being said and written about her. "I feel everyone's love," she says, "I do." With just a few seconds left on the call, I stammer, "The only thing I feel confident of is that Jesus will be there with you tomorrow night. I know he will be." "I know he will be, too," Kelly says as our phone call ends.

On Monday evening, a group of us travel to Jackson, Georgia, to the site of the men's prison that houses the death chamber. Some of our group head to the grounds where a few hundred people will keep vigil, including a handful of women who had been in prison with

Kelly. A few of us go on to New Hope House, a sister community of the Open Door's, that provides hospitality to families who visit men on death row as well as a base on execution nights for loved ones and lawyers, a sanctuary tucked away from the media and crowds where they can receive as much information as the Attorney General's office can provide. The execution is scheduled for 7:00 p.m., but as often happens there are several delays as we wait for the Supreme Court to rule on appeals to the higher courts. Hours later, these last-minute appeals are denied. More hours pass and finally we hear that there might be a complication with the lethal injection. Information is spotty, until finally, close to 11:00 p.m., the Department of Corrections issues a last-minute postponement due to an unidentified problem with the compounded drug. It appears to be "cloudy." All planned executions in Georgia are temporarily postponed and will resume once the analysis of the drugs is complete.

Cheers ring out at the vigil on prison grounds. At New Hope House, we breathe a collective sigh of relief as we take in the news. Inside the women's prison in B Unit, a number of women had gathered around the television praying until the coverage seemed to end. They had dispersed under the assumption that the execution had taken place until a woman who had been listening to the radio bursts down the hall shouting, "She's alive! She's alive!" Waiting in the holding cell next to the gurney, having no idea what is going on, Kelly also hears through the local news that there is "more drama in the Gissendaner case."

The next morning, headlines read, "Religious leaders see delay as an act of God"; tweets proclaim: "Snow. Cloudy Drugs. @GovernorDeal @GA_ParoleBoard @SCOTUSblog call this off before the plagues and swarms of locust arrive!" and editorials ask, "What else must God do?" Months later, as we await another death warrant, Kelly's investigator tells me, "The more I've thought about it the more convinced I've become that Kelly's life was saved that night because of the work you all did to make sure the world was watching. The Department of Corrections didn't have to stop that execution on account of the drugs."

On Good Friday, as I walk across the prison compound with Keisha, she tells me that the delay of Kelly's execution reawakened her faith and gave her back her strength. "It had been so long since I had seen God move," she says. Still reeling from the experience just a few weeks before, I ask—more for me than for her—"What if the worst still happens? How will that affect your faith?" "I've thought about that a lot," Keisha responds. "All I can say is that I needed to know that God is still moving. Now I know."[76]

76. For a more complete story of our advocacy efforts and my experience with Kelly Gissendaner, see Jennifer M. McBride, transcript and audio recording of "Lived Theology on Death Row: The Story of Kelly Gissendaner" at http://www.livedtheology.org/resources/lived-theology-on-death-row-the-story-of-kelly-gissendaner-audio/ (accessed September 24, 2016).

# 8

---

# Pentecost: The Birth of the Discipleship Movement

I still have many things to say to you, but you cannot bear them now.
When the Spirit of truth comes, he will guide you into all truth.
—John 16:12–13

But you will receive power when the Holy Spirit has come upon you;
and you will be my witnesses. . . .
While he was going and they were gazing toward heaven,
suddenly two men in white robes stood by them.
They said, "People of Galilee, why do you stand
looking up toward heaven?"
—Acts 1:8–11

Pentecost traditionally marks the birth of the church when God's Spirit is poured "out on all flesh . . . both men and women" (Acts 2:17–18), adding thousands of people to the small community of disciples in one day. Those who respond to the apostles' preaching do so not merely with cognitive belief but with decisive action. They repent and enter a new way of life characterized by an inclusive community that overcomes seemingly insurmountable cultural and religious barriers and is based on radical economic sharing that meets everyone's need. They are baptized and receive the Holy Spirit.

The power of the Spirit they receive is the same power of the risen Jesus, the revolutionary energy of the resurrection unleashed at Easter. Trinitarian theology affirms this in its basic claim that Jesus and the Spirit are interdependent. Jesus is dependent on the Spirit; he cannot begin his ministry of liberation for the oppressed without the Spirit's presence: "The Spirit of the Lord is upon me, because he has anointed me to bring good news to the poor," Jesus says in his inaugural public address. Conversely, the Spirit is the gift of the risen Christ who energizes discipleship, with the full effect of the Spirit dependent on Jesus returning to the Father. "I tell you the truth," Jesus says to the disciples. "It is to your advantage that I go away, for if I do not go away, the Advocate will not come to you; but if I go, I will send him to you" (John 16:7). In the Gospel of John, Jesus takes great care in explaining to the disciples the integral connection between the coming Spirit and himself. In his physical absence, he does not want them to lose sight of the continued concreteness of discipleship. The disciples have followed Jesus in the most concrete way, literally walking alongside him, but now Jesus is going "to him who sent me . . . and sorrow has filled [their] hearts" (John 16:5-6). What Jesus communicates is that the coming of the Spirit is not an end to their discipleship journey but is the beginning of a movement—one rooted just as firmly in incarnational existence and bodily engagement as before. "I still have many things to say to you," Jesus says as he reinforces the continuation of discipleship, "but you cannot bear them now." The disciples must live into the weight of Jesus's prior claims—those demands of the gospel to make peace, have mercy, do justice, and love enemies. They are to work out his teachings in their social and political context and put them into practice in each new situation, internalizing their meaning as they bear the implications of Jesus's teachings in their embodied and communal lives. They cannot fully comprehend what Jesus's truth will call them into. They do not know the pain and joy that awaits them as they live according to his way. But when the Spirit comes, it will guide them deeper into truth by animating the this-worldly performance of their faith. Echoing this reality, Dorothy Day writes, "I have always felt, with St. Francis of Assisi, that we do not know what we have not practiced, and that we learn by our actions."[1]

In the Acts account, the disciples have to be reminded again, this time by angels, that their concrete discipleship does not depend on the physical presence of Jesus of Nazareth. "While [Jesus] was going and they were gazing toward heaven, suddenly two men in white robes stood by them. They said, 'People of Galilee, why do you stand looking up toward heaven?'" They are not to focus on Jesus's ascension because the this-worldly implications of the gospel remain. Perhaps in that moment, as they are exhorted to live their lives here with courage, the disciples recall Jesus's final teaching, recorded in Matthew 25: whenever you feed the hungry, welcome the stranger, clothe the naked, care for the sick, and visit the prisoner, "you do it to me." In those last days, as Jesus prepares the disciples for his death, resurrection, and ascension, his message is this: Let me go, and then seek my concrete presence in those who are vulnerable and oppressed.

For the Open Door Community, the outpouring of the Spirit is not only the birth of the church but, more specifically, is the beginning of the "discipleship movement," a movement that has specific content based on the life and teachings of Jesus. The term refers back to the earliest Christians who came to understand themselves as practitioners of "the Way" and participants in the Jesus movement. It also refers to a network of contemporary intentional communities that draw inspiration from twentieth-century practitioners like Dorothy Day, cofounder of the Catholic Worker Movement in 1932, and Clarence Jordan, founder of an interracial farm community in Georgia ten years later. Jordan, a Baptist pastor and biblical scholar, named his community Koinonia, the Greek word used for that inclusive community in Acts 2 that contradicted the values and practices of the Roman Empire. With its breach of southern mores, Jordan's interracial

---

1. Dorothy Day, *Dorothy Day: Selected Writings*, ed. Robert Ellsberg (Maryknoll, NY: Orbis Books, 2005), 333.

farm caused great offense to the white Christian establishment of his time and stood as an alternative to the South's segregated way of life. Recognizing faith as discipleship, Jordan called Koinonia a "demonstration plot" for the kingdom of God and deemed Jesus's Sermon on the Mount "the platform" of "the God movement"— teachings that were intended "not to evoke inspiration but perspiration" since they set disciples in motion.[2] Likewise, by appealing to the discipleship movement, the Open Door seeks to emphasize that the Christian life "is not simply a confession of faith, a doctrine, or even justification by faith." Ed says, "To move is not to sit still. . . . A movement is Moses leading the people to the land of milk and honey. A movement is Jesus and his disciples going to Jerusalem through Samaria. And in contemporary parlance, a movement is public action for social change." Alongside *movement* the term *discipleship* is the key qualifier for the Christian life today "because the name 'Christian' no longer means anything content wise," Ed says. "Discipleship is a name with content."[3]

As we have walked through the Gospel narratives from Advent to Pentecost, we have named some of that content and discerned some of the characteristics of a discipleship community. The content includes the teachings of Jesus as well as the specific insights garnered by following him through the Gospel narratives in the particular way we have. The discipleship community understands the inherent social and political character of the gospel, enters new situations and creates spaces that reduce distance between privileged and oppressed people (introduction), yearns for the great reversal and enacts public repentance (Advent), performs creative nonviolent resistance to social evil and meets human need (Christmas), turns toward and welcomes harsh and raw realities with compassion and courage (Ordinary Time), laments and rejects moralism (Lent and Holy Week), participates in Jesus's solidarity with society's victims (Good Friday), engages others out of a disposition of trust, and witnesses to the power of life over

---

2. Joyce Hollyday, *Clarence Jordan: Essential Writings* (Maryknoll, NY: Basic Books, 2003), 31.
3. Ed Loring, e-mail correspondence with the author, September 28, 2013.

death and liberation over oppression (Easter). As the birth of the church and the discipleship movement, Pentecost urges us now to examine the type of communal structure needed to form Christians into disciples who can engage injustice and build right relationships with those who are oppressed. This new communal structure, I argue, should take the form of houses of hospitality that are incorporated into existing congregations, anchoring their identity and mission.

## The Discipleship Community as the Community of the Spirit

By calling Pentecost the birth of the discipleship movement, the Open Door affirms that the discipleship community is the community of the Spirit, as Paul explains in 1 Corinthians 12. The church community is both the "body of Christ"—the physical manifestation of Jesus in the world—and the community that receives the Spirit and participates in the Spirit's dynamic movement. The work of the Spirit revealed throughout the biblical text complements the insights we gained from entering the Gospel narratives, since the work of Jesus and the Spirit are one and the same. This is important to note because distortions readily arise when Christians assume that we possess or have the Spirit at our disposal, such that any work we do as Christians must be of God. As Anglican bishop John V. Taylor says, "Our theology would improve if we thought more of the church being given to the Spirit than of the Spirit being given to the church."[4] Disciples enter into a movement God has already begun, discerning the movement of the Spirit as they follow Jesus in concrete ways.

Just as following Jesus through the Gospel narratives reveals the inherently social and political character of the good news Jesus embodies and proclaims, so, too, is there an inherently social and political character to the Spirit's work. This is seen in a pointed way in the Pentecost narrative in Acts 2, where there are at least three overlapping ways that the Spirit's work has social and political consequence. The Spirit (1) fosters inclusive community or "beloved

---

4. John V. Taylor, *The Go-Between God: The Holy Spirit and the Christian Mission* (London: SCM Press, 1972), 133, quoted in Migliore, *Faith Seeking Understanding*, 268.

community" as King says, (2) fosters freedom from and for—*from* our bondage to sinful attitudes and acts and *for* others—and (3) fosters creative vision and energy for living according to the future God promises to bring. The Spirit's social and political character revealed at Pentecost echoes throughout the biblical text.

First, the communal work of the Spirit is not, as theologian Daniel Migliore says, "the power of mere togetherness of the likeminded or the kinship of people of the same family, race, economic class, or nation. It is the power of new community that unites strangers and even former enemies."[5] In the community of the Spirit, as expressed vividly at Pentecost, division and alienation cease because, as Paul says in his letter to the Galatians, "there is no longer Jew or Greek . . . slave or free . . . male and female; for all of you are one in Christ Jesus" (3:28). In this unifying Spirit, unlikely relationship and mutual transformation are made possible, and through the Spirit's incorporating power, disciples grow in solidarity with their fellow human beings—especially the despised and oppressed. Growth in discipleship is, as Migliore says, "a process of entering into solidarity with ever-wider circles of community. . . . This new spirit of solidarity presupposes a *metanoia*, a repentance or renewal of the mind, whereby we . . . become increasingly conscious of and sensitive to the needs of others."[6] Acute sensitivity and empathy necessarily lead to a struggle against all that causes people harm.

Therefore, the work of the Spirit is also liberating, setting disciples free to resist evil and injustice, for "where the Spirit of the Lord is there is freedom" (2 Cor 3:17). The Spirit liberates us from our bondage to fear of others, to judgment and self-righteousness, to vengeful and punitive impulses, to disregard for our neighbor's welfare, and frees us for the work of God's kingdom. This is the work of building beloved community, ignited in a particular way at Pentecost where the newly formed church uses its resources to enact justice by meeting human need. Throughout the Hebrew scriptures, and especially in the

---

5. Migliore, *Faith Seeking Understanding*, 229.
6. Ibid., 244.

prophetic tradition, the Spirit's liberating power restores justice and enables God's chosen servants to be agents of liberation:

> Here is my servant, whom I uphold,
> my chosen, in whom my soul delights;
> I have put my spirit upon him;
> he will bring forth justice to the nations
> . . . . . . . . . . . . . . . . . . . . . . . . .
> I am the Lord, I have called you in righteousness
> . . . . . . . . . . . . . . . . . . . . . . . . .
> to open the eyes that are blind,
> to bring out the prisoners from the dungeon,
> from the prison those who sit in darkness."
> (Isa 42:1–7)

In the New Testament, as we have repeatedly seen, the Spirit anoints Jesus to proclaim liberty to the captives and freedom for the oppressed, which defines his mission from the start. God's central concern for liberation and restoration, coupled with the reality that God's Spirit "blows where it pleases" (John 3:8), compels us to look for the movement of the Spirit beyond the confines of the church, in the work of peace and social justice in all their myriad forms.[7]

Finally, at Pentecost we see in a heightened way that the work of the Spirit is creative, bringing new life—an alternative way of living—out of the old, stagnant, and oppressive status quo. The Spirit grants disciples the creative vision to live now according to the future that God promises to bring as "first fruits," the "first installment," or "guarantee" of that future fulfillment (Rom 8:23; 2 Cor 1:22; 5:5). The Spirit grants disciples creative vision and energy, which is another way of saying that the Spirit ignites hope. Through the Spirit of the risen Jesus, disciples are "born into a living hope" (1 Pet 1:3). As they live according to the promises of God, their way of life stands in contradiction to oppression, with the hope that is within them causing "not rest but unrest."[8] When historical conditions oppose the kingdom of God and the vision of beloved community, the Spirit energizes the

---

7. This section draws extensively on Migliore, *Faith Seeking Understanding*, 226–35.
8. Moltmann, *Theology of Hope*, 21.

discipleship community to contradict and change these conditions. But "where there is no vision or hope, no discontent or protest against present injustice and evil," writes Migliore, "there is assuredly no presence of the Spirit in the biblical understanding of the term."[9]

As the birth of the discipleship movement, Pentecost gives disciples the power to walk Jesus's way of solidarity, liberation, and creative action. Since the Pentecost passages in the Gospel of John and the Acts of the Apostles reveal that the work of Jesus and the Spirit are the same, they exhort Christians to read the rest of the New Testament (particularly Paul's letters to the early church) in light of the Gospel narratives. God's Spirit incites radical discipleship, calling Christians to dwell continually within the Gospel narratives and walk alongside Jesus as the first disciples did. As explored in the introduction, the Spirit enables Christians to hear Jesus call us out of our "previous existence" into "a new situation" where we must practice Jesus's teachings to love enemies, make peace, have mercy, and do justice in a concrete manner. The Spirit enables the discipleship community to walk with Jesus and respond to his word, which "creates existence anew."[10]

## The Discipleship Movement's New Ecclesial Form

The renewing Spirit of Pentecost calls for a new ecclesial form, for privileged churches in the United States to become new social spaces that make beloved community concrete, however fragile their expressions may be. There is a great need for renewal within the church, evidenced in part by the rapid increase in people who diagnose the church as irrelevant to the needs and concerns of the world and thus see no compelling reason to participate in religious community. The increase of religiously unaffiliated people, the "Nones" and "Dones" as sociologists calls them, is happening across categories of age, gender, race/ethnicity, and class, with the ranks of the unaffiliated growing fastest among millennials. In a 2012 and 2014 Religious

9. Migliore, *Faith Seeking Understanding*, 229.
10. Bonhoeffer, *Discipleship*, 62.

Landscape Study, the Pew Research Center's Forum on Religion and Public Life reported that two-thirds of Nones describe themselves as believing in God, one-third as "spiritual but not religious," and one-fifth say they pray daily.[11] This means that while some Nones self-identify as atheist or agnostic, many more simply do not want to affiliate with organized religion, or, more critically, have been active and faithful practitioners who are now "done"—leaving institutional Christianity, but not necessarily their faith, behind. They are tired of the insularity and exclusivity of many churches; the ideological shape the faith has taken in politics (too often expressed in the fight to reduce civil rights instead of expand the common good); and the focus on right belief instead of just action. The renewal of the church consists in making clear the practical relevance of the gospel in relation to the struggles of our time, which is to say it depends precisely on a discipleship movement. This movement calls privileged Christians to dwell continually within the Gospel narratives as we enter new situations that reduce distance between ourselves and those who are oppressed, be they the incarcerated or the homeless, immigrants or refugees, or people enduring Islamophobia and other forms of racism.

What is needed is a new ecclesial space that itself becomes for congregants the "new situation" that Bonhoeffer argues is vital for discipleship. Recall from the introduction that through the new situation, Jesus calls Christians out of their previous existence into a place where they can develop a faith that has this-worldly redemptive power, a place where they may no longer keep their distance from those suffering within an unjust society. A primary strength of the Open Door is that for decades it has been the new situation for thousands of residential and nonresidential volunteers as they have built relationships with homeless people through their works of hospitality, or have come to know people on death row or the formerly incarcerated. A considerable number of Christians across the United States and even around the world mark their time at the Open Door as the start of their discipleship journey, the moment they truly heard

11. See "Religious Landscape Study," Pew Research Center, 2014, http://tinyurl.com/zvusvfq.

the call to follow Jesus in concrete ways that have social and political consequence. Their responses to that call have led to a variety of works that advance the kingdom of God, the beloved community, in their diverse and particular contexts.

As the new situation, the Open Door manifests the definitive relationship between worship and social engagement, namely, that the worship that is pleasing to God must be tied to works of mercy and justice. Recall God's word through the prophet Isaiah,

> Is this not the fast that I choose
> to loose the bonds of injustice,
> to undo the thongs of the yoke
> to let the oppressed go free?
> . . . . . . . . . . . . . . . . . . . . .
> Is it not to share your bread with the hungry,
> and bring the homeless poor into your house;
> when you see the naked, to cover them?
> (Isa 58:6–8)

As it connects its liturgy with activism in clear and detailed ways, the Community shows that the public engagement of the Christian is not an expression of what has historically, and sometimes derogatorily, been called the "social gospel." It simply is the gospel. By living into the Gospel narratives and extending the sacraments into their works of hospitality, the Open Door Community performs the good news. They demonstrate that worship without justice is empty. "The true holiness of the church is not seen in impeccable conformity to conventional moral rules but in courageous criticism of injustice, acts of solidarity with the poor and outcast, and sharing of friendship and power with the weak and despised."[12] The socially engaged church is not a social service agency, as the Open Door often says; it is a community worshipping "in spirit and in truth" (John 4:23).

The future of the church in North America, suggested sociologist Robert Bellah, lies in houses of hospitality and discipleship communities like the Open Door that are deeply engaged in the work

---

12. Migliore, *Faith Seeking Understanding*, 271.

of justice and peace as core expressions of their faith.[13] The problem, though, is that the Open Door has become unsustainable, and the model of an intentional community of voluntary poverty is not one that can be duplicated broadly. As I write, the Open Door is at a pivotal place, needing to make decisions about how to keep itself going, and so there is an opportunity to learn from their experience, discard what no longer works, and envision a more sustainable model for our time.

## Discarding What No Longer Works

Most significantly, for close to a decade now, the Open Door has had a difficult time finding people to move into the Community and serve as "resident volunteers," much less make a commitment for life as community "partners." The residential element allows for certain kinds of ministry, namely sharing community and home with a small group of people who were previously homeless or incarcerated, who want to participate in the work, and have been invited to be "residents" on an individual basis. The residential component also roots the work of hospitality in a home, reinforcing that the invitation of the gospel is to share one's life holistically, and that the work of the church is to build beloved community, not to be a dispensary of social service programs.

Still, I contend that the residential nature of the Community, rooted in voluntary poverty, is problematic on a number of levels. The residential character is not so vital to the bulk of the work, it seems to me, that the discipline of voluntary poverty could not be altered to meet the needs of people who feel called to give themselves to this work but have understandable reasons for not wanting, or not being able, to move in and practice this discipline. The Open Door could make room, for example, for bi-vocational callings, where some people live in the house and participate in the work but also hold a part-time job. Ironically, many resident volunteers have found residence at the Open Door quite insular, even as the mission is outward moving toward the

13. Robert Bellah, pamphlet from the lecture "American Character and Culture in Conversation," Columbia Theological Seminary, Atlanta, September 12, 1990.

streets and prisons. There is little room or time for relationships and commitments outside the Community, which is difficult especially for volunteers who are single. Their experience stands in sharp contrast to the founders and partners who entered the work married, with emotional support and intimate friendship already built into their lives. Furthermore, although the Community depends on donors and recognizes the need for nonresidential volunteers at the soup kitchen, foot clinics, and major holiday meals, the founders communicate in a variety of ways that residential community rooted in voluntary poverty is a higher call than other forms of Christian living. Their eagerness for residential membership is certainly understandable. They need relief and leadership to meet more needs, like hosting emergency shelters on exceedingly cold nights, or to return to practices common in earlier years, like allowing homeless friends to sleep in their front yard. When there are responsible interns and experienced leaders living in the house, it is easier to accomplish the tasks set before them. Still, to the extent that they communicate, whether unintentionally or not, that residential community in voluntary poverty is the purest form of discipleship, they inadvertently reinforce a monastic ideal about which Bonhoeffer warns.

Bonhoeffer engages the question of the exceptional nature of discipleship while discussing monasticism, the intentional communities of the medieval church. He argues that within the medieval context, as within our own context, Christianity had been cheapened. Costly grace was sought through monastic life but failed to the extent that it presented discipleship as "a possibility for too small a number of people."[14] Bonhoeffer writes,

> The expansion of Christianity and the increasing secularization of the church caused the awareness of costly grace to be gradually lost. The world was Christianized; grace became common property of a Christian world. . . . Here, on the boundary of the church, was the place where the awareness that grace is costly and that grace includes discipleship

14. Bonhoeffer, *Discipleship*, 39.

was preserved. . . . Monastic life thus became a living protest against the secularization of Christianity, against the cheapening of grace. . . . [But in doing so] monastic life became the extraordinary achievement of individuals, to which the majority of church members need not be obliged. . . . The mistake was that monasticism . . . [became] the extraordinary achievement of a few. . . . God showed [Luther] through scripture that discipleship is not the meritorious achievement of individuals, but a divine commandment to all Christians.[15]

Of course, the Open Door agrees with Luther and Bonhoeffer that all Christians are called to costly discipleship. But if discipleship, as an outworking of costly grace, necessitates a monastic life of voluntary poverty in residential community, then it is indeed "a possibility for too small a number of people." Bonhoeffer's words above, which name the tendency for monastic life to become an achievement "to which the majority of church members need not be obliged," is exemplified precisely by the fact that the Open Door continues to have steady financial support from its many donors who clearly value the work, but it can no longer find people to move into the Community and stay "the long haul." The Open Door serves as the place that preserves the costliness of grace—serves as "a living protest" against the cheapening of Christianity—but its weakness is that it exists "on the boundary" of the church.

I propose a different but complementary model that ensures that the call to discipleship is not for the exceptional few—a model whereby houses of hospitality are implemented within our existing congregations in a variety of ways, perhaps similar to what the Open Door founders hoped would occur at Clifton Presbyterian, a "different type of membership in the church" as they originally proposed.[16] Interestingly, Bonhoeffer uses the story of the rich young man, who was told by Jesus that in order to follow him, the young man must first take on voluntary poverty (Matt 19:16–22), to underscore the point that discipleship is in the reach of all Christians—but he rejects the idea that voluntary poverty is a universal calling for Christians. Bonhoeffer

---

15. Ibid., 46–47.
16. Gathje, *Sharing the Bread*, 59.

interprets Jesus's encounter with this man not as the basis for a universal principle about divestment of property but as Jesus's command spoken in the concrete moment to this particular person. In doing so, he anticipates a framework for Christian ethics that he will develop later, where he rejects formulaic rules and universal directives like voluntary poverty in favor of a more dynamic approach that takes into account the particularities of context, personal narrative, and the necessity of agency and freedom for discipleship. Jesus "creates the situation that is called for," Bonhoeffer says, the new situation from which this specific individual could not retreat. "The goal is following Jesus," he says, and the means "in *this* case is voluntary poverty."[17]

A problem with voluntary poverty as practiced by the Open Door is that it does not honor what Jennifer Harvey in *Dear White Christians* calls an "ethic of particularity." An ethic of particularity recognizes that there is "different work required" for those who are privileged and those who are oppressed in overcoming injustice, since each group has a "distinct relationship" to oppression.[18] For example, whereas privileged people need to grow in the direction of increasing simplicity, economically oppressed people need to grow in the direction of upward mobility. At the Open Door, the spiritual discipline of poverty is imposed on all members, which leaves formerly homeless and incarcerated people with little means for economic uplift and, in turn, has implications for power dynamics within the Community. When residents leave the Community or are asked to leave the Community for violating the rules, the vast majority return to the streets. The focus on downward mobility also affects the diversity of its leadership. The Open Door has never had middle-class people of color move into the Community and become "partners." This is especially telling in light of the vibrant work of community uplift happening down the street at Martin Luther King Jr.'s historic Ebenezer Baptist Church, whose ministries today focus as much on the dignity of self-determination as on the necessity of interdependent community.

---

17. Bonhoeffer, *Discipleship*, 73–74. Italics mine.
18. Jennifer Harvey, *Dear White Christians: For Those Still Longing for Racial Reconciliation* (Grand Rapids: Eerdmans, 2014), 59–60.

## From Voluntary Poverty to Voluntary Simplicity and Joy

Instead of voluntary poverty, there is a new generation of socially conscious Christians committed to growth in simplicity. The move from voluntary poverty to voluntary simplicity signals a change from a rule-based ethic, which sets certain demands on everyone in the Community regardless of the particular variables in each member's life, to a virtue ethics approach, which focuses on faith formation through the practice of certain virtues, like simplicity. While a rule-based ethic can be controlling and even infantilizing, a virtue ethic meets people where they are, so to speak. It honors the pace of each person's discipleship journey, personal discernment, and self-determination as each person practices a virtue like simplicity to varying, and perhaps increasing, degrees. As spiritual disciplines, poverty and simplicity are similar in that a life of simplicity is, like voluntary poverty at the Open Door, a practice that fosters solidarity with those who are poor in one's local context. As spiritual disciplines they are also a response to consumer culture and the ecological crisis, a response that recognizes that the majority of the world's population struggles to have their basic material needs met as we in the United States consume a disproportionate amount of material goods.

Growth in simplicity is different, though, in that it is not based on a model of scarcity or stark deprivation. The Open Door finds inspiration for their vows of voluntary poverty in Dorothy Day, who includes "destitution" and "precariousness" as fundamental characteristics of voluntary poverty and even signs of grace, which is to say that she shares in a tradition of Christianity that, one could argue, glorifies suffering. Day herself struggles with this "paradox," as she calls it, of both critiquing and promoting poverty. She says, "Poverty is a strange and elusive thing. . . . I condemn poverty and I advocate it." She condemns it because "God did not intend that there be so many poor. The class structure is of *our* making and by *our* consent, not His, and we must do what we can to change it." Yet she advocates it because "we cannot see our brothers' need without first stripping ourselves. It is the only way we have of showing our love."[19] For Day, voluntary poverty is "the means" through which the Catholic Worker houses of hospitality may help those who are poor, because it is the instrument through which the cycle of sharing begins.[20] As they depend on the gifts of others for their own material need, they draw people with material resources into the act of giving. Day explains, "In an effort to achieve a little of the destitution of our neighbors, we gave away our furniture and sat on boxes. But as fast as we gave things away, people brought more. We gave blankets to needy families. . . . We gave food away and more came in."[21] This same process of giving and sharing happens daily at the Open Door.

Still, I contend that this dynamic is not dependent on voluntary poverty per se. A better way to conceptualize the process described by Day is precisely through the spiritual practice of simplicity. As David Hilfiker argues in *Not All of Us Are Saints: A Doctor's Journey with the Poor*, simplicity is also, in a sense, a more honest depiction of the practice upheld by Day and the Open Door. Hilfiker writes about living and working in Christ House, a medical recovery shelter for homeless people in Washington, D.C., and offers a stinging critique of voluntary poverty, contending that those of us who are privileged socially and economically are "irredeemably middle-class." One's experiences, expectations, education, social networks, healthy sense of pride, basic sense of security from harm, and predictability in relationships all bar one from ever being able to become truly poor. He says, "The poverty of inner-city Washington is not to be sought. The spiritual discipline of 'voluntary poverty' has nothing in common with the oppression and despair of the ghetto. . . . The poverty of the inner city is evil, and we betray those caught in its web by . . . imagining that we—by divesting ourselves of some bits of our privilege—can choose to enter into it."[22] Day and the Open Door would agree to a certain extent that

19. Day, *Dorothy Day*, 109, 111.
20. Ibid., 109.
21. Ibid., 107.
22. David Hilfiker, *Not All of Us Are Saints: A Doctor's Journey with the Poor* (New York: Ballantine Books, 1994), 76–77.

the spiritual discipline that shapes their lives could be understood as simplicity instead of poverty. Indeed, Catholic Worker cofounder Peter Maurin describes voluntary poverty not as lacking all things but as "sharing rather than hoarding" and "going without luxuries in order to have essentials."[23] Still, voluntary poverty is problematic to the extent that it undermines a balance between simplicity and human flourishing, glorifies unnecessary self-deprivation, and imposes the discipline in a rigid manner on all who are in the Community, regardless of their social location.

Finally, insofar as voluntary poverty is based on a rigidly imposed discipline that is functionally unsustainable or inappropriate for the majority of its members, it undermines the flourishing of joy. Day refers to joy as "the duty of delight," a good that one must obediently seek because it is often absent amidst the destitution of poverty and the utter exhaustion of the ever-present work.[24] Trusted sister communities to the Open Door have encouraged the leadership to restructure the life of the Community in ways that allow joy to arise more effortlessly, such that it is less a duty to be sought and more a gift readily received. Certainly there are moments of profound wisdom and insight that come from the lives the Open Door members lead and that produce great joy, some of which the preceding chapters have made manifest. The point, though, is that in a fallen world, when suffering is already built into the life of discipleship (as Jesus warns his disciples when he tells them to "take up their cross and follow me" [Matt 16:24]), there is no need to add more poverty and suffering to the world through rigid deprivation.

The very fact that discipleship already entails some degree of suffering makes the intentional cultivation of joy, playfulness, and flourishing all the more vital for the work. Indeed, there is a wounding that happens when we who are privileged respond to the call to reduce distance and walk further into that call, a wounding that the Open Door partners have experienced for decades, a wounding I have now

---

23. Forest, *All Is Grace*, 114.
24. See Forest, *All Is Grace*, 278.

experienced not only in my deepening friendships with women in prison but also in a particularly intense way in Kelly's execution. Being so close to injustice, evil, and death cannot help but cause harm. The closer one gets to sin and bears it, the more one gets stained and broken by it, as expressed poignantly by death-penalty lawyer and Open Door friend, Bryan Stevenson. In *Just Mercy* Stevenson writes, "My years of struggling against inequality, abusive power, poverty, oppression, and injustice had finally revealed something to me about myself. . . . Being close to [these] didn't just illuminate the brokenness of others . . . it also exposed my own brokenness. You can't effectively fight abusive power, poverty, inequality, illness, oppression, or injustice and not be broken by it."[25] Given that the work of the gospel involves welcoming harsh realities into our lives, opportunities for human flourishing are necessities that must be encouraged and even structured into the discipleship community and the daily lives of its members. While good in and of themselves, these experiences also serve as a safeguard that helps prevent disciples from wounding others out of our own unresolved wounds. Disciples are sustained and healed by palpable joy.

### "Christ Houses" as the New Ecclesial Space and Sustainable Ecclesial Form

The renewal of the church depends on a new ecclesial space that, like the Open Door, becomes the new situation, where Jesus calls Christians out of their previous existence into a place where growth in solidarity and simplicity, where the work of liberation and the building of beloved community, is made possible. Christian renewal depends, in other words, on the church structuring itself in a way that facilitates radical discipleship by creating space in which distance is reduced between those who are privileged and those who are oppressed. The Open Door founders' original intent was that a new ecclesial space—something like a house of hospitality—would exist within their

---

25. Bryan Stevenson, *Just Mercy*, 289.

present congregation at Clifton Presbyterian, but their vision required that the church community be receptive to this new ecclesial form. As we discern the type of communal structure needed for the renewal of the church today, we would do well to return to—and open ourselves up to—this vision, a different but complementary model to what the Open Door became, the model mentioned above, whereby houses of hospitality are implemented within our existing congregations in a variety of ways.

Maurin promoted the idea that houses of hospitality should be rooted within existing congregations. He found inspiration in the fourth-century church father Basil the Great, who developed a "city of hospitality" in Cappadocia where people who were most often despised and feared were instead made welcome. Maurin wanted these spaces of hospitality to be implemented in each parish through a "Christ House," a term he borrowed from another fourth-century church father, Saint Jerome. This vision was applied in the mid-fifth-century North African city of Carthage, where a church council instructed every bishop to have a house of hospitality connected to its parish. The vision of these fourth- and fifth-century Christian leaders replicates the "custom that existed among the first generations of Christians," whose homes often included "the stranger's room" or room for Christ. For Day, the existence and use of the Christ room demonstrates that for the early church, "faith was a bright fire that warmed more than those who kept it burning," meaning that the church community's reach included ever-expanding circles as it intentionally met the needs of neighbors and strangers.[26] Maurin emphasized that this experience of met need and belonging was a primary reason there were so many converts in the early church, even at the risk of persecution by the Roman Empire.[27] What fueled the spread of the faith was the practice of beloved community.

I suggest that houses of hospitality be integrated within existing congregations across the United States, rooting the congregation in

26. Day, *Dorothy Day*, 95–96.
27. Forest, *All Is Grace*, 120–22.

works of mercy and justice that inaugurate beloved community and make visible God's redemptive reign. These "Christ houses" within congregations should not be seen as separate programs or even outreach ministries of the church; rather, they should define the congregation's identity and mission. While these spaces of hospitality that reduce distance may take a variety of forms, and while there are numerous possibilities for creative vision, I lift up four examples of hospitality centered around homelessness and incarceration that may be implemented in congregations in similar ways or may stimulate other constructive possibilities for fostering beloved community: Manna House in Memphis, Tennessee; SAME Café in Denver, Colorado; Magdalene House in Nashville, Tennessee; and New Hope House in Griffin, Georgia. Some of these models could include a residential option on a full- or part-time basis for a few church members; others may be based on nonresidential leadership and volunteers. While none of these initiatives are housed inside a congregation, each exhibits an understanding that "the church must go where the congregation is," and each offers a model for the kind of work that churches could readily undertake.[28] Each is a concrete and constructive response to central questions posed by the gospel, like, what does hospitality to strangers look like in my specific community, or love of enemies, be they real or perceived?

## Models of Hospitality Houses

### Manna House

The vision for Manna House arose from the communal discernment of a small group of housed and homeless individuals. The former had spent various amounts of time at the Open Door and had gotten to know three people from the streets by worshipping with them at Sacred Heart Catholic Church in Memphis. Cofounder Peter Gathje, who was an integral member of the Open Door Community while in

28. Michael Curry, "A Word to the Church from Bishop Curry," video, 3:43, November 2, 2015, http://tinyurl.com/hgph77q.

graduate school and years later established Manna House while serving as a professor in Tennessee, says that the hospitality they came to offer was a direct result of people on the streets "naming their needs."[29] As a nonresidential and scaled-down version of the Open Door Community, Gathje describes Manna House as a "living room," a place of hospitality and welcome for homeless people and others in need, located in an 800-square-foot house on a downtown street, with a secluded backyard filled with colorful picnic tables and an outdoor chapel for meditation. Because a Saint Vincent de Paul Mission was already serving breakfast, Manna House decided to provide a place for conversation and rest before and after the meal, from 8:30 to 11:30 a.m. every Monday, Tuesday, and Thursday. During this time, Manna House offers coffee, bathrooms, showers and a change of clothes, personal hygiene items, and other items of clothing like winter hats, gloves, and coats to their homeless friends. Following the practice of the Open Door, Manna House respects the "humanity and personhood" of their guests and seeks to know them "as persons with names, histories, and hopes." Their aim is not to "'save' people or remake them in [their] own image" but to build right relationships, to share their lives in mutually transformative ways, which includes the founders and volunteers learning to "recognize and repent" of their "racism, classism, sexism, and heterosexism." To do this, Manna House practices an action-reflection hermeneutic and encircles its work in prayer. Volunteers gather for prayer before they serve and gather after they serve to share their experiences and examine how they may improve their practice, which sometimes leads to implementing new forms of hospitality like a monthly foot clinic and weekly dinner for their guests. Their "practices of hospitality, justice, and peacemaking" are rooted in the biblical narrative, in passages like Isaiah 58 and Matthew 25 and in verses like Hebrews 13:1–2, which reads, "Let mutual love continue. Do not neglect to show hospitality to strangers, for by doing so some have entertained angels without knowing it," and 1 Peter 4:8–10, "Be hospitable to one another without complaining. Like good stewards of the manifold

29. Peter R. Gathje, presentations to author and students, Manna House, May 2014 and 2015.

grace of God, serve one another with whatever gift each of you has received."[30]

Like the Open Door Community, Manna House is honest about the limits of hospitality. As the volunteer guide reads, "We abide by the vision and practices of Manna House that are necessary for the good order needed for hospitality. Among those practices is the recognition of the need for boundaries and limitations on what we can offer and when. We affirm that sometimes it is necessary to say 'no' to a request from a guest in order to continue to say 'yes' to those forms of hospitality to which we are committed for the long haul."[31] Manna House cofounders understand that because of these limits, the work of building beloved community requires not only works of mercy but also campaigns to dismantle the structural injustices that create unmet need in the first place. And they understand that sustainable activism is fueled by personal relationships with those who are oppressed.

Depending on the guests' interests and expressed needs, there are a variety of services that could be implemented in a place like Manna House. Similar kinds of ministries offer, for example, community prayer and Bible study, English as a Second Language and Spanish language classes for the homeless and housed alike, and writing, drawing, and painting workshops where participants share their stories and get to know one another across difference through written and visual art. Although Manna House is not the outworking of one particular church, something like it could easily be housed within an existing downtown congregation, with that congregation supporting the work through tithes and parishioner engagement.

## SAME Café

In Denver, Colorado, at SAME Café, the concern for those who are homeless and hungry is located within a larger movement for food justice. Founded by Brad and Libby Birky, Mennonites and former

---

30. All quotes from the Manna House volunteer pamphlet, Peter R. Gathje, "The Practices of Hospitality at Manna House," Memphis, TN, 2015.
31. Ibid.

Catholic Workers who had prior experience with soup kitchens and food banks, SAME Café is the second nonprofit, "pay-what-you-can" restaurant established in the United States. Instead of a cash register, patrons pay into a donation box, with people who have financial resources paying more and people who are homeless or struggling financially paying less. As the website reads, "If you can give more, please do. If you have a little less, pay what you can. If your pockets are empty, exchange an hour of volunteer work at SAME for one of the café's mouth-watering meals." The philosophy behind the restaurant is that "everyone, regardless of economic status, deserves the chance to eat healthy food while being treated with dignity," and is summed up in their name, **So All May Eat**, and in their mission statement, "good food for the greater good." Monday through Saturday, from 11:00 a.m. to 2:00 p.m., the restaurant provides "unique daily menus" consisting of two kinds of soup, pizza, and salad—like butternut squash or strawberry soup, three-cheese or California chicken pizza, creamy carrot slaw or arugula, goat cheese, and bacon salad—all made on-site from fresh, organic ingredients. Ninety percent of the food comes from local farmers in order to support the local economy, decrease their carbon footprint, and provide better-tasting meals than what is served at the average soup kitchen. The restaurant is supported by patron donations and a range of volunteers, who prep food and cook, serve and wait tables, wash dishes and clean, and do maintenance work. "Believing in dignified exchange as a way of life" the intent of the café is "to build a healthy community by providing a basic need of food in a respectful and dignified manner to anyone who walks through the door."[32] Patrons ranging widely in socioeconomic status share a meal together at a common table that facilitates conversation among neighbors and strangers.

---

32. All quotes from SAME Café's website, http://www.soallmayeat.org/ (accessed December 28, 2015); other content from informal presentations of founders to author and students at the café, August 2014 and 2015.

## Magdalene House

Recognizing the neighbor as women who have endured prostitution, trafficking, and addiction, Episcopal priest Becca Stevens founded Magdalene House, a two-year residential program and advocacy service in Nashville, Tennessee. The rent-free program offers housing, medical and dental care, therapy, education, and job training at Thistle Farms, the social enterprise established four years later, which employs residents and graduates of the program and teaches the skills they need "to earn a living wage" and gain "economic independence." Referring to Magdalene House and Thistle Farms as a "sanctuary" and a "movement that celebrates women's freedom," Stevens writes, "We are a community of survivors, advocates, employees, interns, volunteers, and friends . . . [who] want to change a culture that still allows human beings to be bought and sold. We believe that in the end, love is the strongest force for change in the world."[33]

Magdalene House began as one home for four women, who agreed to love themselves and one another without the oversight of residential staff and with the help of "simple principles" that facilitate "living gracefully in community," like "find your place in the circle," "think of the stranger as God," "unite your sexuality and spirituality," "show hospitality to all," and "pray for courage." Rooted in the Housing First model discussed in chapter 1, Magdalene House multiplied into six more homes in Nashville and many more around the country and world. Stevens offers educational workshops where she teaches organizations and churches how to implement the model of Magdalene and shares best practices with groups that want to help women recover and heal from trafficking and forced prostitution.[34] Stevens says, "From childhood sexual abuse, to addiction and distorted views of self-worth, women who have found themselves in prostitution did not get there alone. There are many forces that send a woman to the streets and it will take many forces to help her recover and find her way home."

33. All quotes from Thistle Farms website, http://thistlefarms.org (accessed December 29, 2015).
34. For a list of workshop times and registration details, see http://thistlefarms.org/pages/education-outreach.

A congregation may enter this vital work by establishing its own Magdalene House through which it may build relationships with women who have survived trafficking and grow in solidarity with them as it learns how to fight the systemic powers "that force most women to the streets."[35]

Given the connection between incarceration and trafficking, Magdalene recently expanded its reach inside the prison. "Magdalene on the Inside" offers programs that address the sexual abuse of incarcerated women who have been trafficked and works with the Department of Corrections to parole these women into the residential program in Nashville, where they can begin to heal from wounds that often date back to childhood and rebuild their lives in a supportive community. Magdalene House serves as only one model whose mission has historically focused not on reentry from prison but on welcoming women directly from the streets. Different congregations may foster beloved community with a variety of men and women released from prison through a broad range of houses of hospitality that address reentry needs. Following the model of Magdalene on the Inside, spaces for housing, referrals, or advocacy may be paired with educational efforts inside the prison that could take the form of liberative Bible studies or theology certificates, courses in creative writing and art, or more formal degree programs in partnership with colleges and universities. Any of these would allow congregants to begin to build relationships with those who will reenter society while they are still in prison and to gain a better understanding of the prison system and the struggles incarcerated people endure.

## New Hope House

New Hope House, a sister community in partnership with the Open Door, seeks to foster beloved community with a specific population of incarcerated people: death-row inmates and their families. Founded by Ed and MaryRuth Weir and originally codirected by Lora and Bill Shain,

---

35. http://thistlefarms.org.

the small staff lives at the house on a full- or part-time basis and builds relationships with a number of men on death row through regular visitation. Located in a quiet and peaceful spot in the central Georgia woods just minutes from the prison where male death-row inmates are housed, New Hope's primary mission is to offer hospitality to families during visitation days and scheduled executions by providing companionship as well as free food, lodging, and transportation. They also accompany the defendant's family members to death-penalty trials throughout the state. Mary Catherine Johnson, a former leader at the Open Door who now codirects New Hope House, explains the importance of ministering to the families of death-row inmates. She says, "The violence of the execution deeply affects the offender's family and continues to reverberate in their lives long after their loved one is killed." Describing the pain of one family with whom she got particularly close, Johnson says, "I am convinced that the death penalty would be abolished quicker if people could hear the sound of Marcus' mother wailing at the time of his execution." Support for families includes genuine care for their loved one on death row, so alongside the many members of the Open Door Community who visit in prison, New Hope House staff also build relationships with these incarcerated men. Johnson says, "The death-row inmates we visit are drawn into beloved community through our love and are embraced as children of God. Most of them have done horrible things and have created ruptures in our society that are difficult to mend. But as we get to know them, we see their humanity. We learn that most have suffered addiction and abuse, which does not excuse their violence, but gives context for compassion." Paraphrasing a line from King, she continues, "While abhorring murder, we shall love the murderer. This is the only way to create the beloved community."[36] As a result of knowing "the names and stories" of men and women on death row, New Hope House partners with organizations around the state that are working to abolish the death penalty and hosts prayer vigils at Jackson prison during executions.[37]

36. King, *Strength to Love*, 56.

Each of these models of hospitality cultivates beloved community, which is the core of the good news Jesus embodies and proclaims. As described in the introduction, beloved community is another way of speaking about the kingdom of God made manifest—albeit in a limited and imperfect way—"on earth as it is in heaven." It is a concrete realization of God's intended social order, which requires a dual commitment to the works of mercy and the struggle for justice. The works of mercy that Jesus names in Matthew 25 meet immediate needs and foster human relationships, while the work of justice proclaimed by Jesus and the prophets strives to transform unjust structures that create the need in the first place. Affirming the connection between the two, Day says, "We will never stop having 'lines' at Catholic Worker Houses. But I repeat: Breadlines are not enough. . . . There is much that is wild, prophetic, and holy about our work. . . . But the heart hungers for that new social order wherein justice dwelleth."[38] As Day suggests, the works of mercy drive the work of justice for the discipleship community. As the community fosters mutually transformative relationships with despised and oppressed people, they cannot help but want to enter social movements that seek to systematically change the unjust structures that harm those whom they now love. They cannot help but want to find ways that they—even as a limited discipleship community—may create alternative structures and practices that deliver justice in small but significant ways. The discipleship community's struggles for justice are best rooted in works of mercy, so that the work of justice is energized not by abstract or politically polarizing ideology but by friendship with real human beings. It is precisely friendship with those whom society despises and rejects that makes the work personal and urgent for privileged Christians who would otherwise remain unaffected by social evil and injustice.

As congregations begin to envision the kinds of houses of hospitality that may be implemented within their church communities, they may

37. Mary Catherine Johnson, presentation to author and students, Open Door Community, May 15, 2015.
38. Day, *Dorothy Day*, 252–53.

find comfort in the reality that the way of discipleship unfolds one step at a time. Out of a humble vision and mission, other work will grow as disciples follow Jesus down the path of discipleship and reduce distance between themselves and those who are despised and oppressed. No doubt, these new spaces of hospitality will inaugurate inconceivable personal and ecclesial transformation. The transformation will happen as congregants welcome Jesus into their space in the guise of strangers and enemies, be they real or perceived, and as congregants are drawn out of the confines of the church into the streets, into the prisons, into those uncomfortable spaces where God dwells and where Jesus makes his presence concrete.

## The Gifts of the Spirit: Faith, Hope, and Love

The message of Pentecost is that God has already made available the resources Christians need to perform the gospel and practice beloved community. They are the gifts of the Spirit summed up by the Apostle Paul as faith, hope, and love. From Bonhoeffer, we learned that faith is discipleship, not mere belief. The good news, as the Reformers proclaimed, is indeed God's gift of grace but that grace propels the recipient into action. The good news is the dynamic movement of God and our participation in it, our life with others as we work toward and live into beloved community. "It is grace," Bonhoeffer says, "because it calls us to follow Jesus Christ."[39]

For Bonhoeffer, faith cannot be separated from obedience to Jesus's teachings to make peace, do justice, have mercy, and love enemies. To demonstrate the relationship between faith and obedience, Bonhoeffer places two statements in dialogue, both of which he argues "are equally true" yet when isolated from one another are unfaithful to the biblical witness: "*only the believers obey,* and *only the obedient believe.*"[40] Never denying the central Reformation truth that sinners are justified by God's initiating grace alone and not by human works, Bonhoeffer probes the proper relationship between grace and discipleship.

39. Bonhoeffer, *Discipleship*, 45.
40. Ibid., 63.

Through the claim "only the believers obey," which suggests that belief is prior to obedience, Bonhoeffer affirms that Christians are justified by grace through faith and need not earn God's eternal love and acceptance; thus, in this way, faith and obedience are distinct. God's gift of grace, the call, the givenness of faith remains the driving factor. In the same breath, he hastens to state, however, "that faith is only faith in deeds of obedience," or in the words of James, "faith without works is dead . . . a person is justified by works and not by faith alone" (2:14–26). When Christians speak of obedience as a mere consequence of faith, we split apart what the call of Jesus has united. So he turns to the second statement, "only the obedient believe." The concrete command has to be obeyed so that grace does not become cheap nor faith become self-deceit. Although it is not the work of stepping into the new situation that creates faith and justifies, Bonhoeffer contends that "true faith," faith that is piercing and uncomfortably transformative, is not possible without the newly given situation. Since faith in Jesus Christ is the intended purpose, "the point is to get into such a situation."[41] Now prioritizing obedience over belief, Bonhoeffer signals that some degree of agency is at play. The first step, which places one into a situation of being able to believe, is an external deed sometimes within one's own creaturely power. "Peter cannot convert himself, but he can leave his nets," he can do that "on the strength of [his] human freedom," writes Bonhoeffer. Drawing from a second scene of Peter's discipleship journey, this time where he cannot rely on his own strength but only on his desire to act, Bonhoeffer emphasizes that the call of Jesus may itself be the means of power and grace. "Peter knows that he cannot climb out of the boat on his own power. His first step would already be his downfall, so he calls, 'Command me to come to you on the water.' Christ answers, 'Come.'" Now standing face to face with Jesus, Peter recognizes the inadequacy of belief; he does not have the option of appealing to faith alone, of staying in his present position on the boat and concluding that Jesus knows his heart is pure. No, "the

---

41. Ibid., 67.

step is required. . . . Now that Christ has called, Peter has to get out of the boat" and come.[42]

The energy that gives Christians the courage "to get out of the boat" is the hope that is within us. The hope worthy of the promises of God made known in the Old and New Testaments is a hope for this life, a hope for "a new heaven and a new earth," based on the knowledge that God's Spirit is, at present, "making all things new" (Rev 21:1, 5). As Moltmann writes, "Our true hope" encounters us in the promise that "nothing will be in vain. It will succeed. In the end all will be well! . . . We are called to this hope, and the call often sounds like a command—a command to resist death and the powers of death, and a command to love life and cherish it: every life, the life we share, the whole of life."[43] The gift of biblical hope manifests in an affirmation of this life and a love for every living thing. But where Christians exhibit "social coldness toward the poor and strangers," we demonstrate that we have "no love for their lives."[44]

The mark of the disciple today will be love for the lives of the stranger and enemy, those whom we as a society have deemed guilty and have despised and rejected. The litmus test for the mere believer may be adherence to certain doctrinal claims or the stand one takes on certain politically polarizing issues, but the litmus test for the disciple is love. "Love is the measure by which we shall be judged," Day often said, quoting John of the Cross and paraphrasing the Apostle Paul.[45] "If I speak in the tongues of mortals and of angels . . . and if I have prophetic powers, and understand all mysteries and all knowledge, and if I have all faith, so as to remove mountains, but do not have love, I am nothing . . . I gain nothing," he writes to the church in Corinth.

"What we would like to do is change the world," Day echoes, as she writes about her houses of hospitality and the discipleship movement. "We can to a certain extent change the world; we can work for the

---

42. Ibid., 63–66.
43. Jürgen Moltmann, *The Source of Life: The Holy Spirit and the Theology of Life* (Minneapolis: Fortress Press, 1997), 39.
44. Ibid., 21.
45. Forest, *All Is Grace*, 174.

oasis, the little cell of joy and peace in a harried world. We can throw our pebble in the pond and be confident that its ever-widening circle will reach around the world. We repeat, there is nothing we can do but love, and dear God—please enliven our hearts to love each other, to love our neighbor, to love our enemy as well as our friend."[46]

46. Day, *Dorothy Day*, 98.

# Acknowledgments

In a *New Yorker* essay memorializing Daniel Berrigan, James Carroll shares how this Jesuit poet and peace activist helped him see "language itself as an opening to transcendence." Carroll writes, "What was Creation if not the word of God, and what were human words if not sacraments of God's real presence?" Because of the sacramental character of language, "writing could be an act of worship."

The process of writing this book has been an act of worship for me, albeit, of course, an imperfect one, and the words I received through countless conversations with the women in prison and with friends at the Open Door were a sacrament of Jesus's presence. The act of writing has helped me make sense of some of these shared moments and conversations, the power of which I often recognized in the moment but only on a visceral level. So I have written this book to both worship and better understand. By articulating these experiences, I have sought to honor the women and men whose words fill these pages.

I owe gratitude, then, to a variety of people: to those who created the space for beloved community to take shape in the prison and at the Open Door, to all the people comprising these communities, to people who helped me reflect on what I was experiencing as it was unfolding, and to those who read the manuscript and offered constructive feedback.

A generous grant from Charles Marsh and the University of Virginia's Project on Lived Theology enabled me to spend an intensive year as a full-time participant at the Open Door Community while directing the prison theology program. I am grateful for the Project on Lived Theology's Virginia Seminar and the participants who read sections of this manuscript at our annual workshops: David Dark, Shannon Gayk, Peter Slade, Russell Jeung, Valerie Copper, Vanessa Ochs, John Kiess, and Susan Holman.

The Certificate in Theological Studies is a result of the creative and courageous vision of Elizabeth Bounds, Susan Bishop, and the Atlanta Theological Association (Emory University's Candler School of Theology, Mercer University's McAfee School of Theology, the Interdenominational Theological Center, and Columbia Theological Seminary). The Open Door Community is the result of the creative and courageous vision of Murphy Davis and Ed Loring and the leaders who joined them shortly thereafter, Dick and Gladys Rustay and Nelia and Calvin Kimborough. I am grateful for my friends and companions in the prison theology program who shared these experiences and helped me process them, especially Sarah Hedgis, Cathy Zappa, Heather Bargeron, Letitia Campbell, David Garber, Ingrid Rasmussen, Hannah Ingram, Mary Button, Michelle Ledder, Jessie Smith, Shively Smith, Kristopher Aaron, Crystal McElrath, Lerone Martin, Amy Levad, Andrea White, Thomas Fabisiak, Jerri Haskell, and Nikki Roberts, and for my friends and companions at the Open Door who did the same, especially Mary Catherine Johnson, Emma Stitt, David Christian, David Payne, Terry Kennedy, Jeff Autry, Ralph Dukes, Barbara Shienk, Winston Robarts, Lora and Ed Weir, Quiana Hawkins, David Buer, Susan Evans McQuire, and Robert McGlassen. I am grateful for Jürgen Moltmann, who is present in these pages not only as a theologian from whom I draw wisdom but also as a friend. Through his concern and advocacy for Kelly Gissendaner, he powerfully modeled one of his core theological insights—the political potency of friendship.

I am grateful for friends and colleagues who read the manuscript in its entirety and offered constructive feedback, Karen Guth, Jeffrey Pugh, John McBride, Kit Kleinhans, Derek Nelson, and Mary Gage Davidson, and for those who read parts of the manuscript in draft form, Janel Kragt Bakker, Jonathan Malesic, Paul Lutter, Rick Elgendy, Zachary Thompson, and Peter Gathje.

I am grateful for the support and hospitality of my family, Mary Jane and John McBride and David and Lucy McBride, and for all the playful moments with my nieces and nephews along the way that buoyed my spirits—for Archer, Winnie, Meg, and Caleb.

This book is dedicated to the women in the prison theology program—my teachers, students, sister theologians, and friends—who have encouraged me to write about our time together and whose words are used with their permission and blessing.

# Suggested Reading

## Christian Hospitality and Resistance

Campbell, Will D. *Writings on Reconciliation and Resistance.* Eugene, OR: Cascade Books, 2010.

Gathje, Peter R. *Sharing the Bread of Life: Hospitality and Resistance at the Open Door Community.* Atlanta: Open Door Community Press, 2006.

_____, ed. *A Work of Hospitality: The Open Door Reader.* Atlanta: Open Door Community Press, 2002.

Pohl, Christine D. *Making Room: Recovering Hospitality as a Christian Tradition.* Grand Rapids: Eerdmans, 1999.

## Dietrich Bonhoeffer

Bonhoeffer, Dietrich. *The Collected Sermons of Dietrich Bonhoeffer.* Edited by Isabel Best. Minneapolis: Fortress Press, 2012.

_____. *Discipleship.* Edited by Geoffrey B. Kelly and John D. Godsey. Translated by Barbara Green and Reinhard Krauss. Vol. 4 of *Dietrich Bonhoeffer Works.* Minneapolis: Fortress Press, 2003.

_____. *Letters and Papers from Prison.* Edited by John W. de Gruchy. Translated by Isabel Best, Lisa E. Dahill, Reinhard Krauss, and Nancy Lukens. Vol. 8 of *Dietrich Bonhoeffer Works.* Minneapolis: Fortress Press, 2010.

Green, Clifford J., and Michael P. DeJonge. *The Bonhoeffer Reader.* Minneapolis: Fortress Press, 2013.

Mcbride, Jennifer M. *The Church for the World: A Theology of Public Witness*. New York: Oxford University Press, 2011.

Williams, Reggie L. *Bonhoeffer's Black Jesus: Harlem Renaissance Theology and an Ethic of Resistance*. Waco, TX: Baylor University Press, 2014.

## Dorothy Day

Day, Dorothy. *Dorothy Day: Selected Writings*. Edited by Robert Ellsberg. Maryknoll, NY: Orbis Books, 2005.

Forest, Jim. *All Is Grace: A Biography of Dorothy Day*. Maryknoll, NY: Orbis Books, 2011.

Hinson-Hasty, Elizabeth. *Dorothy Day for Armchair Theologians*. Louisville: Westminster John Knox, 2014.

## Homelessness and Poverty

Hilfiker, David. *Not All of Us Are Saints: A Doctor's Journey with the Poor*. New York: Ballantine Books, 1994.

National Alliance to End Homelessness. http://www.endhomelessness.org.

Stivers, Laura. *Disrupting Homelessness: Alternative Christian Responses*. Minneapolis: Fortress Press, 2011.

## Martin Luther King Jr.

Burrow, Rufus, Jr. *God and Human Dignity: The Personalism, Theology, and Ethics of Martin Luther King, Jr.* Notre Dame: University of Notre Dame Press, 2006.

Harding, Vincent. *Martin Luther King: The Inconvenient Hero*. Maryknoll, NY: Orbis Books, 2008.

Jenkins, Willis, and Jennifer M. McBride, eds. *Bonhoeffer and King: Their Legacies and Import for Christian Social Thought*. Minneapolis: Fortress Press, 2010.

King, Martin Luther, Jr. *Strength to Love*. Philadelphia: Fortress Press, 1981.

_____. *A Testament of Hope: The Essential Writings and Speeches of Martin Luther King, Jr.* Edited by James M. Washington. San Francisco: Harper & Row, 1986.

Wills, Richard Wayne, Sr. *Martin Luther King Jr. and the Image of God*. New York: Oxford University Press, 2009.

# Prisons

Alexander, Michelle. *The New Jim Crow: Mass Incarceration in the Age of Colorblindness.* New York: The New Press, 2010.

Davis, Angela Y. *Are Prisons Obsolete?* New York: Seven Stories Press, 2003.

Gilligan, James. *Violence: A National Epidemic.* New York: Vintage Books, 1996.

Griffith, Lee. *The Fall of the Prison: Biblical Perspectives on Prison Abolition.* Grand Rapids: Eerdmans, 1993.

Marshall, Christopher D. *Beyond Retribution: A New Testament Vision for Justice, Crime, and Punishment.* Grand Rapids: Eerdmans, 2001.

Stevenson, Bryan. *Just Mercy: A Story of Justice and Redemption.* New York: Spiegel & Grau, 2015.

Sullivan, Winnifred Fallers. *Prison Religion: Faith-Based Reform and the Constitution.* Princeton: Princeton University Press, 2009.

Sweeney, Megan. *Reading Is My Window: Books and the Art of Reading in Women's Prisons.* Chapel Hill: University of North Carolina Press, 2010.

Zehr, Howard. "Restorative Justice." In *Capital Punishment: A Reader*, edited by Glen H. Stassen, 23–33. Cleveland: Pilgrim Press, 1998.

# Peacebuilding

Schirch, Lisa. *The Little Book of Strategic Peacebuilding.* Intercourse, PA: Good Books, 2004.

Sharp, Gene. *Waging Nonviolent Struggle: 20th Century Practice and 21st Century Potential.* Boston: Porter Sargent Publishers, 2005.

# Racism and White Privilege

Harvey, Jennifer. *Dear White Christians: For Those Still Longing for Racial Reconciliation.* Grand Rapids: Eerdmans, 2014.

Segrest, Mab. *Born to Belonging: Writings on Spirit and Justice.* New Brunswick, NJ: Rutgers University Press, 2009.

Shelton, Jason E., and Michael O. Emerson. *Blacks and Whites in Christian America: How Racial Discrimination Shapes Religious Convictions.* New York: New York University Press, 2012.

Tatum, Beverly Daniel. *Why Are All the Black Kids Sitting Together in the Cafeteria? And Other Conversations About Race.* New York: Basic Books, 1997.

## Theology and Social Ethics

Barth, Karl. *The Word of God and Word of Man.* Gloucester, MA: Peter Smith, 1978.

Berkhof, Hendrik. *Christ and the Powers.* Scottdale, PA: Herald Press, 1977.

Cannon, Katie Geneva. *Katie's Cannon: Womanism and the Soul of the Black Community.* New York: Continuum, 2003.

Cone, James H. *God of the Oppressed.* Maryknoll, NY: Orbis Books, 1997.

Girard, René. *I See Satan Fall Like Lightning.* Maryknoll, NY: Orbis Books, 2009.

Guth, Karen V. *Christian Ethics at the Boundary: Feminism and Theologies of Public Life.* Minneapolis: Fortress Press, 2015.

Migliore, Daniel L. *Faith Seeking Understanding: An Introduction to Christian Theology.* Grand Rapids: Eerdmans, 2004.

Moltmann, Jürgen. *A Broad Place.* Minneapolis: Fortress Press, 2008.

_____. *The Source of Life: The Holy Spirit and the Theology of Life.* Minneapolis: Fortress Press, 1997.

_____. *Theology of Hope.* Minneapolis: Fortress Press, 1993.

Park, Andrew Sung. *The Wounded Heart of God: The Asian Concept of Han and the Christian Doctrine of Sin.* Nashville: Abingdon Press, 1993.

Weaver, J. Denny. *The Nonviolent Atonement.* Grand Rapids: Eerdmans, 2011.

Williams, Delores S. *Sisters in the Wilderness: The Challenge of Womanist God-Talk.* Maryknoll, NY: Orbis Books, 1993.

Williams, Rowan. *Resurrection: Interpreting the Easter Gospel.* Cleveland: Pilgrim Press, 2004.

# Index of Names and Subjects

Advent, 2, 4–6, 25–27, 29–31, 33–36, 38–39, 41–42, 46–47, 50, 55–57, 64, 72–73, 76–77, 102, 119, 232

Alexander, Michelle, 50–53, 56, 61–62, 267

Anselm, 152–53

Ash Wednesday, 129

Autry, Jeff, 62, 262

baptism, 39, 108, 116–17

Barth, Karl, 71, 123–24, 127, 268

beatitudes, 27

Bellah, Robert N., 7, 238–39

belonging, 2, 87, 117, 126, 137, 143–46, 147, 198, 247, 267

beloved community, 8–11, 20, 23, 37, 41, 46, 73, 83–85, 96, 100, 108, 112, 114–16, 146–47, 152, 159, 160–61, 168, 189–90, 195, 198, 204, 213, 233–36, 238, 239, 246–48, 250, 253–56, 261; as God's intended social order, 9, 12, 28, 36, 39, 41, 72, 196, 255. *See also* Kingdom of God

Berkhof, Hendrik, 74, 268

bibliotherapy, 209

black Christ, 163, 165–66, 168

blindness, 37, 57, 10–102, 123, 151, 168, 189–93, 195–96

bodies, 4, 20, 22, 58, 76, 94–96, 99–100, 128, 135, 139, 144, 159, 198; embodiment, 6, 22, 29, 73, 76, 180, 186, 233, 255

Bonhoeffer, Dietrich, 1–17, 22, 29, 30, 33–36, 39–43, 46, 73, 84–86, 98, 106, 111–12, 122–25, 129–30, 135, 138, 162–68, 172–73, 190, 197, 199, 201–2, 207, 216, 221, 237, 240–42, 256–57, 265–66; cheap grace, 12, 15, 39, 112, 214, 241, 257; costly grace, 12, 15, 39, 240, 241; *The Cost of Discipleship,* 14–15; *Letters and Papers from Prison,* 1, 265; new situation, 13–16, 18, 22–23, 142, 145, 232, 236–38, 242, 246, 257

Cahill, Lisa, 189

Calvin, John, 43, 152

Campbell, Will, 214, 265

Cannon, Katie, 154, 189, 201, 268

capital punishment. *See* death
penalty

Catholic Worker Movement, 19,
42–43, 140, 231, 244–45, 251, 255

certificate in theological studies, 2,
21, 31, 108, 160, 200, 202, 204,
209, 223, 253, 262. *See also* prison
theology program

Chesnut, Mary, 126–27

Christian, David, 99, 262

Christmas, 1–2, 26, 71, 72, 73, 76–78,
80–84, 94, 157, 218, 221

church, 5, 7–10, 12, 14, 18, 19, 28,
34–35, 44–45, 78, 96, 97, 108,
116–17, 131, 139, 142–43, 149,
150–52, 161, 165, 182, 192, 199,
200–201, 205, 207–8, 212–13, 220,
229, 231, 233–38, 240–42; church
community, 3, 7–8, 13, 40, 45,
66, 80, 87, 110, 206, 233, 247;
ecclesial space, 6, 117, 236–37,
246–47; identity and mission of,
16, 20, 41–42, 122–26, 130–31,
136, 193–94, 233, 239, 248, 251,
253–54, 256; worshipping
community/congregation, 2–3,
8–11, 16–19, 21, 28, 31, 34, 78,
115–16, 139–40, 142–43, 163, 178,
184, 238, 248, 261; black
churches, 10, 13, 44, 117, 165,

192; white churches, 28, 45, 66,
97, 125, 131, 242

Cone, James, 174–81, 184, 201, 268

Cook, Randy, 137

cross/crucifixion, 22–23, 26, 33,
40–41, 72–74, 76, 96, 122, 128–29,
149, 151–57, 159, 160, 163–64,
166, 168, 172–73, 177–78, 186,
190, 192, 221, 226, 245, 258

Davis, Angela, 92–93, 211–12, 275

Davis, Murphy, 17–19, 34–35, 38, 51,
62, 72–73, 77, 80–82, 102–3,
113–14, 119, 120, 138, 198, 214,
262

Day, Dorothy, 19, 41–42, 95–96,
113–14, 202, 231, 243, 247, 255,
259, 266

death penalty / capital
punishment, 2, 20–21, 63, 113,
138, 149–51, 156–58, 214, 246,
254, 267

death row, 21–22, 30–32, 77–78, 80,
82, 84, 86, 109–10, 116, 150,
154–55, 157–78, 219–20, 223,
227–28

discipleship, 5–8, 11–12, 14–18,
21–22, 26, 29, 40–42, 76, 85,
96–97, 138, 191, 197, 216, 240–43,
245–46, 256–57, 265; discipleship
movement, 83, 85, 87, 104, 114,
123, 136, 173, 202, 229, 230–31,
233–39, 245, 255, 258; radical
discipleship, 4, 6, 10, 23; as

standing with the guilty, 22, 151; versus mere belief, 14–15, 22, 197, 256

Douglass, Frederick, 215

Du Bois, W. E. B., 126, 166

Easter, 122, 146, 156, 187–89, 191, 196–97, 201, 203, 214, 216, 230, 238, 268

Eichenberg, Fritz, 140

eschatology, 9, 11, 38, 112, 179–80

Eucharist, 78–80, 100, 108–16, 130

faith seeking understanding, 26, 35, 199, 219, 233–35, 238, 268

Fortune, Marie, 131

Francis of Assisi, 231

Frye, Marilyn, 49, 59

Gandhi, 88

Gilligan, James, 88–92, 212, 267

Girard, René, 154–57, 159, 172, 268

Gissendaner, Kelly, 31, 33, 78–80, 82, 108–13, 116, 122, 129, 184, 191, 196, 217–28, 246, 262

Good Friday, 122, 151, 177, 228, 232

Good Samaritan, 44–45, 64

gospel/good news, 4, 6, 16, 22, 23, 29, 34, 37, 38, 72, 73, 75, 85, 101, 102, 104, 110, 116, 167, 168, 169, 188, 191, 208, 214, 216, 230, 233, 238, 255, 256; social and political character of, 5–6, 11–12, 14, 27, 38, 73–74, 76, 84, 96, 104, 110, 122, 124, 151, 177, 188, 191, 197, 230, 232–34, 238

Gospel narratives, 4, 6, 10, 14, 16, 23, 28, 35, 39, 44, 163, 232–33, 236–38

Gudorf, Christine, 58

guilt / the guilty, 1, 2, 22, 27, 29, 30, 39, 40, 43, 45, 48, 50, 52, 58, 67, 89, 122, 124, 131, 136, 137, 151, 155, 157, 158, 159, 160, 161, 164, 171, 172, 173, 200, 234, 238, 247, 255, 256, 258; guilt and innocence, 22, 30, 36–47, 52, 89

Gutierrez, Gustavo, 11–13

Gutterman, Melvin, 210–11

habitus, 98–99

han, 130–36, 138, 159, 164, 268

Harvey, Jennifer, 242, 267

Hawkins, Quiana, 142, 262

Herod, 38, 71, 73–74, 81, 94, 96

Hilfiker, David, 244, 266

Hill, Warren, 114

Holy Spirit, 19–20, 35–36, 96, 101, 153, 187, 199, 229–36, 256–58

Holy Week, 121–23, 125, 138, 140–45, 163, 232

homelessness, 2, 5, 19, 21, 23, 27, 30, 45, 64–68, 72, 93, 96, 107, 122, 126, 130, 138, 139, 140, 143, 147, 188, 192, 214, 248, 266; people who are homeless, 3, 19, 21, 67–68, 107, 116, 121–22, 131, 137, 140–41, 143, 145–46; the streets,

5, 9, 21–22, 67, 77, 94–99, 105–6, 114–18, 137–39, 146, 170, 182, 248–49, 252–53, 256

hope, 9–10, 26, 31–32, 39, 45, 62, 64, 72–73, 82, 86–87, 90–91, 95–96, 102, 113, 117, 123, 127, 131, 136–38, 158–59, 175, 181–82, 191, 194–96, 199, 206, 209, 213, 218, 221, 223–25, 227, 235–36, 241, 249, 256, 268, 266

hospitality, 5, 19, 77, 85, 94, 114–15, 140, 160, 227, 237–39, 248–50, 252, 254, 271; Christ Houses, 244, 246–48; houses of, 16, 147, 246–48, 250–51, 254–56, 258

Hugo, Victor, 131

image of God, 9, 42–44, 56, 106, 209, 266

incarnation, 11, 76, 81, 84–85, 88, 94, 96, 100, 106, 110, 163–65, 180, 230

Jesus Christ: commands of, 12, 14, 37, 43, 84, 93, 151, 160; as convicted criminal, 22, 41, 149, 161, 167, 172, 174–77; as incarcerated Christ, 4, 152, 168–74; as Prince of Peace, 71, 73, 75, 83, 86; as representative of humanity, 41–42, 84, 163–64, 167, 175, 179, 190; as the second Moses, 13

Jim Crow, 50, 53, 106, 125, 125; new Jim Crow (see mass incarceration)

John the Baptist, 9, 17, 25, 27, 29, 46, 38, 116–18

Johnson, Mary Catherine, 145, 254–55, 262

Jordan, Clarence, 231–32

justice, 2, 9–11, 14, 17, 18–19, 40, 44, 50, 72–73, 83, 87–88, 95, 99, 103, 112, 114–15, 117, 137, 156, 179, 206, 214, 216, 225, 230, 234–36, 238–39, 248–50, 255, 256; restorative, 11, 63, 136, 199, 212, 226, 267; retributive, 54, 62, 64, 90, 136, 212–13. *See also* commands of Jesus

Kimborough, Calvin, 72, 146, 262

Kimborough, Nelia, 28, 37–38, 78, 94–97, 99, 116–17, 262

King, Martin Luther, Jr., 8–11, 17, 41, 44–46, 49, 56–57, 64, 85–87, 91, 93–95, 102, 114–17, 131, 158, 192–95, 202–3, 206, 209, 214–16, 234, 242, 254, 266

Kingdom of God, 6, 9, 17, 22, 25–26, 28, 35–40, 44, 46, 68, 73, 76, 79, 87, 113, 127, 137, 156, 160–61, 167–68, 178, 180, 189, 194, 196, 198, 232, 234–35, 238, 255. *See also* beloved community lament, 47, 121–40

Lent, 3, 121, 122, 129, 130, 136, 140, 232

liberation, 11, 13, 17, 32, 34, 78, 108, 112, 118, 161–63, 173–80, 184, 186, 190–91, 198, 201, 203, 213–14, 216, 230, 233, 235–36, 246 ; as mutual, 13, 204, 206, 213, 234, 249, 255

liturgy, 4, 10, 16, 26, 78, 82, 238; liturgical space/seasons/work/ calendar, 4–7, 21, 23, 25–26, 76, 81, 102, 118, 177

lived theology, 3, 8, 228, 261–62

Loring, Ed, 17, 19, 23, 77–78, 81, 95–96, 107, 114, 137–39, 142, 188, 214, 232, 262

love, 6, 10, 14, 20, 30, 34, 39, 51, 74, 77–86, 89, 91, 92, 95, 103, 111, 113–16, 120, 124–26, 131, 135, 153, 154, 157–58, 163–65, 172–73, 182–85, 191–94, 196, 207, 214–16, 219, 225–26, 244, 252, 254, 256, 266; nonviolent love, 73, 81, 84, 88, 100; for strangers and enemies, 6, 10, 14, 84, 145, 151, 214, 230, 234, 236, 248, 256

Luther, Martin 43, 110, 136, 153, 162, 172, 201, 241; the hidden God, 110, 162, 165, 168

Lutter, Paul, 136–37, 263

Magdalene House, 248, 252–53. See also Becca Stevens

Magnificat. See Mary, mother of Jesus

Manna House, 248–50

Marshall, Christopher, 54–55, 64, 88, 210, 212, 267

Mary, mother of Jesus, 25, 27–30, 33–36, 44, 46, 53; great reversal, 27, 28, 30, 34, 36–37, 42, 44, 46, 55, 64, 232; Magnificat, 28–30, 33–34, 46, 53, 72; Mariology, 29

mass incarceration, 2, 21, 27, 50–56, 61, 63, 68, 126, 130, 162, 172–74, 208, 214, 267; as the New Jim Crow, 50, 51, 52, 53, 56, 61, 62, 267; criminal justice system, 51, 52, 54, 132, 212

Maurin, Peter, 43, 245, 247

mercy, works of, 2, 17, 43, 103, 115, 238, 248, 250, 255

Moltmann, Jürgen, 26, 196–97, 199–201, 219, 223, 235, 258, 262, 268

morality/moralism, 38, 74, 115, 123–25, 127, 129, 131, 150–51, 173, 184, 209, 212, 232

Mounier, Emmanuel, 43

Myers, Ched, 35

New Hope House, 227, 248, 253–54

Nicodemus, 45

nonviolence / nonviolent resistance, 10, 21, 54, 73, 76, 77, 81, 84–85, 86, 88, 90, 94–97, 100, 107, 140, 154, 206, 232, 267, 268.

*See also* peace/peacemaking/ practices of peace

O'Connor, Flannery, 105
Open Door Community, 1–23, 27–28, 30–31, 33–41, 51, 60–62, 67, 71–73, 76–78, 81–85, 94–99, 103–4, 106, 109, 111–12, 115–16, 121–22, 129, 137–42, 145–47, 149–50, 157, 188, 231, 238–46, 248–50, 253–55, 262, 265; Clifton Presbyterian Church, 17–20, 241, 247; *Hospitality* newspaper, 60, 62, 84, 207–8; Southern Prison Ministry, 18, 214
oppression, 9, 13, 30, 34, 46, 48–49, 59, 65, 67, 74, 76, 83, 102, 113, 115, 125–26, 131, 137, 157, 163, 166, 176–77, 184, 190, 203, 207, 233, 235, 242; oppressed people, 4, 9, 13, 17, 18, 27, 34, 36, 37, 44, 59, 69, 84, 101–4, 118, 122, 124, 131, 163, 165, 168, 174–76, 178, 179, 189–91, 193, 195, 199, 215, 230–35, 237, 238, 242, 246, 250, 255, 256, 268
ordinary time, 101–5, 113–14, 117–20, 232

Palm Sunday, 138
Park, Andrew Sung, 130–31, 268
Paul the Apostle, 20, 48, 74–76, 80, 87, 102, 110, 113, 151–53, 159, 160, 163, 172–73, 190–91, 194,

202, 233–34, 236, 257–58; as Saul, 187, 189, 190, 191, 195–96
peace, 13–14, 34, 40, 71–77, 79, 80–81, 83–88, 94–96, 99, 100, 103, 104, 142, 214, 230, 235–36, 239, 254, 256, 259, 261; peacemaking, 74, 76, 78, 84–85, 94, 249; practices of, 69, 72, 76, 100
Pentecost, 4–6, 26, 229, 232–36, 256
personalism, 42–44, 107, 266
Peter the Apostle, 15, 121, 123, 124, 196, 249, 257–58
powers and principalities, 11, 26, 30, 35, 38, 72–78, 80–82, 85, 87, 92, 96, 102, 113, 128, 162, 165, 172, 179, 191–92, 194–95, 210, 214, 222, 253, 258, 266, 268
prison, 1–4, 31–32, 47–64, 88–94, 108–13, 118–20, 130–36, 160–62, 168–86, 188, 198–228, 235, 252–56; imprisonment, 5, 23, 32, 40, 49–50, 55–57, 90, 93, 102, 188, 211–12
Prison Fellowship Ministry, 204, 211; Colson, Chuck, 211; reentry from prison, 52, 62, 66, 253 *See also* mass incarceration
prison theology program, 1, 7, 118, 191, 199, 205–6, 223, 262–63. *See also* Certificate in Theological Studies
privileged Christians, 4–6, 9–10, 13, 16, 23, 27–28, 34, 36, 41, 66, 68, 87, 115, 123–24, 126–28, 137, 140,

167–68, 178, 189, 191–93, 207, 232, 236–37, 242, 244–45, 255

racism, 10, 34, 45, 50, 66, 102, 115, 130, 192, 194–95, 237, 249, 267–68

redemption, 11, 13, 26, 39, 41, 45, 50, 97, 102, 108, 110–12, 114–16, 125, 128, 136, 172, 205, 226, 228, 232, 275

reducing distance, 4, 5, 7, 14, 16, 18, 23, 32, 35–36, 43, 69, 72–76, 81, 84–85, 88, 92, 94, 96, 127, 232, 237, 245–46, 248, 256

Religious Landscape Study, 237

repentance, 6, 16, 17, 25–26, 27, 28, 36–42, 46, 64, 68, 115, 129–30, 152, 154, 156, 160–61, 172, 174, 191, 198, 208, 223, 229, 232, 234, 249; accepting guilt / taking responsibility, 27, 41, 132, 164, 172, 175, 193; *metanoia*, 12, 41, 234

restrooms, 98, 105–8, 118, 140

resurrection, 11, 26, 32, 96, 122, 156, 163–65, 175–77, 189–92, 195, 197–99, 203, 212–14, 224–25, 230–31, 268

Rustay, Dick, 140, 262

sacrament, 104, 108–9, 111, 113, 115–18, 122, 129, 140, 143, 238, 261; of baptism (*see* baptism); of Eucharist (*see* Eucharist)

SAME Café, 248, 250–51

Segrest, Mab, 125–28, 137, 267

Sermon on the Mount, 10, 29, 37, 43, 84–85, 123, 232

sin, 6, 11, 13, 15, 17, 19, 22, 26, 38–40, 42–43, 45, 48, 73–74, 110, 112, 122–24, 129, 130–32, 135–36, 141, 152–53, 158–60, 164, 172–73, 176–77, 179, 192, 198, 207–8, 216, 219, 234, 246, 256; injustice, 8, 10, 18, 27, 30, 40–41, 44, 45–46, 49, 59, 64, 67, 74, 87–88, 90, 93, 115, 123, 124, 128, 130–31, 133, 137, 166, 168, 171, 176, 189, 193, 194–95, 206, 213, 233, 234, 236, 238, 242, 246, 250, 255; social sin or structural evil, 16, 28, 41, 43, 48, 50, 67, 122, 123, 129, 154, 162, 173

*Shalom*, 88, 137

shame, 63, 89–92, 116, 119, 132, 182

Solzhenitsyn, Aleksandr, 48–49, 52, 56

Stevens, Becca, 252. *See also* Magdalene House

Stevenson, Bryan, 246, 267, 275

Stitt, Emma, 157, 262

Stivers, Laura, 64–66, 68, 192–93, 266

Stringfellow, William, 38–39, 74

substitutionary atonement, 152–60

Sullivan, Winnifred, 210–12, 267

Sweeney, Megan, 202, 209–10, 267

Taylor, John V., 233

Thurman, Howard, 30

transformation, 22, 40–42, 47, 55, 64, 68, 75, 87, 147, 160, 165, 172, 179, 204, 206, 256; personal, 6, 12, 17, 41, 91, 96, 99–100, 218–20, 223–34; social, 6, 12, 41, 45, 96, 99–100

victim(s), victimization, 4, 46, 48, 56–58, 63, 89, 123, 130, 132–33, 135–36, 151, 152, 154–63, 166–67, 172, 174, 177, 179, 190–91, 193, 194, 202, 206, 220, 232; of crime, 57, 63, 151, 158, 220; of social harm, 4–5, 46, 48, 56, 57, 123, 151–52, 162–63, 166, 172, 177, 190–91, 194, 206, 232; victim mechanism, 154–59; victim–oppressor cycle, 48, 57–58, 89, 130, 132–33, 135–36, 152, 156, 157, 159, 160–61, 163, 165, 172, 179, 193, 202

voluntary poverty, 239–45

vulnerability, 66, 105, 111, 125, 128–30, 134, 137, 204

War on Drugs, 50, 51–56, 172

Wellons, Marcus, 82–84, 157–59, 191, 254

Williams, Reggie, 165–66, 266

Williams, Rowan, 156, 159–60, 172, 190–91, 218, 268

Wink, Walter, 74–75

women in prison (names changed): Ashley, 119; Carla, 119–20, 134, 168–73, 191, 207–8; Denise, 133–34; Erika 135, 161–62; Gail, 134; Janet, 119, 174–75; Keisha, 132–33, 184–85, 204, 228; Kristi, 135, 162; Natalie, 1–2, 51, 132, 135, 177, 188, 204; Neka, 118, 134; Patricia, 133; Sarah, 135, 200, 204; Sierra, 119, 129, 134, 176–78, 180–85, 188, 191, 203; Tahjae, 118–19, 135–36; Terri, 61, 135

worship, 3, 8, 9–10, 16–17, 19, 21, 28, 31, 34, 78, 81, 115, 116, 139, 140, 142, 146, 163, 178, 184, 206, 238, 248, 261

Yoder, John Howard, 11–12, 74

Zehr, Howard, 63, 136, 267

# Index of Scripture

Genesis
1:27 ...... 9

Psalms
27:13 ...... 196
42:1 ...... 181
118:17 ...... 196
146 ...... 38

Isaiah
9 ...... 39–40, 72
9:2–7 ...... 71, 73
42:1–7 ...... 234
53 ...... 153
58:6–12 ...... 17–18, 238

Matthew
2:9–12 ...... 81
2:16–18 ...... 71
3:1–2 ...... 25, 37
4:17 ...... 37
6:9–13 ...... 79
6:10 ...... 196
7:1 ...... 123

7:7–8 ...... 31
10:7–8 ...... 37
10:42 ...... 98
11:2–6 ...... 37
16:24 ...... 122
18:20 ...... 110
19:16–22 ...... 241
19:24 ...... 168
25 ...... 43, 122, 255
25:31–46 ...... 17, 20, 33
26:20–28 ...... 110
28:19 ...... 22

Mark
2:14 ...... 14
12:41–44 ...... 84

Luke
1:15, 44 ...... 36
1:34 ...... 35
1:46–55 ...... 25
3:4–5 ...... 29
3:8 ...... 37
3:11 ...... 37

4 . . . . . . 168, 189

4:16–21 . . . . . . 101

4:18 . . . . . . 34

7:34 . . . . . . 19, 22

10:25–37 . . . . . . 44

18:1–7 . . . . . . 225–26

22:62 . . . . . . 121

23:33 . . . . . . 149

23:34 . . . . . . 192

23:39–43 . . . . . . 178

24:9–11 . . . . . . 187

John

3:8 . . . . . . 235

4:23 . . . . . . 238

6:19 . . . . . . 197

6:39 . . . . . .

10:1–10 . . . . . . 20

13:1–20 . . . . . . 116

15:12–17 . . . . . . 19

16:5–6 . . . . . . 230

16:7 . . . . . . 230

16:12–13 . . . . . . 229

Acts

1:8–11 . . . . . . 229

2:17–18 . . . . . . 231, 233

2:45 . . . . . . 20

8:1 . . . . . . 190

8:1–9:18 . . . . . . 187

8:3 . . . . . . 187

Romans

8 . . . . . . 20

8:23 . . . . . . 235

12:1 . . . . . . 95, 144

12:2 . . . . . . 194

15:13 . . . . . . 196

1 Corinthians

1:18–25 . . . . . . 149

12 . . . . . . 20, 233

12:8–10 . . . . . . 80

2 Corinthians

1:20 . . . . . . 197

1:22 . . . . . . 235

3:17 . . . . . . 234

5:5 . . . . . . 235

5:21 . . . . . . 153, 172

Galatians

3:13 . . . . . . 153

3:28 . . . . . . 113, 234

6:2 . . . . . . 129

Ephesians

1:10 . . . . . . 26, 196

5:15 . . . . . . 102

6:12 . . . . . . 11, 74

Philippians

2:12–13 . . . . . . 17

Colossians

1:15–20 . . . . . . 74

1:20 . . . . . . 196

Hebrews
13:1–2 . . . . . . 249

James
2:14–26 . . . . . . 257

1 Peter . . . . . . 196
1:3 . . . . . . 235
4:8–10 . . . . . . 249

1 John . . . . . . 125
4:20 . . . . . . 125
5:19 . . . . . . 197

Revelation
3:20 . . . . . . 33
21:1 . . . . . . 258
21:5 . . . . . . 26, 196